A Year of Hope

devotional

hope✱books
collections

Edited and Published by hope*books © 2025 hope*books with contributions from over 200 writers.

Published by hope*books
2217 Matthews Township Pkwy
Suite D302
Matthews, NC 28105
www.hopebooks.com

hope*books is a division of hope*media

Printed in the United States of America

The authors of individual contributions retain copyright to their respective works. By contributing to this collection, each author has granted hope*books a non-exclusive license to include their work in this publication and in future print or digital editions.

All rights reserved. Without limiting the rights under copyrights reserved above, no part of this publication may be scanned, uploaded, reproduced, distributed, or transmitted in any form or by any means whatsoever without express prior written permission from both the author and publisher of this book—except in the case of brief quotations embodied in critical articles and reviews.

Thank you for supporting the author's rights.

First edition.
Hardcover ISBN: 979-8-89185-406-2
Library of Congress Number: Application submitted; number pending

All Scripture quotations are from The ESV® Bible (The Holy Bible, English Standard Version®), © 2001 by Crossway, a publishing ministry of Good News Publishers. Used by permission. All rights reserved.

Table of Contents

Foreword v

January 1

February 37

March 67

April 105

May 139

June 173

July 207

August 245

September 279

October 311

November 345

December 379

Foreword

By Brian Dixon

When we first dreamed of *A Year of Hope Devotional*, I imagined what it might feel like to hold a devotional that meets you right where you are – in the early mornings, in the quiet moments, and in the seasons when life feels like too much. I wanted it to feel like a friend's voice reminding you that hope is still alive.

As I read through these pages, I found myself doing exactly that – exhaling. Each devotion feels like a conversation between heaven and earth, an invitation to pause, breathe, and remember that God is near. These stories are honest and human. They don't rush past the pain or the waiting; instead, they show us that hope is not the absence of hardship but the steady light that shines through it.

You'll read about God's faithfulness in unexpected places – in hospital rooms, in answered prayers, in long seasons of waiting, and in the quiet courage it takes just to keep believing. Every page testifies to the same truth: God is still writing redemption stories, and yours is one of them.

This book is more than a devotional. It's a movement of voices – each one echoing the same promise that anchors us all: "Hope does not disappoint." My prayer is that as you read *A Year of Hope Devotional*, you'll not only find encouragement for today but also courage for tomorrow. Because no matter what season you're walking through, God's story for your life isn't finished yet.

Brian Dixon
Founder, hope*books

To learn more about the authors, scan the QR code below.

hopebooks.com/ayoh-authors-2025

January

January 1

The Edge of Hope
By Tara L. Banks
Today's Scripture: Romans 15:13 & Jeremiah 29:11

Doesn't the first day of January seem like anything is possible, as if you're standing on the edge of something incredible, just waiting for it to appear? For some, it's a time to get started on goals, open new journals, and set sights on lofty intentions. Others peer into the beginning of January, relieved and ready for a different kind of year to start—a better one. Regardless of how you enter or what you face, January can hold hope.

When I start something new, especially at the beginning of the year, I don't want to start empty. I want to start from a place where I am filled with the power of the Holy Spirit, so that I can do the work that He has for me with confidence. This requires a step of faith. Faith to start. Faith to keep going. Faith to believe God will be with me as I navigate everything the year will hold.

Confident hope means that we look through eyes of faith at our situation and draw our strength for whatever may come our way from the source of hope, our loving and faithful God. As we learn to trust Him and He fills us with His power, we can then boldly step into a new year overflowing with hope.

Right here, at the top of the year, let's commit to believing the best about the Lord and His plans for us and allow that hope to carry us into everything new we will face. Remember, He is for us. Let's embrace the "anything is possible" work the Lord wants to do in our hearts and lives this year.

Prayer

Lord, only You can do a new thing in us. As we fully put our trust in You on January 1st, standing here on the edge of hope, would You fill us with Your Spirit so that we can be empowered to live a life that honors You? Fill us with the confident hope that only you can offer.

January 2

Take A Leap of Faith
By Reverend Doctor Juana Jordan
Today's Scripture: Proverbs 3:5-6

My father used to do this thing that would drive my mother crazy; he would ask questions he already knew the answer to. Jesus did something similar. In John's Gospel, he asked, "Do you want to be healed?" (5:6) and "Whom do you seek?" (18:4,7). One of my favorites is in Mark, "What do you want me to do for you?" (10:51).

We know Jesus knew the answers, but I wonder if the questions are more about whether we know what we want. Are we brave enough to speak them aloud and make the ask?

I had been the appointed pastor to my church for 2 ½ years when it became apparent that it was not a good match. Two of my closest colleagues suggested I ask for an appointment change. I had been wrestling with the decision for some time and prayed about it. Then, one morning, I heard, "Juana, what do you want?" Without any hesitation, I said, "I would like to take a year off. Have a reset."

On this day in 2022, I was two days into my reset.

I had never taken a leap or jumped without a net before. I had no concrete plans for monetary support, yet I felt an overwhelming sense of peace. That's the byproduct of following the Proverb writer's wisdom to "Trust in the Lord with all your heart, and do not lean on your own understanding." I stepped away from ministry – a path I "understood" well and one that the church had "understood" and affirmed as my calling. It was an act of not leaning on that understanding.

That's the challenge – to take ourselves out of it. Faith requires that we place our deep-seated confidence in God's character and promises to the extent that even when the path is crooked, we will submit to God's way and take the leap!

Prayer

God of the Leap, Thank You for the courage to ask for what we want and the faith to jump towards it. Give us the strength to trust You with all of our heart, even when we can't see the way. Guide our steps as we lean into Your promises and find peace in your faithfulness.

January 3

Divinely Directed The Beauty of God's Guidance
By Dr. Jasmine Rosetta Gordon
Today's Scripture: Psalm 37:23, Exodus 13:21

Life is filled with choices, crossroads, and detours. Each day, we make decisions —some small, some life-changing —that shape our journey. While we often seek advice, wisdom, or even our own instincts, there is no greater assurance than knowing we are divinely directed by God.

To be divinely directed means our path is not random, our struggles are not in vain, and our steps are not without purpose. This means to surrender our control to God. It is to invite God into the driver's seat of your life, trusting that He knows where He is leading you. You do not have to see the whole map. God's direction may not always align with your plans, but it will always align with His purpose.

When God is driving, He leads us toward His purpose, even when the road feels uncertain. The Holy Spirit is our divine navigator. He speaks through Scripture, prayer, inner peace, and even closed doors, redirecting us toward His best. Think about the Children of Israel in the wilderness. They did not wander aimlessly; the cloud by day and the fire by night were visible reminders that God Himself was leading the way. In the same way, God has promised to guide you, not just in monumental moments, but in everyday steps.

Our understanding is limited, clouded by emotion, fear, or impatience. God's direction cuts through confusion and brings clarity. God often shows us the next step, not the entire journey. Clarity does not always mean detail. The more we lean on God, the less burdened we are by uncertainty. Clarity comes through trust.

Prayer

God, Thank You that my life is not left to chance. Thank You for ordering my steps and directing my path. Please help me to trust Your lead, even when I do not understand it. Teach me to surrender my plans and depend fully on Your wisdom. May I walk daily in peace, knowing that I am divinely directed into Your perfect will.

January 4

Filling Up My Failures
By Amy Leigh Hughes
Today's Scripture: 2 Corinthians 12:9

As a new year begins, many of us hold the hope of new possibilities. The slate has been wiped clean; we can start over with the best of intentions. I am always convinced that this will be the year I finally get myself together and that I will be able to muster the discipline to just change my lifestyle overnight.

Yet, here we are on day four. I have undoubtedly already failed to become the kind of person who gets up at 5am to do yoga and bake bread. At this point, I usually throw in the towel and decide I'll try again tomorrow, or next month, or even next year. I name myself an utter failure for not being able to do what I ought.

My heart and my flesh are so weak. I start confidently down one path and abandon it as soon as I meet challenges. I don't like to do difficult things, and I often don't believe I'm capable of overcoming them.

There's good news and bad news. The bad news is that failure is inevitable. My mistake is assuming I have the power within me to continually improve until I have perfected myself. In my humanity, I will inevitably fail. The good news is that my failure makes a way for Christ to come in and show his power. He empowers me with his Spirit in a way that I could never achieve on my own. Whenever I recognize my own shortcomings, it is an opportunity for Him to come into my life.

This means that I CAN do hard things, but not because I am so strong and capable. It's only because of the power of God working in me, filling up my failures with His perfect ability.

Prayer

God, Thank You for not leaving me to my own devices. I pray that You would come into my brokenness and show Your wholeness, that You would come into my failure and show Your power. Please remind me today that I have the power of Christ resting upon me, and that Your grace is sufficient to cover my weakness.

January 5

What if the Key to Forever Love is Letting Go?
By Dr. Shelley Kemp, Ed.D., SHRM-SCP
Today's Scripture: Psalm 56:3-4

What if the only way to find lasting love... is to let go of your need to control it?

Fourteen years ago, on January 5th, I went on a first date that almost didn't happen. I canceled once. Rescheduled. Got scared. Even tried to talk myself out of going while getting dressed.

But I went.

And that single, ordinary evening turned into the beginning of something extraordinary.

At that point in my life, I had already experienced failed relationships—ones I had entered without truly inviting God in. I had made choices from a place of fear, loneliness, and self-reliance. And each time, the result was brokenness.

But before this date—this man—I had finally done something different.

I surrendered. I told God, "I trust You to choose. I trust You to lead. And I trust You to change me into the woman I need to be." And when I met him, something felt different.

He was everything I had asked God for. Strong where I was weak. Calm where I was anxious. Wise where I lacked direction. For all of our imperfections, we are perfectly matched.

Today marks fourteen January 5ths together. Fourteen years of learning that love doesn't last because of feelings or compatibility. Love lasts when both people surrender—daily—to God's will, God's wisdom, and God's way.

So let me ask you...
What if the future of your relationship isn't built on chemistry, but on Christ?
What if true security comes not from passion—but from shared surrender?
What if the greatest love stories don't begin with fireworks—but with a quiet, "Yes, Lord. I trust You."

Here's the truth: when God writes the love story, the chemistry is real, the passion is present, and the fireworks? Unforgettable—because His plans are worth the wait.

Prayer

Lord, Thank You for being the Author of love stories that last. Teach us to surrender our hopes, fears, and timing to You. Help us wait well, love well, and trust Your wisdom over our wants. Whether single or married, may we always seek You first—knowing Your plans are better than our own.

January 6

Crossing Bridges By Sarah Fry
Today's Scripture: Matthew 6:34

Hi. My name is Sarah, and I'm a bridge crosser and a worrier. In my defense, let me say: it's not entirely a bad thing! One way I deal with hard things is by planning ahead. I pack my backpack with helpful tools and face challenges head-on.

But sometimes, I prepare for problems that don't even exist yet—and that uses up emotional and mental energy I need for other things.

Years ago, early in our ministry, I shared some fears with a wise older woman as my husband and I prepared for a move. She gently said, "Sarah, God gives us grace for things when we get there. You don't need the grace for that now—you're not there yet!"

I've had to choose to surrender to that truth many times. And it helps.

Jesus said it perfectly:
"Therefore do not be anxious about tomorrow, for tomorrow will be anxious for itself. Sufficient for the day is its own trouble" (Matthew 6:34).

He's right. Each day usually has plenty that needs my attention. So why is it so easy for me to borrow trouble?

Well, I've seen a lot of grief. I've carried many heavy stories with people. My imagination knows a thousand ways things could go wrong. Worry gives me a sense of control—but it's an illusion. I'm not in control. But my Abba is.

Lately, He's been gently saying:
"Sarah. Just stay with Me."
When I'm pulling ahead—solving, pre-grieving, building protections—He reminds me:
"It's not up to you. I'm here. Stay close."

I've been hyper-focused on bridges I may never cross. But He's turning my heart to what I have now.

I have Him.
A pool of living water.
Refreshing grace.
Right here. Right now.
I think I'll just sit and soak for a minute.

Prayer

Abba, Thank You for knowing me so well...that in my tenderness I often become fearful. Please teach me to stay right beside You so I can learn to trust. Continue to retrain my brain to remember that You are always, always good. And that the deep antidote to the pain of the world is You! I rest in You today.

January 7

Hanging onto Hope in Your Single Years
By Abigail Ruth Miller
Today's Scripture: Psalm 62:8

I first discovered this verse in college, in my devotional time. It was right after I found out my fellow freshman friend had died over the winter break from brain cancer. I had a lot going on in my mind, and the fact that the God of the universe would want me to "pour out my heart" to Him meant so much.

This pouring continued in other areas of my life. I never had a boyfriend to talk to in college. Being without 'my person' until I was 38 was the hardest thing I've ever gone through. For 25 long years, I poured out my heart and prayers to God. God didn't bring me a man during that time, but He brought me Himself.

I learned to seek Jesus in a very personal way, knowing that a man DID exist who wanted to hear all my thoughts and feelings. How LOVED we are by the One running the cosmos! He REALLY wants to hear all about what's happening in your heart.

I'm a verbal processor, so having someone who will sit and listen to me share is one of the ways I feel the most loved. When I realized GOD wanted to do that for me, I took Him up on His offer and never stopped.

Friend, you can tell Jesus anything and express all your emotions to Him. If you are mad, or sad, or glad, tell Him. He can handle it all, and He LOVES to hear your heart. I encourage you right now to get a piece of paper and pour out all your thoughts and feelings to the God who made you and your beautiful heart!

Prayer

Father God, Thank You for sending Your precious son, Jesus to live on this earth and experience what it's like down here. Thank you for the GIFT of being able to pour out our hearts to you and for meeting us in our most vulnerable moments. Please help us tell you ALL the things and trust you always!

January 8

Power in His Name
By Linda Lowe Erley
Today's Scripture: Psalm 138:1-2

After receiving news of a dear friend's death, I fell to my knees and sobbed. In the stillness that followed, I lifted my tear-stained face and called out to God, desperate to cling to who He promises to be.

"God," I cried, "You are El Roi–the God who sees me and my precious friend's family right now. You are Yahweh Nissi–the Lord my banner–and I hold it high as I raise my hand, knowing You are here with us in this pain. I trust You, Yahweh, to get us through."

In moments like this, trust feels fragile unless it's rooted in truly knowing God. We only trust deeply when we know someone deeply. We must spend time with them. God waits for us to invite Him into our lives, to discover who He is to us, to know His promises that are always 'Yes' and 'Amen'

"For all the promises of God find their Yes in him. That is why it is through him that we utter our Amen to God for his glory." -2 Corinthians 1:20

Do you long to know God more deeply? How unfathomable that the one true God has so many names–each revealing who He is to you. When you don't know how to pray, call out and praise Him for who He is in the middle of the pain. Ask the Holy Spirit to engrave these names on your heart. As these names take root in there, they become both life-changing and life-giving. The tempter flees in the presence of God's names.

There are many books and studies on the names of God. Let our prayer below be filled with a few–for, oh hallelujah, there is power in His Name!

Prayer

Dear God, Thank You for revealing who You are through Your many names. I ask to know You in a deeper way through these attributes. I praise You that You are El Elyon – God Most High (Genesis 14:17-20). You are El Roi – The God Who Sees Me (Genesis 16:7-16). You are Yahweh Shalom – The Lord is Peace (Judges 6:22-24). And You are Yahweh Nissi – The Lord My Banner (Exodus 17:8-16).

January 9

God as Our GPS By Melissa Lindsey
Today's Scripture: John 10:27

My daughter recently moved from Massachusetts to Colorado. The distance is over two thousand miles. She crossed flat plains and mountainous terrain. She endured pouring rain and scorching heat. There were a few areas with no cell reception at all.

We are fearless about traveling these days. Punch the address into our GPS and go! It's liberating. We have the security of "the voice" telling us where to turn or if there's a detour ahead.

Life is often like travel. We aren't sure of what lies ahead. We can encounter twists and turns, which can be overwhelming. We may find ourselves facing uncertainties and not knowing what decision to make. In these moments, knowing God's voice provides us with direction and offers comfort and reassurance.

Even the most advanced GPS cannot match our guidance from God. Unlike electronics that can lose signal on remote roads, God's direction is always accessible. His voice stays constant, whether we're exploring new places or pausing at a crossroads, unsure which way to turn. The real issue isn't the signal's reliability—it's our willingness to listen, to slow down, and to tune our hearts so we don't miss a single word or gentle nudge.

In John 10:27, we are encouraged to listen for His voice and follow Him. Sheep recognize their shepherd's voice and can distinguish it from other sounds. For sheep, this comes naturally, but for us, it requires intentional effort. If you're not used to listening for God's voice or are still building trust in what comes from Him, be patient with yourself. Keep reading scripture. Pray. Reflect on whether your feelings bring you peace or anxiety. While God may prompt us to step outside our comfort zone, His guidance should always reflect His written word and ultimately lead to lasting peace.

Prayer

Dear Lord,
Thank you for the gift of your voice. You love us and want the best for us. Please help us seek your guidance in every part of our lives. Help us recognize your voice as sheep recognize their shepherd and follow the right path. May we move forward confidently, shining our light and encouraging others to do the same.

January 10

Abiding in Jesus
By Sabrina French
Today's Scripture: John 15:1-17; Psalm 91; Galatians 5:16-26; Matthew 13:1-9, 18-23

A few years ago, I purchased a snap pea kit. I didn't know at the time that snap peas were vines. As my snap peas started to grow, it didn't take long for me to learn I needed to support them. I set out to create a trellis out of skewers and twine, and I was thrilled to watch as the vines began to flourish.

Diligently, I cared for it, providing sufficient sunlight and only watering it when the top of the soil was dry. Carefully, I clipped yellow and dead leaves to prevent disease, help it breathe better, and ensure its efforts were put into pod production rather than keeping fading leaves alive. It was my joy to tend to it. In the tending of my little plant, my heart was full of hope for its continued growth and hope for it to nourish my family.

Likewise, it is our Father's joy to tend and care for you so you can produce fruit that nourishes His family, the Body of Christ. But for Him to tend to you, you must abide in His Son, Jesus, the true vine and our first love. Abiding in Jesus is ongoing. All day. Everyday. A branch cannot grow apart from the vine, and neither can you.

When you abide in the Vine, the Father knows how to tend to you, and better than I did my snap peas. He knows the proper season in which you will produce the most fruit, when you need extra support, how much sunlight and water you need, and when to prune you so you don't get sick. As you abide in Him, there is fullness of joy and hope against hope.

Prayer

Father, teach me to abide daily in your Son, Jesus. Restore first love in my life. I yield myself to being tended by you, Father. May the seed of your Word planted inside me grow. Prune what needs to be pruned in my life so I can bear the fruit of your Spirit. Amen.

January 11

The God of the Eleventh Hour
By Shannon Floyd
Today's Scripture: Isaiah 60:22

It was almost 11 p.m. on December 30th when my phone lit up: "The basement is ready. You can move in tomorrow morning." I had been packing to leave my Airbnb the next morning, with nowhere to go. Every door had closed, but I knew God would make a way somehow.

Just ten days earlier, my hosts had offered their downstairs apartment. The tenants had moved out unexpectedly three days before Christmas. It needed renovations. With the holidays in full swing, finishing it in time seemed impossible.

But then the message came. The basement was ready early! God had shown up in the 11th hour.

Have you ever felt like time was running out, a prayer answer wasn't coming, and hope was growing dim? Let me remind you, the eleventh hour is God's specialty.

Scripture is full of last-minute rescues and divine interventions at the brink of despair: the Red Sea didn't part until Israel was trapped between Pharoah's army and the water (Exodus 14:21-22), Lazarus wasn't raised until death had fully settled in for four days (John 11:38-44), and the thief on the cross found salvation in his final breath (Luke 23:39-43).

God often chooses to move in the 11th hour. Not because He's late, but because He's intentional. The 11th hour strips away our self-reliance. It stretches our faith and deepens our trust. It's where miracles are unmistakable and testimonies are born. God delights in showing His power when hope seems lost, so that no one can boast, and all can marvel.

If you're in that hour - waiting, weary, wondering - don't give up. Keep praying. Keep believing. Keep standing. He is the God of the eleventh hour.

Prayer

Lord, I trust You even when the clock is ticking and the pressure is rising. I believe You are the God of the eleventh hour, so I will wait with a heart full of expectation—even if the hour may be late.

January 12

An Escape Plan
By Terrie Stevens
Today's Scripture: Luke 15:20

I had screwed up my life – broken all that was good. I had failed in my marriage and chased away my friends. And just this week, I lost a job I loved.

Everything was gone.

Now, sitting in the back corner of the sanctuary, I perched cautiously on the edge of a hardwood pew – chosen for its proximity to the exit, just in case I needed an escape. The wood beneath me stirred memories of childhood Sundays – similar pews, but usually closer to the altar, when I'd sit eagerly, waiting to hear stories and songs about a loving God.

But time had passed. I had chosen a path that led away from Him, determined to live by my own rules.

And yet... something told me it wasn't working. I was a terrible guide in my own life.

The choir sang as people moved through the sanctuary, greeting one another with warmth. Their faces glowed with peace – something I couldn't remember feeling.

An older man stopped beside me. "Can I pray with you?" he asked, voice shaking with age. I nodded. He took my hands in his.

I don't remember his words. But calm and security wrapped around me like a grandmother's quilt. The troubles still haunted me, but the grip they held began to loosen. Tears welled up, but I smiled. He squeezed my hands gently before walking away.

That day, God welcomed me home. He didn't list my failures. He didn't shame me. He just wanted me back. Like the prodigal son, God fetched the fatted calf and laid before me a feast of forgiveness and redemption.

Prayer

Dear Jesus,
Thank You for Your constant love and devotion, even when we run from it.
Thank You for the patience it takes to welcome us back into Your loving embrace when we have strayed.
Please help us to remain warm and safe in Your arms.

January 13

Biblical Friendship
By Wendy Cookson
Today's Scripture: Hebrews 10:24-25

My mom met her dearest friend in 1962. Margaret moved in next door with two little girls, the same ages as my sister and me. At the time, Margaret was expecting baby number three. What began as a simple invitation to come over for coffee grew into a daily tradition. Their friendship endured for 50 years, until Margaret passed away to be with the Lord in 2014.

It wasn't until I became an adult that I realized the impact of Godly relationships. I often wonder if my mother and Margaret knew they were living out the biblical principles of friendship. Their bond reflected loyalty, honesty, kindness, forgiveness, sacrifice, and accountability—qualities exemplified in Scripture through examples such as Naomi and Ruth, David and Jonathan, or Shadrach, Meshach, and Abednego. Each of these friendships was brought together by God for His glory.

Do you have that friend who will lift you up in a crisis? Who holds you accountable with love and forgiveness? Who helps restore you with compassion and strength? Who celebrates your successes and is never jealous? That kind of friend is a treasure.

If God has sent someone like this into your life—the one who brings peace, love, joy, patience, kindness, and faithfulness—you are truly blessed. And if you do not yet have such a friend, I encourage you to pray and ask God to send one to you. James 4:2 reminds us, "You do not have, because you do not ask."

My mom developed Alzheimer's and, in the end, did not know most of us. Yet she always remembered her dear friend. On the second Friday in January, exactly three years after Margaret went home to the Lord, my mom joined her friend in heaven.

Prayer

Heavenly Father, Thank You for the blessing of true friendship. Teach us to love well, forgive freely, and encourage faithfully. Help us reflect Your heart in every relationship and surround us with friends who draw us closer to You. May our lives honor You as we carry one another's burdens with grace and joy.

January 14

The Blessing of Overflow
By Elizabeth Clark
Today's Scripture: Matthew 14:20

When faced with difficulty, we often focus on our limitations. We see the five loaves and two fish and feel overwhelmed by the needs around us. This passage from Matthew 14 teaches us that what we offer to the Lord, no matter how small, becomes a source of limitless provision in His hands.

The story of the feeding of the 5,000 shows us that God is more than enough. He is not limited by our circumstances or what we have to offer. The blessing is always greater than the offering, and the surplus is greater than the need. The twelve baskets of leftovers show that Christ is inexhaustible and that His blessing is an abundant overflow.

I was in a season of emotional and spiritual exhaustion when the needs of others felt overwhelming, and I felt I only had five loaves and two fish to offer. I was reminded to offer what I had, no matter how small. I prayed, "Lord, I give You my brokenness and my little bit of strength. Use it." And He did. My small offering met the needs of others and brought satisfaction to my own soul, with a surplus remaining.

Don't be discouraged by the smallness of your offering or the magnitude of your needs. Your Heavenly Father knows your needs and can meet them, even in a desert place. The key is to offer what you have to Him. Let Him break it and watch as He multiplies it. Live with the courageous faith of one who knows the Author of life is also the God of more than enough.

In your life today, what are the 'five loaves and two fish' that you feel you have to offer? What needs in your life or in others' lives are you anxious about?

Prayer

Lord Jesus, we thank You for being our life supply and for Your unlimited provision. We confess our anxiety and lack of trust in Your ability to meet our needs. We offer what we have to You, however small, and ask You to multiply it, that we may be satisfied and live in the reality of Your abundant overflow.

January 15

In the Waiting
By Tyann Beenken
Today's Scripture: Psalm 37:4-5

Like many young girls, I dreamed of the day I would get married. I imagined the dress, the flowers, and the music. As I grew older, the dreams changed slightly, but the desire remained. Deep in my heart, I wanted to get married and have a family, but it did not happen when I thought it would. I waited for a while, and waiting for something you want is hard.

I waited through college, graduate school, and beyond. During those seven-plus years, I participated in many weddings, but none of them were mine. There were times during that season of singleness when I became discouraged, wondering if God would ever answer my prayer. I remember journaling out my frustrations one time and hearing God whisper to my heart, "Do not look for someone else to fulfill these desires...seek Me—be filled by Me—be complete in My Perfect Love."

In Psalm 37:4-5, David tells us to delight in the Lord. To "delight" in something means to take pleasure in or enjoy it. David also tells us to commit our ways to God and to trust Him to act. How often do we find ourselves wishing for the next season, pursuing the next dream, trying to make things happen in our own strength, while neglecting to delight ourselves in the One who gave us the dream?

Do you find yourself in a season of waiting? Trust God, surrender your dreams to Him, and watch expectantly for Him to move. While you wait, delight yourself in the Lord. As we spend time in His presence, our hearts begin to look like His, and when our desires align with His, He takes great pleasure in giving His children the desires of our hearts.

Prayer

Abba Father, You are a good Father who gives good gifts, but the gifts will not satisfy the deepest longings of my heart. Help me to seek You first, above all things. Help me find my greatest joy in Your presence and to trust You to fulfill the desires of my heart in Your perfect time.

January 16

Learning to Pray Small
By Carla Herndobler
Today's Scripture: 1 Peter 5:7

Are you ever hesitant to pray about small problems because you don't want to "bother" God? I have to answer that question with an embarrassed, yet convicted, "yes." I don't always pray over little things like the keys I've misplaced (again), the sore throat that threatens to keep me away from a celebration in my preschool classroom, or the special meal I've been asked to cook for a family gathering. Those things seem trivial in light of all that's going on in the world, but I end up worried and frustrated trying to handle it all on my own.

At times like that, God is gracious, whispering the words of 1 Peter 5:7 to my soul, calling me to cast all my anxieties on Him. He draws me to Himself, reminding me that I am so precious to Him that He has even numbered the hairs on my head (Luke 12:7)! A love like that--a love that sent His Son to the cross for me is solid assurance that He cares about even the slightest worries of my life. And often He also gives grace to see how He makes a way when the keys remain lost, a sore throat morphs into the flu, and even when the meal is a flop.

I'm learning that small prayers about small worries exercise my faith muscle and wire my brain for deeper trust in the Lord for all things. It's a practice of dependence on an omnipotent God who tends to overwhelming burdens as well as little bumps in the road. His answers for small asks stand alongside His help with heavier burdens as signposts in my faith journey, pointing to the One who is ever faithful in every circumstance.

Prayer

Dearest Lord, Your word assures me that you are a good and loving father who calls me to lay all of my burdens, no matter the size, at your feet. Please help me to remember your faithfulness and to trust you with everything. Thank you.

January 17

Unashamed
By James Hatcher
Today's Scripture: Romans 1:16

Let's be honest, the world wants to make living like a Christian not seem just "un-cool," but worse. This world praises popularity, self-expression, and tolerance of everything but absolute truth; following Jesus is and always will be swimming upstream. People will call you judgmental, weird, boring, old-fashioned, or, in today's world, unaccepting.

When we are ridiculed, excluded, and misrepresented, we turn to the encouraging words of Paul. Even as he was facing these same problems himself, Paul writes in Romans 1:16, "I am not ashamed of the gospel..."

Why should we not be ashamed of the Gospel? Because it's not just a belief system, it's the testimony of God's love. The Gospel isn't confined just to a church service; it's the eternal rescue message. Paul didn't wear it just as a label. He gave us an example of how to incorporate scripture and its loving message into our whole lives.

When doubt and trials come, we are to remember the Gospel means we've been forgiven, loved, and saved, and there's nothing shameful about that. But the world doesn't always see it that way. Jesus actually warned us this would happen.

"If the world hates you, know that it has hated me before it hated you."
-John 15:18

So, if people look down on you for your faith, remember that you're in good company. We, in Christ's righteousness, are not to be loud, rude, or aggressive in our testimony.

But we do have to be brave.
Brave enough to be kind when others mock.
Brave enough to say no when others say everyone is doing it.
Brave enough to live unashamed, in the life Christ set us apart for.

Remember, you're walking the same road Jesus did, and He never let the crowd define Him.

Prayer

God, give me courage to live unashamed. Help me have the humility to live in the midst of persecution. Give me confidence in who You are and who I am in You. Lord, use my life as proof of Your love, even when the world doesn't understand it.

January 18

Hope Beyond Tears
By Mary Grace Johnson
Today's Scripture: 2 Corinthians 5:8-9

My sister Jeanne was a wonder. As the eldest of 5, she carried a motherly strength, especially after our daddy died when she was just 14. Organized, competent, and intelligent, she also had a joy that spilled from uncontrollable giggles to tears of joy.

When Jeanne was diagnosed with breast cancer in 2003 at the age of 46, she faced it with courage. Later, Stage-4 ovarian cancer was discovered; yet, even through exhausting treatments, she showed grace. Her selflessness gave us more than inspiration—she gave us a future. After expensive genetic testing, she was found to have the BRCA-1 gene mutation. Because of her sacrifice, several family members, including me, were tested and took preventative measures that likely saved our lives.

When she had to stop working, Jeanne felt she had lost her identity. Yet her worth was never in what she did. It was in whom God made her to be. When the doctor told her she had only weeks left, our hearts broke. That Christmas, we laughed and reminisced as a family, treasuring memorable conversations. In January 2009, Jeanne entered hospice. Surrounded by loved ones, she passed peacefully into the presence of Jesus at age 51.

Jeanne's life reminds us that identity is not found in work but in Christ. She lived with courage through suffering, and though death came too soon, it did not have the final word. Because of Jesus, she stepped from pain into His eternal presence. For those of us left behind, God promises His nearness and comfort when grief feels unbearable.

Prayer

Lord, thank You for the gift of loved ones and the memories that remain. When grief feels heavy, remind us You are near to the brokenhearted, and in Christ, we have eternal hope.

January 19

The Escape Plan
By Richard Dubay Jr.
Today's Scripture: 1 Corinthians 10:13

We've all heard it before—the well-meaning reassurance: "God will never give you more than you can handle." These words are often offered in times of struggle, meant to comfort and inspire hope. But what if everything you've believed about that statement is a lie?

Today's scripture has got to be one of the most misquoted verses ever. Still, it's easy to see where the misunderstanding comes from. 1 Corinthians 10:13 says, "God is faithful, and he will not let you be tempted beyond your ability..." Taken at face value, it would seem that Paul is actually saying that God won't give us more than we can handle.

Except that isn't what he's saying at all.

Paul isn't saying that God won't give us anything we can't handle. The verse specifically addresses temptation. It says that He won't allow us to be tempted beyond what we are able. We also tend to forget that there is a comma in that sentence and skip the last part of the verse. 1 Corinthians 10:13 continues, "...but with the temptation he will also provide the way of escape, that you may be able to endure it."

This last part is crucial: the "that" changes everything.

On our own, the temptation we face is going to be too much for us. God can and will give us more than we can handle. But how good is our God that, in our temptation, God will provide a way for us so that we can bear it. With Him, we can handle whatever comes our way.

Prayer

God, thank You that when we are at our weakest, You are most strong. Thank You for providing a way for us when we can't see a way. Thank You for taking our heavy things and making them an easy yoke and a light burden. You are so good.

January 20

Radical Generosity
By Mary Thissen
Today's Scripture: Proverbs 19:17

Throughout my teenage years, my relationship with my maternal grandmother was complicated, primarily due to my being a hormonal tween and teenage girl. My attitude toward her was one of disdain. Though looking back on it now, it doesn't make much sense. I felt that my paternal grandmother and I had a closer relationship because we shared a more similar personality.

As I grew up, I became less irritable in my relationship with her, and I realized the multitude of gifts she had and the lessons her life taught me. The lesson that sticks with me most is that she was radically generous, even in a world that had not been good to her.

My grandmother never knew a stranger and was able to engage anyone in conversation. Our holidays at her table were filled with friends who would otherwise have spent the day alone. As a five-year-old, I witnessed her give her last cash to a hungry, homeless person.

At the time, I couldn't understand the impact of this generosity. Later in life, I came to know the extent of her suffering. Abused and with no other choice, she filed for divorce, only for life to become troublesome in keeping a roof over her and her children's heads and making a living. The events I had witnessed as a young child made a great deal more sense to me all those years later.

Now, in my own life, I ask myself how I can be more generous to those God surrounds me with, even when I feel I don't have much to give. I thank God for all I have and ask how he wants me to show the radical generosity that my grandmother's example may continue to radiate God's love in the world.

Prayer

Lord, please reveal to me the people in my life who need to know your love through radical generosity. May my words and actions be a blessing to them. Teach me to give radically to the point of sacrifice, as your Son did on Calvary.

January 21

Gathering Fruit: Love (Agape in Greek)
By Gerald L. Chafin
Today's Scripture: Galatians 5:22-23; 1 Corinthians 13; Mark 12:29-31

First Corinthians 13 is an excellent place to begin contemplating the Holy Spirit's fruit of love. It's certainly well-known that this is referred to as The Love Chapter in Scripture. I've often read this chapter for numerous wedding ceremonies. (And, here's a quick 'note' of information: A musical setting of The Love Chapter was sung for Sonja and me at our wedding ceremony. I can still hear the music in my mind as we celebrate our 40th anniversary this year!)

Beginning in verse four, there are sixteen characteristics of love mentioned in most translations. A shocking item, definitely for me, reveals that the number of "love is not" statements is more than the number of "love is" statements! (I made a chart in a journal using several translations just to follow all the references.)

And, in addition, if you go back and study the first three opening verses of First Corinthians 13, there are three instances of the phrase "but have not love...." Yikes! Maybe we should begin to be hyper-aware of what aspects of love we are not doing well in our lives, so that we can learn to become more loving!

Here's an idea for us to consider in seeking to gather the fruit of love in our lives: Begin exercising toward the elimination of what love is not. This will undoubtedly be an exercise that's not easy! In addition, as we study the descriptions of what love is not, note which items in the list are internal, affecting our personal lives, and which items are external, affecting others.

Jesus, in Mark 12:31, combines the love of one's neighbor with the love of oneself. That's certainly an interesting connection to the internal and external items in First Corinthians 13. Maybe a "what-not-to-do" list could help us better love ourselves and our neighbors?!!

Prayer

Lord, help me to love You with all my heart, soul, mind, and strength. Please grant me Your grace and mercy to love my neighbor and myself.

January 22

Gathering Fruit: Joy (Chara in Greek)
By Gerald L. Chafin
Today's Scripture: Galatians 5:22-23; Nehemiah 8:10; Isaiah 12:2-3; 51:11; 55:12; Luke 15:1-10; James 1:2-3

Can you fill in the blanks to these songs?
"I've got the _____, _____, _____, _____ down in my heart! Where?"
Or,
"_____ to the world, the Lord is come."
Or,
"The _____ of the Lord is my _____."

Excellent, dear friends! Thank you for sharing today's dive into the fruit of joy! That fill-in-the-blanks exercise should easily cover our understanding of the second fruit of the Spirit. Have a great day, everyone! ... Okay, hold on! It's not exactly that simple or easy! Actually, in all honesty, joy is the fruit of the Spirit that is the most complicated for me. To be fully confessional, joy is probably the fruit of the Spirit that I personally struggle with the most and (...gulp) find most difficult to live.

Seems strange, doesn't it? Joy should easily be a cake-walk! Yet, I'm reminded of a statement that goes something along these lines: "Happiness depends upon what happens around us." Thus, happiness is an outer experience. Joy and happiness are not the same qualities! Here's where things become really obvious - joy, as a fruit of the Holy Spirit, is an inner quality that can radiate outwardly.

Therefore, and this is a crazy take-away: When things are spinning out of control around you, like in the passages listed from Luke 15, allow the fruit of joy, which comes through the Holy Spirit from within, to bring calm and joy and guide your life!

Prayer

Lord, help me to resonate Your joy. Joy that You have placed inside me. May Your joy within me become my strength, no matter what I'm dealing with in any circumstance. Help me to share Your joy with others, especially when they are facing difficult circumstances.

January 23

Gathering Fruit: Peace (Eirene in Greek)
By Gerald L. Chafin
Today's Scripture: Galatians 5:22-23; Psalm 34:14; Isaiah 26:3; Isaiah 26:12; Philippians 4:6-7; Matthew 11:28-30

Peace. God's perfect peace.

To be completely honest with you, peace is the fruit of the Holy Spirit that I need - and desire - most in my life. There are undoubtedly numerous reasons. I'm sure I've been going too fast and too hard at things for too long. And because I'm a hyper-creative-type personality, I do tend to live in a unique "world-of-my-own." (Which is definitely something people who know me would easily confirm.)

Isn't it interesting that Philippians 4:6-7 contrasts worrying, or being anxious, with peace? That's quite the pendulum swing, isn't it? But that's what can happen when we work at leaning into God's perfect peace. That's when peace creates a sacred space for our lives.

For me, peace begins to rest within me when I find a sacred space. Sometimes that's an early morning walk near a lake or listening to the sound of a stream of water as it passes over rocks. I sense God's peace when my wife and I stand quietly, gaze into the night sky. and marvel at the Lord's intricate creation.

A final thought to enter a space of peace: The word "rest" has connected me to the fruit of the Spirit's peace. As you read the Scriptures listed above for today's devotion, linger with Matthew 11:28-30. Notice how Jesus uses the word "rest." That is indeed where we can find a sacred space for our souls to breathe.

Prayer

Lord, my greatest desire is Your perfect peace. Help me to keep my mind on You. To trust in You with all my heart - not leaning or relying on my own understanding. In all my ways help me to acknowledge, recognize, and know You, so that You direct my path.

January 24

Gathering Fruit: Patience (Makrothumia in Greek)
By Gerald L. Chafin
Today's Scripture: Galatians 5:22-23;
Isaiah 26:8; Genesis 8:1-17

Patience is listed as the fourth fruit of the Spirit. Therefore, here is a good moment in our journey to share that the nine fruits of the Spirit are sometimes thought of - or divided - into three groups or areas. Thus, there are three fruits for each grouping. The method is sometimes thought of in this way: Love, joy, and peace are a direct connection from God to you. "North to South," if you will! From God to the individual.

Patience, kindness, and goodness are connections between ourselves and the people in our lives. "East to West," if you will, connecting to others around us.

Next, faithfulness, gentleness, and self-control are connections explicitly directed to each individual. "Internal" and centering within ourselves.

Now let's take a quick plunge toward the fruit of patience. Indeed, patience often implies waiting. However, consider Isaiah 26:88 and connect it with the narrative of Genesis 8. Noah was, without question, dealing with a lot; so much! Yet... in reading Genesis 8, even though there is no mention of the word patience in the chapter, we can undoubtedly sense that Noah displayed the fruit!

Prayer

Lord, I confess that patience is often not my best quality, especially at the pace at which life often goes. Help me to display patience toward myself and toward others. I pray for calmness within my life that comes directly from the Holy Spirit.

January 25

Gathering Fruit: Kindness (Chrestotes in Greek)
By Gerald L. Chafin
Today's Scripture: Galatians 5:22-23; Proverbs 12:25; Ephesians 4:32; 2 Timothy 2:23-24

We've been enjoying a group Bible study at our home with a bunch of friends. Interestingly (and intentionally!), the writing of these devotionals about the fruits of the Spirit has coincided with our group's several weeks of study and discussion on this amazing topic. (Or should I say "topics" since there are nine fruits of the Spirit. And, remember that three unique categories were described in the section on patience!)

One evening, sitting outside around tables, we handed out notecards. The group was asked to write a statement commenting on any of the fruits of the Spirit that came to their attention. Flipping through the cards, here are three statements from our group that interpreted the fruit of kindness. May these thoughts resonate with us and help us inspire sharing kindness from our lives to others:

Kindness is a selfless act to uplift someone's day! The Lord reminds me daily that kindness has the power to inspire others to be kind. And, third, here's a quote shared by a group member who recalled a statement attributed to Mother Teresa:

Let no one ever come to you without leaving better and happier.
Be the living expression of God's kindness;
Kindness in your face,
Kindness in your eyes,
Kindness in your smile.

Prayer

Lord, create in me a kind heart. Help me in difficult circumstances to be kind to others, and may my kindness be the support they need. I pray that kindness may become a natural part of me and that it be evident to those I encounter.

January 26

Gathering Fruit: Goodness (Agathosune in Greek)
By Gerald L. Chafin
Today's Scripture: Galatians 5:22-23,
Galatians 6:9-10, Luke 19:45-48, Micah 6:8

Goodness. It sounds so, well, good. And, it is. And, personally, I've typically connected goodness and kindness together. It seems that the words 'goodness' and 'kindness' are so similar. And, they are. And yet, there is a startling difference between these words.

The discovery of this startling difference came to me through researching the Greek word for goodness, agathosune. In addition, this is best understood by a comparison with the Greek word for kindness, chrestotes.

Chrestotes helps. Chrestotes (kindness) greatly desires to provide help. Agathosune (goodness) goes further, in a 'good' way - when needed. Agathosune will correct, discipline, and even rebuke! Theologian William Barclay's listing of the fruit of the Spirit guides readers to the role of goodness that Christ provides, as seen in our passage from Luke 19.

Indeed, may this remarkable bundle of patience, kindness, and goodness direct every step in our relationships with the people around us.

Prayer

Lord, Thank You for Your goodness. I want to pray this very sincerely: Thank You for Your goodness! And, therefore, I most sincerely ask that You would provide agathosune toward me when You know I need correction and redirection. May Your good and gracious Spirit always direct my life in the way I should go.

January 27

Gathering Fruit: Faithfulness (Pistis in Greek)
By Gerald L. Chafin
Today's Scripture: Galatians 5:22-23,
Psalm 119:30, Proverbs 17:17, Romans 12:9-18

We are now entering the homestretch, the third category, which is about the fruit of the Spirit. It was back in the devotional about the fruit of patience where a telescope view of the fruit of the Spirit was provided. To review: 1.) the first three fruits are from the Lord to the individual, 2.) the next three fruits connect us with others. Now we begin our microscope study of faithfulness, gentleness, and self-control. A focus on these fruits of the Spirit becomes very personal. The focus is internal; within ourselves.

The Greek word for faithfulness is pistis, which means trustworthy and reliable. And, in all honesty, I am not always trustworthy or reliable. We know that God is! The absolutely beautiful phrases in Lamentations 3 share that His mercies/compassions never fail and great is His faithfulness. And, of course, this Scripture reference serves as a reminder of the beautiful hymn "Great Is Thy Faithfulness." Yes, God is indeed so very faithful to us. And now comes the tough, internal question: How faithful are we to God, to others, and to ourselves?

Yes, that's a huge question! As we read the Romans 12:9-18 passage, let's be honest and consider how faithful we are in all the areas listed in the passage. (And there are a lot listed!)

Going back to our home Bible study gathering that was first mentioned in the fruit of kindness, here's a statement that was shared on one of the notecards:
Faithfulness is the biggest test in human life, but it always reaps the greatest rewards.

Prayer

God, this is a unique prayer and a huge request. Help me to internalize faithfulness. Help me live a life of faithfulness to You, to others, and, yes, to myself.

January 28

Gathering Fruit: Gentleness (Praotes in Greek)
By Gerald L. Chafin
Today's Scripture: Galatians 5:22-23,
1 Kings 19:11-16, Philippians 4:5, 1 Peter 3:15

My wife Sonja and I thoroughly enjoy and absolutely love visiting "The Low Country!" For those not familiar with that phrase, it's in South Carolina. We especially enjoy visiting all the various places in and around the Charleston area.

Lots of things resonate with me every time we go. I am uplifted to linger near and gaze at the ocean, as well as the opportunity to do a walk/run across the iconic Ravenel Bridge. It would be easy to keep listing unforgettable moments and places. Yet there's one 'tree'mendous place in particular where we have visited that I have to share with you.

Called The Angel Oak, it is a Live Oak Tree (Quercus Virginiana species, be impressed!) that is located on Johns Island just south of Charleston.

Why share this with you? Because, without question, the fruit of gentleness is the total and absolute vibe that I sense every time I walk around this tree. By the way, the tree is incredibly huge! The limbs stretch far out. And here's the amazing takeaway: This tree resonates with gentleness! It has a calmness that echoes the phrase "a low whisper" that we read about in 1 Kings 19:12.

Prayer

Lord, may gentleness resonate within me. Indeed, may the gentleness that resides within me literally branch out and extend into the way that I live and be a blessing, a gentle whisper, to others.

January 29

Gathering Fruit: Self-Control (Egkrateia in Greek)
By Gerald L. Chafin
Today's Scripture: Galatians 5:22-23, Matthew 7:24-27, Romans 8:5-11

It really was a situation without self-control. My wife Sonja and I went to a restaurant for dinner. It was a completely fantastic meal. Definitely enough to eat. Then, as we were leaving, I glanced over toward the counter, and there it was. A magnificent display - an artistic display, actually - of brownies and cupcakes! Yes, it's true...I was absolutely compelled to purchase a brownie to take home. (Side note, after we arrived home, I measured the brownie. It was a perfect square, 4x4. And, yes, that's a large brownie.)

Indeed, self-control is a very internal matter. About food, that is certainly one aspect that counts as an issue for self-control. But there are many, many more. YET, (notice the massive emphasis here: all caps, italicized, and underlined) there are definitely considerable areas of life in which self-control matters hugely and impacts our relationship with ourselves as well as with others! May we allow the Lord to grant us a hyper-awareness of these areas, and may we invest ourselves daily in the practice of self-control.

Thus, the question that naturally arises from the fruit of self-control is this: In what areas of my life do I need to be more vigilant in the practice of self-control? As a grand finale to these nine devotions of walking through the garden of God's gift in the fruits of His Spirit, let us graciously receive James 1:21b as our prayer.

Prayer

Lord, help me to "receive with meekness the implanted word" (James 1:21b) for it truly has the power to save our souls.

January 30

The Best Father in the World
By Tara Brueske
Today's Scripture: 1 John 3:1

God calls Himself Father. Do you ever think about what characteristics a good father has? Features like trustworthy, good, compassionate, slow to anger, a provider, a protector, generous, and one who loves me.

I grew up a pastor's daughter, and as a small child, I felt loved by my dad. But as I grew older and the demands of the church pulled him there, I noticed his absence at home and didn't feel close to him.

I now realize that my view of my father began to shape my view of my Heavenly Father. Though I sought God by reading His word and praying, I'm not sure I understood that He loved being with me.

When I was 21 years old, I went to Last Days Ministries. It was a Christian retreat where we learned to know God intimately. And it was where my heart was awakened to see the beautiful, fatherly traits of God.

While there, I searched the scriptures and found SO MANY verses that show God's character. Features like compassion (Psalm 103:13), slow to anger (Nahum 1:3), a provider (Psalm 23:1), and good (Psalm 31:19).

And...this God called Himself my Father and claimed me as His child. So, though my earthly father didn't have all of these traits, my Heavenly Father did! I could look to Him for the things I thought were lacking from my earthly dad.

The best part was realizing that as His child, I could go to Him for everything. Little children who are loved know that they can run to their daddy at any moment. They feel safe, protected, delighted in, and special! We can be the same with our heavenly Papa.

Today, may you know that what you long for in a father is completely found in God!

Prayer

Papa, You said that I am Your dearly loved child. Open my eyes to see Your true character—that what You've planned for me is from a very good, perfect Father's heart. You are my hope, Lord! I rest today knowing you're my daddy who loves me tenderly and that I can always run into your lap.

January 31

You Can't Live for Both
By James Hatcher
Today's Scripture: James 4:4

You can't chase two things at once, just as you can't face two directions. You can't run after Christ and run after the world. James doesn't soften it. He says it plainly:

"Therefore whoever wishes to be a friend of the world makes himself an enemy of God." - James 4:4

That sounds harsh, but James knows it's not about God rejecting you. It's about you choosing where your loyalty lies.

This verse isn't saying you can't enjoy life. It doesn't mean you should avoid people who don't follow Jesus. It's about your deepest allegiance. Where is your true home?

The world wants you to follow your feelings, not your faith, or choose popularity over purpose, or worse, build an image, not a character. However, Christ calls you to deny yourself, not define yourself. Christ wants us to serve, not perform, so that we can live set apart, not blend in with the world. You get to choose: do you want to look great in the world's eyes? Or be great in God's?

James is challenging us to ask ourselves hard questions. Where am I being pulled to "fit in" instead of standing out for Christ? Have I tried to make peace with a world that doesn't care about God? Do I care more about being liked…or being loyal?

As believers in Christ, we need to be on our knees, asking ourselves these things, and letting the Holy Spirit challenge our flesh so that we may be renewed in the grace that Christ's sacrifice has given us.

Prayer

God, I don't want to chase the kind of greatness that fades. I want to pursue the things that proclaim the greatness of your testimony
Help me not to blend in when You've called me to stand out.
Give me the courage to say no to what distracts me,
and the strength to say yes to You, every time.

February

February 1

A Legacy Heart Remembers With Gratitude
By Gwen Christeson
Today's Scripture: Hebrews 6:10

Today, February 1st, is a significant day in my legacy story. A legacy heart remembers all God has done with gratitude. I celebrate this day with gratitude; it is the day I opened my law office. I have not always celebrated this special day.

Just before my 15th anniversary, three people within one week told me how well I was doing as a new business. As I told them I had been in business for almost 15 years, I realized my anniversary was quickly approaching. It was time to celebrate this important milestone. A press release ran in our local paper, "Jackson Attorney Celebrates her 15 Year Anniversary."

When my 20th anniversary approached, I hired a business strategy coach. When I shared about my passion for legacy, she was the person God used to tell me, "You should write a book." She also told me she would not buy a book written by an attorney about estate planning. Her honesty forced me to write the legacy book God wanted me to write, teaching my readers how to leave a legacy gift of love, faith, hope, and gratitude.

I remember with gratitude all God has done in my life and business. When I rented my first office, I was pregnant with my son. My son will soon join me as a licensed attorney. I rejoice in the plan God has had for my business, as he joins me to continue helping God's people with financial stewardship by crafting their own legacies through estate planning.

Do you have a significant day you need to acknowledge and thank God for? God has plans for your life and a purpose for your legacy. When you take time to reflect and remember with gratitude all that God has done, He will give you a heart for legacy.

Prayer

You gave each one of us unique personalities and talents to qualify us to do the life's work You created us to do. We are grateful for Your plans for our lives and purpose for our legacies. Help us remember with gratitude what we've seen and heard, and what you've done for us, so we can remember your good works.

February 2

Enlargement: Make Room for Growth
By Dr. Jasmine Rosetta Gordon
Today's Scripture: 1 Chronicles 4:10

For your spiritual, professional, personal, and social life to experience enlargement, you must first make preparation. If you want to enlarge your ministry or business, you must be willing to prepare. To hold an increase, you must prepare for it.

How? You must strengthen your foundations, including your character, prayer life, relationships, and your stewardship. To prepare for enlargement requires faith. This faith prepares in expectation, not in reaction.
Noah built an ark before a drop of rain fell. Abraham walked into a land he did not know. The widow gathered jars before the oil started to flow. Enlargement begins before the increase arrives. You must sow before you reap.

When you step into enlargement, you step into greater influence, fruitfulness, and legacy. God's enlargement is never just for you. It is for others. He blesses you to be a blessing.

Enlarged vision produces impact. Enlarged faith inspires generations. Enlarged capacity allows you to carry more of God's purpose.

Think of Jabez, who prayed, "Oh that you would bless me and enlarge my border," (1 Chronicles 4:10). God granted his request, not just to give him more land, but to expand his influence and legacy. Pray bigger prayers. Ask God for more than what feels possible. Invest in your growth. Read, learn, and seek mentorship that stretches you. Build habits of prayer and discipline. Prepare for capacity. Make room for an increase.

God's enlargement does not always look like instant promotion. It often feels like a season of stretching, pruning, and preparation. Be encouraged. If He spoke it, He will perform it. Just as Jabez prayed, you too can boldly ask God to enlarge your territory. Trust God to shape you for the blessing before He releases it.

Prayer

Heavenly Father, help me to see beyond my limitations and trust in Your promises. Stretch my faith, expand my vision, and prepare my heart for what You are bringing into my life. I declare that I will not hold back but will lengthen my patience and strengthen my faith. Lord, fill the space I prepare for Your glory.

February 3

Jesus and Spurs
By Katrina Mintz
Today's Scripture: Hebrews 10:24-25

Love in community isn't always comfortable. Scripture calls us to "stir up one another," but that doesn't mean constant ease. Sometimes encouragement feels like a warm embrace. Other times, it's a nudge—or even a push—toward growth.

In the round pen with a horse, and in life, pressure is a tool. Trainers use the principle of "Air, Hair, Skin, Muscle"—starting with the lightest cue and increasing only as needed. The goal isn't punishment—it's communication. The same applies to our words and actions. When used with wisdom, pressure becomes guidance.

Jesus didn't wear spurs, but He did challenge, correct, and call people forward. He knew when to speak gently and when to flip tables. That's the tension we're invited into: grace and accountability, comfort and correction.

Some days, we need soft love. Other days, tough love is the only way forward. Wisdom is knowing which is needed—and having the courage to offer it.

Spurs aren't meant to wound. They're intended to encourage forward motion. In the same way, believers are called to apply the right kind of encouragement—sometimes gentle, sometimes firm—to help one another grow in love and truth.

Hope doesn't always come softly. Sometimes it arrives with grit, with boundaries, with the kind of love that says, "I won't let you stay stuck."

So we spur one another on—not with force, but with faith. Not with fear, but with love.

Prayer

Lord, Teach us to lead with courage and listen with compassion.
Let us offer gentleness when it heals, truth when it strengthens.
May we never confuse comfort with kindness, nor correction with condemnation.
Let us create arenas in life where grace and accountability work in tandem, spurring others forward in love. Keep us humble, empathetic, and bold—tender when needed, firm when called.

February 4

Unlimited Cake
By Amy Leigh Hughes
Today's Scripture: Matthew 7:9-11

How often do you go to God first with your thoughts, cares, and desires, instead of using him as a last resort to get what you want? We expect him to just immediately grant our every wish, and then get angry with him when it doesn't go our way, as if not giving us what we wanted means he doesn't love us.

If my toddler had all the cake he wanted, he would get very sick. His body would not have the necessary nutrients to grow and thrive. I know better than he does, so I don't give him unlimited cake (even though he cries as though the world is ending). How much more we can trust in the infinite wisdom of a God who knows everything!

God could just give us whatever we need all the time. Instead, he invites us into the process. He wants us to ask, tell, praise, and be in his presence. He allows us to feel our need for Him, so that we may be comforted with the only true comfort that comes from Him alone. He whispers to our hearts that he sees us, he knows us deeply, and he cares for us. Then he gives us what we truly need, even if we can't understand it yet.

The Holy Spirit is always interceding for us– even when we forget to ask. He takes our imperfect prayers and the deep groanings of our hearts, and presents to God a request that is fully in line with his will. Prayer is interactive between the persons of God. Let it fill you with wonder and awe today that he wants you to be a part of it, and that by his grace, you have unrestricted access to the heavenly throne room!

Prayer

God, help me to continually seek your presence in all that I do, that I would learn to pray without ceasing. Thank you for loving me beyond what I could even imagine. I pray that the desires of my heart would increasingly align with your will as I walk with you each day.

February 5

A Life Surrendered to Jesus
By Michelle Barringer
Today's Scripture: Exodus 15:13

On February 5, 2002, my heart despaired as I searched for truth, understanding, and love. Is divorce the answer?

Hours after I'd left my home and my husband, I walked through a bookstore. I stood by a bookshelf of Bibles. I picked one up. I can't buy this. We don't have enough money right now. A voice whispered, "This may be the best gift you ever buy yourself."

Later, alone in a hotel room, I lay crumpled on the bed, tears streaming from pure agony. That's where God met me and revealed His holiness as never before. In those holy moments, I surrendered my life again to the One who saved me three decades earlier when I was just seven years old.

I surrendered to Jesus again. This time as an adult woman. One who had lived through pain and trials. He helped me see the Truth, and He led me home that night in more ways than one. Just after midnight, as I tucked into my own bed in my home, Jesus whispered, "Welcome Home."

Today, a quarter century since I purchased that gift, I page through my old Bible, smoothing its page corners, gently turning loose pages, and reading the annotations. My soul floods with gratitude. He was right. This is the best gift I've ever bought myself because God Himself has used it to teach, rebuke, correct, and train me in righteousness. Pressing the worn Bible into my chest, I can smell the fragrance of a life changed by its Author.

Are you also searching for truth, understanding, and love?

What will your life (and Bible) look like in 25 years? Will it show evidence of a life redeemed and strengthened by a Holy God? Perhaps it's time to surrender to Jesus and let Him guide you home, too.

Prayer

Father God, redeem and strengthen me. Bring Your Truth, understanding, and love into my soul. Teach, correct, and train me in Your ways. I surrender to You. Save my life, Lord, and may You guide me home to You again.

February 6

Leaving the Pig Pen
By Cynthia Bennett
Today's Scripture: Luke 15:20

My childhood held simple gifts: picnic lunches on a laundered sheet by our farmhouse, brothers racing up from the pond, and warm eggs from the henhouse. Then my dad left. Still, Mom made sure we caught the church bus each week. My faith formed early, drifted in high school, and sat on a shelf in college.

In 1999, the Lord met me in a New York hotel and turned me homeward. Back in Michigan, humbled and searching, a family invited me to church. I heard about knowing Jesus as a friend and Father. His kindness led me to repentance.

After months of wrestling, my 'yes' came. On February 6, I knelt on my living room floor between my cats, Jasmine and Belle, and prayed a prayer. I surrendered to Jesus. Since then, He has met me in laundry piles, long days, and holy moments, teaching me to trust, forgive, and see His goodness.

I'm reminded of the lost son who wasted his inheritance and, when famine hit, ended up feeding pigs, so hungry he longed for carob pods—substitutes sweet enough to distract, never enough to nourish.

I know the pig pen. The place we settle when life hurts. I've had my own pods: hurts, habits, fears, the next thing. Why do we linger here? It's familiar; humility is hard; pain makes us question if God is good. We leave the pen by getting up and following the porch light back to the Father.

God's love keeps inviting me out of the pig pen, away from carob pods that never satisfy, and into the arms of a Father who restores, forgives, and calls me His own.

If your heart feels far, name one carob pod when you're ready. Place it in Jesus' hands and whisper yes to coming home. Begin small. Begin again.

Prayer

Jesus, Thank You for drawing me with kindness and walking with me in ordinary days. Help me lay down carob pods—every substitute—and admit my need for You. Grow mustard-seed faith. Strengthen me to forgive, steady my steps in peace, and anchor my heart in Your Word. Light my yes for Your glory; use it to point weary hearts to You.

February 7

Welcoming Strangers
By Margaret Ellis
Today's Scripture: Hebrews 13:1-2

My earliest memories growing up are of my grandmother living with us, and my mom's brother often staying with us for short periods as he needed. From family and friends to complete strangers, my amazing parents' home was an open door of generosity, compassion, and love.

Between the ages of 10 and 13, we lived in Japan on an Air Force base. I remember one night flying into the base airport and finding a man sleeping on the floor. His flight had been delayed, and he had nowhere else to go. So off he came with us to our very modest apartment on base.

My parents had a way of making everyone feel seen—even strangers. They did the very thing Hebrews 13:1-2 tells us to do. Their faith in God was strong. How are you showing up for the "strangers" in your life?

One of my most memorable experiences occurred when my sister and I were teenagers. My mom frequented a movie rental place called Blockbuster several times a week. While there, she befriended two male employees with distinctive accents. They were on a work exchange from New Zealand. Just before Easter, my mom asked the two young men if they had plans. They did not, so of course, my mom invited them over to our house for Easter dinner. From that brave and generous invitation came a lifelong friendship. One of the young men, now a grown man with teens himself, just visited us for a week. I got to meet his wife and sons.

Their friendship is incredibly special, and it is all because my mom opened her heart and her home to a couple of young men with nowhere to celebrate Jesus' resurrection. What a beautiful picture of Hebrews 13:1-2. In what ways could you show compassion to strangers in your life?

Prayer

Dear God,
Let me not forget that love is often lived out through simple invitations – a place at the table, a space on the floor, a warm conversation. Open my eyes to see those around me who need a touch of Your kindness through me. Let my life reflect Hebrews 13:1-2.

February 8

Close to the Brokenhearted
By Angie Hanson
Today's Scripture: Psalm 34:18

Grief anniversaries have a way of sneaking up on us, even when we see them on the calendar. February 8th holds the weight of two losses in my family – my late husband Jack and my father-in-law. The days leading up to it are often filled with quiet heaviness, and the day itself can feel like the air is too thick to breathe.

It's on days like this that I hold tight to Psalm 34:18. God's Word doesn't say He stands at a distance, waiting for us to get ourselves together. It says He is close. Right here. Present in the quiet moments when words won't come and in the loud sobs when the ache becomes too much.

There were times after Jack's passing when I couldn't imagine how the next day – let alone the next year – would look. But each sunrise brought a small reminder that I wasn't walking this road alone. God's presence didn't take away the pain, but it kept me from being swallowed by it.

If today is a day when loss feels fresh for you, take heart – God is not only aware of your pain, He is with you in it. The same God who holds the universe holds every tear you cry, and He will give you the strength to keep moving forward, even when it feels impossible.

Prayer

Father, Thank You for staying near when my heart feels heavy. Remind me that I'm never alone in my grief. Hold my tears and breathe Your peace into my soul. Give me strength for today and hope for tomorrow, trusting that You will carry me through.

February 9

Hope in Rest
By Ashley Meador Bryan
Today's Scripture: Psalm 121: 3-4; John 1:14

We are stuck in the middle of what I like to call "Winter-Gloom." Even on a sunny day in Charleston, South Carolina, where I call home, Winter can still feel defeating. The days are shorter, there's less sunshine and Vitamin D to soak in, and my medical clinic is chock full of folks who are fighting "gloom" they can't explain.

I'm a special-needs mom and medical provider. Momming this kind of kid means I've lived through my share of trauma. I resonate with the aching in one's heart that is hard to describe, and tossing and turning through the nights. But we cannot leave it at our broken hearts; we must not lose our hope.

God does not need to sleep or slumber. He teaches us to rest, but He does not "need" the rest. His power does not stop when we close our eyes (Psalm 121:3-4). I can sleep because He does not. I can close my eyes even when my workload is too much, even when I've just received bad news, and I can rest at 2 am when all I can think about are really, really hard things. I can sleep because my all-powerful God does not.

I can also sleep because I know God came to earth in the form of Jesus (John 1:14). Knowing what God's word says about Jesus, I understand the Father's character. Who is this all-powerful, never-sleeping God? Is He a God who really cares for me? I know that Jesus was a God-man who was and still is for the broken, for the hurting, for the aching, for the children, for the outcast, for the paralyzed, poor and broken boned.... For you and for me.

Prayer

God, I can't always feel how much you care. Remind me. Give me hope and peace. Let me rest in your greatness and power despite this broken world. Put your truths on repeat in my head and heart as I rest tonight.

February 10

Carrying Legacy, Claiming Victory
By Sharon F. Fleshman
Today's Scripture: 1 Corinthians 15:54-58

In 1956, 21 African-American teachers in Elloree, South Carolina, sat in the conference room and listened. The ultimatum was clear – "Renounce the NAACP or lose your jobs." Given the organization's role in civil rights, the teachers knew what was at stake. The choice for them was clear – they resigned and became known as the Elloree 21. One of those teachers was my mother, Laura Pickett Fleshman. Years later, she would support and advocate for older adults as a social worker. She would demonstrate God's love to me before I fully understood it.

In 2025, I watched my mom tug at her hospital gown like she was trying to pull it off. I did all I could think to do; I prayed for a miracle. My hope was that she would be healed on this side of heaven, but it was not to be. I had little time to sit with my broken heart as I planned my mom's funeral. When I chose 1 Corinthians 15:54-58 as one of the Scriptures to be read, I reflected back on my mom's fidgeting with her gown. Perhaps she was just uncomfortable. But what if she was waiting for her ultimate wardrobe change? I pictured her preparing to wear the imperishable. I imagined that she was ready to put on immortality. While I miss her so much, I remind myself that in Christ, she had victory over death. I rejoice that my mom's labor in the Lord was not in vain.

Today is my mom's birthday. While I grieve her absence, I also celebrate her presence through her legacy of love, justice, and courage. I envision her smiling, making a victory sign with one hand and holding a torch in the other, saying to me, "Take this and run your race."

Prayer

God of Hope, when we wrestle with grief, remind us of the legacy that has been left behind. Strengthen us to move forward with victory, knowing that Jesus has led the way. May Your love, joy, and peace keep us as we trust in You day by day.

February 11

Beloved Surprise
By Kristy Mabe
Today's Scripture: Ecclesiastes 11:5

My husband sat in our bedroom as I entered the bathroom. Minutes later, the test lay on our vanity, and a timer was running. When his phone beeped, I looked. Two clear lines appeared. My emotions seesawing between fear and elation, I announced, "Happy Father's Day! You're going to be a dad."

With ten years pre-wedding, plus two years of medical issues, God's timing had come to fruition. Our family was notified, and we started learning about pregnancy. Though we recognized that only God knew all the details.

After an appointment where our due date was set late, we delighted in learning she adored music, preferred nighttime, and enjoyed jabbing my organs. My baby girl's first flutters occurred on a drive home from work. Then came the day she didn't move. By dinner, I was in tears. Thankfully, an hour later, she shifted. Relieved, I couldn't soothe the fear that something would go wrong.

I waddled into our last month, anxious to see our baby in person. Regulars in childbirth class, we were thankful for the lessons. Nesting followed, and our bag was packed, including the birth plan.
God had other plans. At a week overdue, detecting a complication, my doctor sent me straight to the hospital. Meds induced hours of contractions. Ultimately, the doctor ordered a C-section, something that was definitely not in my birth plan.

Inside the freezing operating room, my husband stood in space garb holding me during the epidural. Hearing our baby's warbling cry, he dropped his camera. Then he kissed me and shifted to her side. Elated but exhausted, I thanked God as the doctor sewed me up.

In a picture taken while I was separated from them, he sat in a rocker holding our baby girl snuggled close. I realized we'd come full circle. He truly was a dad now.

Prayer

Dear Lord, help us to trust in God's timing and not assert our own agenda. Only he knows the intricacies of life and the master plan for our future. We believe God works for the good of those who love him, so help us to be patient and have faith in him.

February 12

Visible Faith in a Watching World
By Shannon Floyd
Today's Scripture: 1 Peter 2:12

In a world where faith is often misunderstood, misrepresented, or even mocked, Peter's words offer both challenge and hope: "Keep your conduct among the Gentiles honorable..." The way we live among those who don't share our beliefs matters deeply.

Our lives are meant to be visible testimonies to those who don't yet know God. We're not on display for applause, but for impact and God's glory. Consistency in living out the gospel can soften hearts and open eyes.

Living with integrity, love, mercy, grace, and courage is how we reflect Christ. It means choosing kindness when it's inconvenient, forgiveness when it's undeserved, and truth when it's unpopular. Your choices can shape someone else's view of Christ.

Accusations may come. You might be judged unfairly, mocked for your convictions, or misunderstood for your choices. But notice the promise tucked into the verse: "...so that when they speak against you as evildoers, they may see your good deeds and glorify God on the day of visitation."

Honorable behavior has a way of silencing critics and pointing hearts toward God. When believers respond to hostility with humility and kindness, it disrupts expectations. It forces people to look again. And sometimes, that second look leads to a glimpse of God.

One day, Scripture says, those who once doubted may give honor to God. You may not change every heart, but your consistent goodness plants seeds. And one day, those seeds may grow into praise for the God who empowered you to love in a world that didn't.

Prayer

Lord, help me live a life that reflects Your goodness. When I'm misunderstood or misjudged, help me respond with grace. Let my actions speak of Your love and mercy. May others watching my life be drawn to you. Strengthen me to live boldly and let my life be a witness that brings you glory.

February 13

The Lord is My Husband
By Lisa Todd Wilkins
Today's Scripture: Isaiah 54:20

It was nearing the six-year anniversary since my husband had left. I sat alone on my sofa, crying over all the loss, navigating life as a single parent in my late forties. My heart felt heavy with grief and loneliness.

Through my tears, I cried out to God: "I need a husband." In the quiet of that moment, I heard His calm, assuring voice say, "I am your Husband."

Immediately, memories flooded me—how He had provided for me over the years. He had been my Husband in every way that mattered: providing food, shelter, purpose, and meaning. I realized that even in seasons of loss, God had never left me alone. He had been faithfully caring for me, guiding me, and sustaining me every step of the way.

The Lord is our faithful Husband. He provides, protects, and loves us in ways that exceed human understanding. Even in our deepest loneliness, He is present, caring for our every need, and delighting in us. When we cry out, He answers, often in ways we may not expect but perfectly meet the longings of our hearts.

Prayer

Lord, Thank You for being my faithful Husband. Help me trust Your provision, recognize Your constant presence, and rest in Your love, knowing You will always supply what I truly need.

February 14

Everlasting Love
By Jane H. DeLong
Today's Scripture: Jeremiah 31:3

The year was 1986. As a newly engaged couple, we were deciding on a date for our big day. Like most young couples, we were anxious to start our life together. Out came the calendar for 1987, and the search for the perfect Saturday began. We noticed that Valentine's Day fell on a Saturday that year, but both agreed it was too sappy for us. So we looked into March. We chose March 14.

However, when we announced it to our families, a major conflict arose, so we had to adjust our plans. We decided to move the date up rather than back. Valentine's Day!

Valentine's Day may seem like a romantic day to get married, but in reality, it isn't; places are overcrowded, and gifts are overpriced. In our society, we often equate love with romance, depicted as candlelight dinners, soft music playing, and tiny boxes wrapped in pretty bows. True love isn't that at all.

True love is sacrificial in nature, prioritizing the other person's needs over our own. There is no love on earth comparable to God's love for us. His love is everlasting - not fading, not dependent on performance, not breakable by failures.

God's love is deeply personal. He knows every part of us - the broken, the hidden, the weary - and still, He chooses to draw close. He isn't waiting for us to be "better" before He lavishes us with love.

Receiving God's love quiets fear, heals wounds, and invites us to rest. We don't have to strive for God's approval; we already have His heart.

So today, let God romance you with His love. Breathe in the truth:
You are fully known and fully loved by the God who created you.

Prayer

Father God,
Thank You for romancing me with Your everlasting love. Help me receive Your love today with an open heart. Remind me that Your love never leaves, never changes, never gives up. Teach me to rest in that love. Let it shape the way I see myself and others. May I overflow with that same love to those around me.

February 15

Growth Happens, Even in Winter
By Sasha Abele Katz
Today's Scripture: Psalm 34:18

From Thanksgiving to New Year's, everything just kept crumbling. My health. My business. My marriage. My two dear children were the only part of my world that was not spiraling out of control. Some time that winter, it occurred to me that my life, all of it, was just too much to carry. I could no longer tone down or turn off my tears of desperation. Wise sisters gathered around me and suggested a therapist.

In February 2017, I sat down with Dan, a biblical, licensed therapist, for a two-year journey that helped me transition out of winter into a season of flourishing. One of my greatest pains of February was the spiritual silence I felt in my dark winter. I came to learn that, even when God feels silent, He is still speaking. God is close to the brokenhearted. When we are crushed, He speaks all the more. That truth opened my eyes to see sprouts making their way through the ground, which God was nurturing and growing within me.

In time, I learned to communicate in my marriage. With bravery, I asked my husband for what I needed. He began to see me in a new light, too. I grew faith that God had my back when it came to family income. I came to understand that raising teens and running a business are moving targets beyond my control. These lessons transformed me.

God was near in my time of winter. He is near to you, too. He is never silent, even when you can't hear Him speak. He is singing over you and making a way for you to grow through frozen ground. Sprouts of life are breaking ground because you have a Father who will always come through for you, even in winter.

Prayer

Jesus, hold your child in their season of winter. Open their ears to your kind voice. Help them see that you will not just be with them through this harsh season, but you will show them all the ways you are orchestrating their life for good. Graciously lead them to growth and into a season of flourishing.

February 16

Forgiveness Heals
By Stephanie Gavel
Today's Scripture: Matthew 6:12

I would imagine that we have all been in a position where we have needed to ask for forgiveness and a position where we have needed to forgive. Although these words are uttered every time we pray the Lord's prayer, we most likely do not stop long enough to realize what we are saying. These words, "forgive me God the way I forgive", are not meant to just ask for forgiveness, but instead to foundationally change who we are.

Forgiveness is hard. God knows this. He knows that some hurts are so severe that they can alter one's life permanently. He knows that forgiveness has a cost and that we must look past our pain to Him, just as He looked beyond all our mistakes, imperfections, and sins to forgive us. He also knows that forgiveness is healing. Forgiveness heals our hearts.

When Jesus shared this prayer with the disciples, he knew what he was doing. This line is sandwiched between the requests to give us what we need each day and for our protection. We want the blessings, but do we really know what we are asking?

We are asking God to change our hearts and to trust that He always has our best interests in mind. Unforgiveness was never a burden that we were designed to carry. Our hearts were made for Him. Just as Jesus went to the cross with nothing but love for us, God wants us to go to the cross and lay down our unforgiveness because our hearts are so full of love for Him that we can't bear to allow anything to separate us from Him.

Prayer

Lord God,
I confess to you that I have unforgiveness in my heart. I want to let it go. I want to lay it down, but it is hard. If Jesus said this is how I am to pray, then God I want to fully forgive _____ and release my unforgiveness to you, because I do not want anything to separate me from you.

February 17

What's In Your Glove?
By Sandi Banks
Today's Scripture: 1 John 4:13

Floppy the rabbit was no ordinary puppet. He was my globetrotting sidekick—a quirky, fun, adventurous ministry partner who served with me in various parts of the world. With my two hands working inside, every inch of Floppy moved, and he seemed to bring joy to kids of all ages.

On February 17th in Switzerland, at our annual Bible conference, Dr. Charles Ryrie took the stage to speak. Floppy had just finished doing his "thing," which included a lively dance, a sing-along with finger cymbals, and a few improvised corny jokes with audience participation.

"Well, that's a tough act to follow," Dr. Ryrie began as he reached the podium. Then, turning to Floppy, he said, "I hope to have a photo op with you later, Sir." A gracious man. An unforgettable moment.

It's been years since Floppy went into retirement, and I happened upon him the other day. He was but a lifeless bundle of fur. Useless. Obsolete. Then I put my hands inside...and he "came to life."

Instantly, I recalled what Corrie Ten Boom taught us about the glove and the hand. She explains that we are like gloves, created for purpose but unable to move on our own. It's only when the Holy Spirit fills and moves within us that we can truly live out God's work.

Prayer

Father, Thank You that we don't have to be a "glove," struggling to do what You long to do in and through us. We can invite Your "hand," Your Holy Spirit, to come in and reside—and show us all the plans and adventures You have for us. And we will give You all the glory and praise!

February 18

Cracked Halos and Reluctant Hope
By Katrina Mintz
Today's Scripture: James 1:2-4

Following Christ doesn't always feel like a victory lap. Sometimes, it feels like collapsing in the stall, begging for rest, and wondering if God still sees you.

I've been there. Maybe you have too.

There are seasons when the ache is so deep, the darkness so thick, that even breathing feels like a battle. When prayers feel unanswered and hope feels unreachable. When you whisper, "I quit," and mean it.

But God doesn't quit on us.

He sees the soul that doesn't want to live. He sits with us in the stall, in the ER, in the broken places. And sometimes, He sends a mirror—a soul who reflects our wounds and reminds us that healing is possible, even if it's slow.

We rise with cracked halos. Not because we're perfect, but because we're loved. Not because we're strong, but because He is.

Hope doesn't always arrive joyfully. Sometimes it shows up reluctantly, with scars and stitched-up places. But it shows up. And when it does, we learn to live again—not because it's easy, but because God is faithful.

So if you're tired, if you're angry, if you're holding on by a thread—know this: you are not alone. You are not forgotten. And you are not finished.

God is whispering: "This won't be easy. But we will do it together. I am your strength. Hold on."

Prayer

Lord, When breathing feels heavy and hope feels far, remind us You are near. Give us strength to rise with cracked halos, courage to live when joy feels distant, and grace to trust You in the scarred places. You are our healer, our companion, and our light in the dark. We are not alone.

February 19

A Journey Full of Hope
By Mary Thissen
Today's Scripture: Jeremiah 29:11

I sat on the bed, crying, spent from trying anymore. Marriage was supposed to bring joy and togetherness as we journeyed with my husband toward Heaven. But I felt it was doing anything but this. Through the years, we had tried counseling, prayer, date nights, and getaways, but nothing seemed to work.

I was raised in an environment that saw marriage as a lifelong commitment, as a sacred covenant. Still, I knew of other devoted Christians who had divorced. On this particular day, I came to the awful conclusion that I, too, would be a divorced Christian. This decision was not made hastily or lightly; we had been together for over 15 years, with 13 of those years married. We had two beautiful children- what would this do to them? Yet, I felt the Lord leading me on in the next step of this journey. I prayed, "Lord, please let me know that this is from you and not from my own sinfulness. Please show me this is the right thing to do."

And I heard a still, small voice after my pleading. "Mary, this is what I am calling you to now. This part of your life is over. It does not mean you are any less of a Christian or any less my daughter. I will be with you; the future is full of hope."

While I cannot know what will come tomorrow, I know that the Lord leads my hand through this valley, and that I am good and pleasing to him if I seek to follow his ways. As the Lord told the Babylonians in exile, his plans for us will always prosper us and never harm us.

Prayer

Lord God, thank you for leading me to where you have led me. I know you have always been with me and will continue to be with me, no matter the difficulties life may bring. Please help me to always know and believe you will prosper my future with hope.

February 20

When I Can't find My Way
By Sara Copley
Today's Scripture: Jeremiah 33:3

Sometimes God speaks through the smallest, most ordinary moments of life.

In parking lots, I usually choose the same area to park. It's a habit, so I rarely think twice about it. But recently, distracted with my AirPods in and my mind elsewhere, I parked quickly and went inside. I thought I was close to my usual spot, but when I came out of the store, I was completely turned around. I wandered for a bit, then had a moment of panic, convinced I could figure it out on my own. Finally, I remembered my key fob and pressed the button. The faint beeping sound guided me straight back to where I needed to be.

That simple moment reminded me of how often I treat life the same way. I face challenges, determined to handle them on my own strength, only to find myself circling, frustrated, and unsure of which way to turn. But God never designed us to navigate life on our own. He invites us to call on Him.

What an incredible promise. God hears us when we call. Not only does He answer, He gives wisdom and guidance far beyond what we could discover on our own.

Maybe today you feel a little lost or distracted, unsure of where you're headed. Instead of trying to figure it out on your own, pause and call on Him. Just as that beeping led me back to my car, God's voice will always guide you back to where you need to be. He is faithful to answer.

Prayer

Father, Thank You that You are always near and ready to hear when I call. Forgive me for the times I try to find my own way. Heavenly Father, I put my trust in You and You alone. Through all the distractions of life, my prayer is that I continue to draw near to You. Today, I surrender my plans and my wandering heart to You. Guide me, Lord, and help me trust that Your voice will always lead me home.

February 21

Waiting With Hope
By Colleen van Nieuwkerk
Today's Scripture: Romans 8:25

God has often planted a desire for something new in my life in the month of February. He has also asked me to wait on Him as He works out the details of those desires.

Waiting is hard, but as this Scripture verse, written by Paul the Apostle, says, we are asked to wait on God's timing with patience and composure—to be steadfast despite opposition or difficulty, with a calmness of mind and bearing.

God called me into full-time ministry to the children in our church in February 1994. We had no position on our church staff for that calling. I did not have a Bible College degree to claim qualification for such a position. I had a lot of volunteer time and previous experience that had prepared me to be considered. I did not understand God's leading, but I did surrender to this calling. I said, "Yes, Lord."

I chose to continue volunteering and growing in my skillset, focusing on the children's spiritual well-being and staying faithfully in a place of expectation. There were, however, many prayers, tears, and longings as well as discussions about the validity of this change in our church structure that could meet the needs of our people.

God honored that calling in September 1997, over three years later.

Where is God asking you to wait today? Do you find yourself willing to stay in expectation as you wait for what will be for your good and for God's glory?

Prayer

Father, Thank you for the opportunities you present to us, as we surrender to your perfect will. Please help us to trust your timing, giving us patience and composure in our thoughts, words, actions, and reactions. Enable us to choose today to rest and hold fast to you.

February 22

Choosing a Different Story
By Rose McCombs Jordan
Today's Scripture: Deuteronomy 30:19–20

I was only eighteen when I found out I was going to be a mother. I loved my family deeply, but there was no denying the brokenness that had shaped us for generations. Patterns of pain, fractured relationships, and wounds that were never healed seemed to pass from one life to the next.

While I was pregnant, a thought rooted itself in my heart: It stops here. I didn't want my child's story to be marked by the same patterns that had marked mine. I wanted him to grow up free, secure, and loved.

That decision began with forgiveness—sometimes offered daily—and a quiet pursuit of God in the little ways I knew how. I couldn't undo the past, but I could choose differently for the future. Over the years, I learned that choosing life is rarely a one-time decision. It's in the small, everyday choices to forgive again, to speak words of blessing, to lean on God when old wounds ache.

Now, my son is grown. He still had to live with my imperfections, but by God's grace, it was always in the process of being healed. My heart aches for the moments I couldn't love perfectly, yet I've watched God fill the gaps with His perfect love. Choosing life that day was more than a decision for my son—it was a turning point for me. And it's a choice God invites each of us to make, one day at a time.

Prayer

Lord, Thank You for offering life and blessing. Help me to choose You daily—to love You, listen to You, and hold fast to You. Heal the places that are still broken, and let Your love flow freely to the generations that follow.

February 23

Dive Deep
By Hallie Turner
Today's Scripture: Psalm 42:7

On this day in 2021, my grandpa passed away. The grief I felt was deep. So deep that four years later, almost exactly to the date, I found myself overwhelmed with conflicting feelings of sadness and hope. It's like my spirit knew what day it was before I did. I decided to lean in, let the emotions wash over me, and bring it all before the Lord. That's when it hit me. The love my grandpa had for me was the closest thing I will experience to the Lord's unconditional love this side of Heaven.

I am blessed to have several people in my life who love me, but there was something special about my Granddaddy's love. He had a twinkle in his eye when he laughed at my shenanigans and a tear in his eye when he listened to me share my latest achievement. After he passed away, I often found myself thinking of him when I did something that felt significant; my brain would immediately surface how proud he would be of me. I couldn't imagine him ever looking at me with anything other than love. And the deeper truth behind that is that the Father is the same way.

Maybe for you, it's not the loss of a loved one. A variety of factors can lead us to those deep places. And it doesn't have to be one of sorrow. Deep reflection, deep peace, these experiences where we tap into something further down inside of us... They're meant to lead us to Jesus. That deep longing is ultimately for our Savior. And the good news? He can go to those depths with you. In fact, He wants to. Dive deep and let the Lord surprise you with just how deep His love, His joy, His healing is for you.

Prayer

Lord, meet me in the depths of my being. My deep calls to your deep. Help me to surrender all that I am carrying, to trust You with my circumstances, and to find hope in your favor over my life. Show me the depths of Your love. Wash over me with Your waves of mercy and grace.

February 24

Good Answers
By Erica Lewis
Today's Scripture: Matthew 7:7-11

It's easy to start listing every seemingly unanswered prayer when we hear "ask and it will be given to you." I think there is a misunderstanding that leads to this list. Jesus declared that when we ask, we will receive good things from a good Father; however, He never guaranteed that we would always receive the exact thing we asked for.

In my life, there have been times when His answers were easy to identify because they were what I'd asked for. Then, there are other prayers that I must look a little harder to see the fulfillment.

For example, I'm praying for God to bless me with a godly husband and a wonderful marriage. I could look at my life and say He's ignoring my prayer since I'm single. However, the truth of the matter is that everything He's teaching me in this season is preparing me to be able to have a healthy marriage someday. God is responding in a different way, and He's planning for a future answer (marriage).

Similarly, the Israelites struggled with negative perspectives in the Old Testament. They cried out to God to be rescued, and when God was in the process of their rescue (the plagues), they complained because they felt like their prayer was being ignored. Yet, we know from Scripture that God heard them and was answering all along. Sometimes all it takes to see God's answer is changing from insisting on a specific outcome to seeking God's goodness.

I encourage you to make a list of all the prayers you've felt were unanswered and intentionally seek out God's answers. See what good He did. Write down the goodness (God's answers) you've found. Continually expand and reread your list as a reminder that He hears you and is still working.

Prayer

God, Thank You that You always hear my prayers, and not one is left untouched. Open my eyes to see Your goodness in every answered prayer. Remind me daily that I am heard and seen by You, and that You are always giving me good answers, even when they look different than what I imagined.

February 25

I Will Be With You
By Tyann Beenken
Today's Scripture: Isaiah 43:2

I was a freshman in college, just 19 years old, when my dad lost a brief but hard-fought battle with cancer. The depth of heartbreak and grief that accompany the death of a loved one is hard to put into words, and the emotions can threaten to overwhelm you. But at a time when the world around me was falling apart, I was held up and held together by a strength and a power not my own.

As Christians, we are not promised a life free from trials and sufferings. What we are promised, however, is God's presence and strength with us as we go through them. In the book of Isaiah, God told the Israelites that when the floodwaters of trial and hardship came, they would not be consumed; He would be with them. Time and again, throughout Scripture, He has demonstrated His faithfulness to this promise. I wish I could sit across from you and tell you the whole story of God's presence and sustaining strength with me the day my dad passed away. In the moment, His hand was hard to see, but now looking back, I can clearly see that He was with me the entire time, holding me up when my strength threatened to fail.

Are you facing a difficult situation and navigating the waters of uncertainty, grief, heartbreak, or disappointment? Are the waves threatening to overwhelm you? If yes, then take courage, you will not go through them alone. God has promised you His presence. His strength is sufficient to hold you firm, even when your strength may fail.

Prayer

Abba Father, You say in Your Word that You are near to the broken-hearted and to those crushed in spirit. You know the tears that have been shed. I pray, even now as I pass through the waters, that I would sense Your presence with me and feel the strength of Your everlasting arms holding me and carrying me through.

February 26

Faithfulness Formed in Everyday Rhythms
By Katherine Hall
Today's Scripture: Daniel 6:10

I've read this verse many times, but the phrase "as he had done previously" stood out to me recently. Daniel's habit of prayer was not a reaction to the crisis in front of him, but the steady rhythm of his everyday life.

Daniel, an Israelite taken into Babylonian captivity, advanced to a position of authority. Living as a foreigner in a land that did not honor God, Daniel remained faithful. When new laws were enacted that restricted him from praying, Daniel remained steadfast. His decision to honor God despite the cost is what ultimately landed him in the lions' den.

Yes, Daniel faced lions, but he also fell on his knees. His identity was not shaped by a single moment of courage, but by the continuous act of turning to God day after day. His strength in Babylon did not come from resisting culture in a single dramatic stand. It came from a lifetime of choosing faithfulness, prayer, and worship again and again.

And notice this: even in such a hard situation, Daniel gave thanks. With a death sentence hanging over his head, he still found reason to thank God. Gratitude was part of his daily rhythm, too.

Daniel's consistency prepared him for this moment of opposition, and his daily practices gave him the strength to remain faithful when it mattered most.

The same is true for us. Our daily habits of reading Scripture, praying, giving thanks, and meditating on God's Word may not feel dramatic. Still, they shape us into people who can stand firm. Like Daniel, we are not defined by our culture, but shaped through the everyday ways we choose to encounter God.

Prayer

God, we're thankful for Daniel's example of steady faith. Let our time in prayer and in Your Word shape us into people who are both faithful and courageous. Help us cultivate habits that continually draw us back to You.

February 27

The Cheering Life Within
By Elizabeth Clark
Today's Scripture: Matthew 9:17

We often see Jesus as our Savior and King. This passage reveals another beautiful truth: He is the new wine, the dynamic Spirit that invigorates our souls. The Christian life can seem like a collection of dull duties, like an old, brittle wineskin that can't hold anything new. But this vibrant life cannot be contained by our rigid ways; we must become new wineskins to receive Him.

The Christian life isn't a chore, but a joyful, vibrant experience. This new wine is a profound source of hope. It assures us that our joy doesn't depend on outward circumstances. Christ is our inward enjoyment, a wellspring of life that strengthens and energizes us from within.

For some time, my Christian life felt like a chore. I was trying to live on my own strength, following rules, and feeling like a dry wineskin. But as I opened my heart to Christ as the cheering wine, a quiet, bubbling joy began to fill me. I realized my spiritual life wasn't about trying harder, but about enjoying Him more. He is the joy that energizes me from within.

Don't be discouraged by any dryness you feel. You have a new, vibrant life ready to fill you. Stop trying to live the Christian life in your own strength or old ways. Open your heart and receive Him as the new wine. Let His cheering life work within you, stirring your spirit, strengthening your resolve, and filling you with contagious joy.

What are the 'old wineskins', the habits or ways of thinking, in your life that are preventing you from fully receiving Christ as the new, cheering wine?

Prayer

Lord Jesus, Thank You for being the new wine. We open our hearts to You and ask that You fill us with Your life-giving, cheering spirit. Help us to put away our old ways and receive You as our strength, energy, and joy.

February 28

This Is The Day
By Hannah Louise Cox
Today's Scripture: Psalm 118:24

Today is my birthday, marking the beginning of a new chapter, and it could be for you too, because every day is an opportunity to start anew. I have a bad habit of believing that the page turns of my life begin when the clock strikes midnight on New Year's and when I blow out the candles on my 7-Up cake. But birthdays are reminders that we are alive and we have a life worth living. Right now, this life is here for us to take, and we get to do with it what we want.

A new age and phase of life can bring about natural changes, and God has His way of bringing about new adventures. However, beginnings and fresh starts are available anytime we choose to step out in faith and move forward. The choice is in our hands, will we decide to move, start, and believe that today is the day the Lord has made? Today is a good day for a fresh start, and it's your choice to take it and walk in it with eyes and hands open to what God has for you.

Don't wait for your birthday or the new year to begin what you feel called to do. Start today. One small step at a time. It won't be perfect, but I believe it will be beautiful as you move through your days in faith, because God is with you. I don't know what this year holds for me or for you, but I do know God is holding us in this chapter of our lives. The question is, what will we do with this beautiful life we've been given today?

Prayer

God, Thank You for this life, it's beautiful, messy, and sometimes complicated, and You love all of it because You love me. Help me be courageous when I'm scared, even when I want easy comfort, and to live each day knowing You made me for this moment.

March

hope✶books
collections

March 1

What if the Greatest Example Was Right in Front of You All Along?
By Dr. Shelley Kemp, Ed.D., SHRM-SCP
Today's Scripture: Proverbs 31:28-29

Have you ever looked back on someone's life and realized they were quietly shaping your strength the whole time?

Today would've been my mother's birthday.

She's been gone for some time now, but her impact remains in everything I do. My mother was the very definition of a Proverbs 31 woman—humble, wise, steady, and faithful. She worked at the same company for over 45 years. After retirement, she started a new job as a tax preparer for another 11 years. She taught Sunday School, volunteered at my school, and still made time to plan birthday parties, take me to piano lessons, and host sleepovers.

She didn't just raise me—she raised everyone around me. My friends called her "mom," too.

We traveled together. We laughed together. And though I didn't always recognize it then, she was pouring out her best into me, every single day. She didn't wear a cape, but she was a quiet kind of superhero.

Now, as a mother myself, I see her sacrifices more clearly. I understand her strength. I feel the echo of her wisdom every time I choose service over self, or calm over chaos.

And I just wish I had told her "thank you" more when I had the chance.

So let me ask you...

What if the greatest role model you're looking for isn't found on a stage or a screen—but right in your own family?

What if the best way to honor her is to become her?

And if your mother is still here—what if today's the day to remind her what a gift she truly is?

Because the greatest women don't always make history. Sometimes, they make daughters.

Prayer

Lord, thank You for the women who shape us with strength, wisdom, and love. Thank You for my mother's life—her quiet sacrifices, her steady faith, and her joyful heart. Help us honor the mothers in our lives while we still have them, and carry their legacy forward with grace. May we love like she did: selflessly and fully.

March 2

Where Else Would I Go?
By Megan Carlton
Today's Scripture: John 6:66-68

This scripture comes directly after a series of miracles. Jesus feeds the five thousand, then withdraws to be by Himself. That evening, He walks on water to meet the twelve disciples. The next day, the hungry crowd searches for Him, crossing the sea by boat. Jesus tells them He knows why they followed Him—not because of the miracles He performed, but because He fed them and they were satisfied. They wanted more of what He offered, not more of who He is.

Jesus explains that the bread they seek will only temporarily satisfy, but that He Himself is the Bread of Life. The sustenance available through a relationship with Him is everlasting. At this, the crowd was confused and offended. With the challenge of His message in their hearts and no loaves for their stomachs, many walked away. His response didn't meet their expectations. He offered an invitation to something deeper, but they declined. Jesus then looks to His twelve closest friends, essentially asking, You aren't going to leave me, too, are you? Peter's response feels etched on my heart, and I continue coming back to these words: "Lord, to whom shall we go? You are our only hope."

Hope is what sustains us. But what do we do when we don't feel hopeful? I've asked God that many times—in grief, in sadness, during job transitions, after hard conversations, and when doors I thought He opened slammed shut. That's when I cling to verses like these. Scripture reminds me that hope is not a feeling based on circumstances, but a confident expectation in the One who meets us within them. Through prayer and returning to Him again and again, we find our true hope. Hope is a Person, and His name is Jesus. Where else would I go?

Prayer

Jesus, you are my hope. When I'm overwhelmed, I hear you whisper, "Come sit with me." When hope feels hard, my dreams feel far, or my circumstances look nothing like I thought, I hear you calling me by name, saying, "I'm with you." Over and over I return to you, again and again you respond. I love you, Lord.

March 3

Living With Purpose: Pray, Listen, Move
By Amber Bishop Mornes
Today's Scripture: Jeremiah 29:11

We spend so much of our lives searching for meaning. But here's the truth: God already created you with a purpose. He placed unique gifts inside of you—not to keep hidden, but to share with the world.

So how do you discover your gift? Scripture tells us the Holy Spirit gives each believer spiritual gifts. Some are easy to recognize, while others take time and prayer to uncover. The best way to find your purpose is to talk to God, trust His guidance, and begin using what He's already given you.

Your calling isn't just a career, a title, or a role. It's a way of living—loving God, loving others, and shining His light in the ordinary moments of life.

Here are three steps to finding and using your purpose:

1. Pray
Ask God to reveal His plan for you. Lay your dreams, your talents, and even your uncertainties before Him. His Spirit will guide you when you seek Him first.

2. Listen
God often speaks through Scripture, through wise people around us, and through the gentle nudges in our own hearts. Pay attention to those whispers—your everyday life is where His calling often unfolds.

3. Move
Purpose isn't something you wait around for; it's something you step into. Take one small step of obedience today—volunteer, encourage someone, or use your talents in meaningful ways.

Remember, purpose isn't a checklist you complete. It's a journey with God— full of surprises, challenges, and opportunities to grow. Even the smallest steps matter.

Walk with Him, and your purpose will come alive day by day.

Prayer

Lord, thank You for creating me with purpose. You know the plans You have for me, even when I can't see them clearly. Open my eyes to the gifts You've placed inside me, and give me the courage to use them. Help me pray, listen, and move with You so that my life may shine Your light and bless others.

March 4

Marching Forth
By Abigail Ruth Miller
Today's Scripture: Philippians 3:13–14

Here are two of the poems I wrote during difficult moments of waiting on God during my later single years.

Trust in the LORD with all your heart

LORD-it hurts
This stripping away
This inability to keep anything
In my grasp
It's all like sand
Slipping, slipping, slipping
Through my fingers
These idols I think I need
That I believe I have a right to have
You say "No"
Because you love me
Too much
To let me have
That which will harm me
LORD, with all my heart I trust you
You are good
All the time
Please hold me now
I will die without you
Take it all away
If only I can have
More of you

March FORTH
She's got her Father's DNA in her bones
She is full of His grace and glory
And she will march forth
For His name- for the cause
Of truth, righteousness, and love
That all may know what it means
To be His precious child- His beloved
She marches forth

Since 2003, I have had a dream of being married on March 4th, marching forth down the aisle for His glory. I have had several painful breakups before then, but FINALLY, on March 4, 2022, Ryan and I walked down the aisle after our wedding, praising God for His good plan and perfect timing. God brought us together in the most beautiful way. God had put a special love for Israel on both of our hearts before we met. Then one day, Ryan was in the park and met a man from Israel. His niece was my friend and marched straight up to him and asked, "Are you interested in dating anyone? Because I have a friend..." God moves in mysterious ways, and his timing is perfect!

Prayer

Jesus, you see my friend. You will work out all the details for her story. Please help us not to live in fear, but to march forth confidently in faith, wherever YOU lead us. You are a good Shepherd who loves us perfectly and will give us everything we need to move forward in confidence. Help her not be afraid.

March 5

When Hard Seasons Become Hope Stories
By Rose McCombs Jordan
Today's Scripture: Romans 8:28

One ordinary morning, my husband Brandon was on duty as a paramedic when he called to say, "I'm in the ambulance... headed to the hospital. I've had a seizure."

Tests revealed a mass in his brain—cancer. Overnight, our world shifted from familiar routines to hospital rooms, biopsies, and treatment plans. For months, Brandon couldn't work, drive, or process information clearly. I became his driver, his advocate, and at times, his voice.

It was hard—harder than I can describe. But even in those hardest days, we saw God's hand. Every bill was paid, sometimes in ways that could only be explained as miraculous. Our marriage grew stronger. And the very illness that forced Brandon to stop working opened the door for him to finish his degree, with me driving him to every class.

Through it all, we began to notice the quiet ways God was working far beyond our own needs. Loved ones who had kept their distance from faith began leaning toward Him. Friends and even strangers told us our journey gave them hope. What felt like our private battle became a testimony of His goodness.

We still pray for complete healing. But even if it doesn't come from this side of heaven, we trust Him. His goodness has surrounded us—in provision, in relationships, and in the hope He's planted in others through our story.

Romans 8:28 says, "And we know that for those who love God all things work together for good, for those who are called according to his purpose." He has proven it.

Prayer

Lord, You are faithful in every season. Thank You for bringing light into our hardest days. Help me trust You when I cannot see the outcome, and to notice Your goodness in the midst of hardship. Use my story to bring hope and point others toward You.

March 6

Eyes Fixed on the Eternal
By Sherrie Williams
Today's Scripture: 2 Corinthians 4:18

On this day in 2020, I had a pivotal day in my journey with God. While the world was glued to their TVs, learning about a virus that would mark the days to come, I knelt before God, crying out to Him to change my reality. Alcoholism had flipped my world upside down, leaving me with a newborn and four young children—including one not yet diagnosed with autism—all looking to me for direction.

The next several years were overwhelmingly filled with homeschooling, working, experts, and special needs therapies. I was overfunctioning, with little time to process what was happening around and to me. With each tear-soaked prayer, He drew me closer, reminding me that He guides us through the valley, that He alone provides peace and still waters. It was in this season I heard His whisper through Paul's words in 2 Corinthians 4:18: "as we look not to the things that are seen but to the things that are unseen. For the things that are seen are transient, but the things that are unseen are eternal."

It is easy to lose ourselves in our hardships. We, in our humanness, can become fixated on our pain and struggles, thinking that is all that will ever exist. But we love and serve a God bigger than our suffering. He promises provision, healing, peace, and joy. He is not bound by this world but is eternal, and so are his gifts.

Today, as we move through our suffering, we must heed Paul's instruction. We need to turn our eyes from the troubles of this world - finances, schedules, sickness - and instead speak of what God has infused into our story: His provision, His healing, His peace, His joy.

When we fix our eyes on Him, He draws us out of our suffering, for He alone can redeem our broken hearts in the eternal.

Prayer

Heavenly Father, Your word reminds us that You are an eternal God. Your word says that you are a God of provision, healing, reconciliation, comfort, and joy. Today, Holy Spirit, come and open my eyes to where your hand is at work in my suffering. Help me keep my eyes fixed not on my struggles, but on you and your eternal gifts.

March 7

Lace Up Your Hiking Boots
By Linda Lowe Erley
Today's Scripture: Psalm 84:5

I was invited to walk the Camino de Santiago pilgrimage in Spain. March of that year marked my 70th birthday, and the timing felt right. With both excitement and a trembling awareness of the unknown, I said yes. As I prepared, I reminded myself: courage is not the absence of fear—it is the willingness to take bold steps despite it.

The truth is, wherever you are in life, you too are on a pilgrimage—a life change, a decision, raising children, a season of pain, or stepping into an empty nest. You don't need to board a plane or travel across the world. So, ask yourself: are you opening your heart today to the journey God invites you to, or digging in your heels?

The only way to take that first step is through the power of God. The psalmist further writes in Psalm 84:7, "They go from strength to strength..." If God calls you, He will equip you. He is always at work, bringing newness to our lives. May we meet Him with open hearts.

As I walked mile after mile through rain and rugged terrain—just as the Jewish people once did on their pilgrimages—I began to hear the steady crunch of gravel beneath my boots, and God met me in ways I never expected.

Are you ready to lace up your boots, accept His invitation, and set your heart on pilgrimage? Listen for the crunch of gravel beneath your boots. What might God be asking you to lay down, to make more room for Him in this season of your life?

Turn to Psalm 84:5-7. Let these words wash over you and fill you with hope.

Prayer

Dear Jesus, what pilgrimage are You inviting me on? Open my heart to receive this journey with you. Show me what I need to lay down—fear, doubt, worry, anger, hopelessness, or unforgiveness—to make more room for You in my life. Help me go from strength to strength. I'm ready to lace up my hiking boots and walk with You awhile, Abba Father.

March 8

Showered in His Power
By Mayda L. Cobban
Today's Scripture: Isaiah 61:3

Four days after a double mastectomy, I was about to face myself in the bathroom mirror for the first time, and I was terrified. My husband was with me to remove the binding, to warn me of what I was about to witness, to catch me should I faint.

As the mirror became foggy from the shower steam, I thought, "Maybe a blurred visual will make it easier to take in". A buffer to the real me. As the binding was pulled away with hands trembling, my husband gently tugged at pieces of gauze stuck with dried blood still on my chest. His eyes lowered. "Babe, it's not pretty."

Stunned by his loving honesty, I looked. It was true, it was extremely "unpretty". It felt like I was witnessing a terrible accident. In reaction, I cried out, "Oh my God," "Oh my God"! Quickly, I stepped into the shower, hiding from my husband, hiding from myself. This felt like the darkest moment of my life.

As I was crying out to God, He showed up! In my shower, as a loving yet firm Father, his presence quieted my sobbing and brought me to stillness. Standing on what felt like the edge of life and death, he spoke to my spirit. "You will not step out of this shower loathing yourself, you are more than flesh". "You are whole". I created you whole before you became flesh. In wholeness you will live". In the days that followed, I felt deep peace. God surely designed me with intention.

I had given too much validity to insecurities and how others viewed me. I asked God, "Why am I being destroyed?" What I know now is that he was reminding me I am who HE says I am, meant to live boldly without shame. He showed up to wash away false labels with the divine pouring of his love. I am whole, and it has nothing to do with soap and water.

Prayer

Lord, there is no wound you can't heal. No brokenness you can't make whole. Your promises remain even when we forget. May we take you at your word, seek you, and know that you are closer than our breath, waiting to provide the peace that is rightfully ours.

March 9

Trading What No Longer Fits
By Sarah S. Brown
Today's Scripture: Isaiah 61:3

As a child, one of my favorite traditions was shopping for a new Easter dress with my mom. By springtime, I had usually outgrown what I wore the previous year, and my idea of what was in style had changed too. Some years I wanted flowers and lace, while other years I chose something more simple and grown-up. There was an excitement that came from donning something new, leaving behind what no longer fit, and stepping into Easter morning with fresh confidence.

God offers us a similar exchange on a far greater and eternal scale. In Isaiah 61:3, He promises beauty for ashes, joy for sorrow, and praise for despair. God doesn't just patch up what is torn or polish what is broken. He makes us new. He takes what is worn and ill-fitting and trades it for what He has lovingly prepared in Christ.

We all outgrow seasons and mindsets. The ways we once thought, coped, or even defined ourselves may have served us for a time, but eventually our old ways of thinking and living no longer fit who we are becoming in Christ. In time, the "garments" of shame, fear, or grief hang heavy on our shoulders and no longer belong to us. Yet, letting go of those old garments can be hard. We may cling to familiar things, even if it keeps us stuck in the past. But just as I couldn't wear last year's too-small dress, we cannot fully embrace the new life God has for us while holding tightly to the old.

What "old garment" might God be inviting you to lay aside so He can clothe you in something new today?

Prayer

Lord,
Help me release mindsets and old ways of thinking that no longer fit the person I am becoming. Grant me the courage to embrace the new life You are clothing me in—beauty instead of ashes, joy instead of sorrow, and hope instead of despair. Teach me to walk confidently in what You've prepared.

March 10

I Was Lost, but Now I'm Found
By Susan DiParisi
Today's Scripture: Psalm 34:18

I was 23, a grad student living in the Columbia University apartments with four other female students. My life in New York City had been a blur of lectures, late nights, and whirlwind outings through Manhattan. I had chased the energy of the city—its culture, excitement, the high life—but beneath it all, an emptiness had begun to grow inside me.

Despite the constant motion, I felt lost. I had no real sense of purpose, no anchor to hold me steady, and the thrill of the city no longer masked the darkness inside. Caring for myself, managing school, and navigating that fast-paced life left me drained and directionless.

One morning, utterly exhausted and feeling very low, I stood in front of the bathroom mirror, brushing my teeth mechanically, staring at my own reflection. Pale sunlight streamed through the window, spilling across the tiles, but it did little to lift the heaviness I felt inside. Desperation poured out of me, raw and trembling.

"God," I whispered, my voice shaking. "I... I need You. Please save me from destroying myself. Lift me out of this darkness. I can't do it on my own."

My heart pounded, and for the first time in weeks, a strange calm settled over me. In that moment of utter surrender, I made a promise: "Jesus, if You rescue me, if You carry me out of the depths of my despair, I will dedicate myself to You. I will be Your faithful servant for the rest of my life."

It wasn't dramatic or flashy, but it was real. As I finished brushing my teeth, I felt a small, unshakable flicker of hope—an unspoken assurance that I had been heard, that I was no longer alone, and that a new chapter, guided by purpose and faith, had quietly begun.

The next time I stepped outside, everything appeared brighter, more vivid than ever before.

Prayer

Dear Father,
Help me to stay close to You in everything I do. Help me to seek You in all things, everywhere. May I seek and desire intimacy with You as passionately as You love me.

March 11

Every Good Gift
By Angie Hanson
Today's Scripture: James 1:17

There's something sacred about birthdays – they're a celebration not just of a date on the calendar, but of the life, laughter, and love that person brings into the world. March 11th is one of my favorite days of the year because it's my daughter's birthday. From the moment she entered the world, she has been a reminder to me of God's goodness.

When you've walked through profound loss, joy can sometimes feel complicated. There were years when my grief whispered that celebrating was somehow disloyal to the ones I missed. But God has been gently teaching me that joy and sorrow are not enemies – they can hold hands. We can honor the people we've lost and still delight in the gifts God has given us today.

On my daughter's birthday, I see the evidence of God's love wrapped in her smile, her humor, her dreams. She is a living testimony that even in the hardest chapters, God is still writing beauty into the story.

If you're in a season where joy feels hard to find, ask God to show you the gifts He has placed in your life right now. They may be as small as a shared laugh or as big as a miracle you prayed for – but each is a reminder that your Father is still in the business of giving good things.

Prayer

Father, thank You for the gift of life and the people who bring light to my days. Help me see Your blessings, even in seasons of sorrow. Teach me to celebrate without guilt, knowing that joy honors You. May my heart overflow with gratitude for every good gift You've given.

March 12

God's Palm Tattoo
By Chanda Husser Rigby, Ed.D
Today's Scripture: Isaiah 49:16

Though the entire Bible can be seen as an enormous love letter to us, one of my favorite love notes is found in Isaiah 49:16, where it says that God has engraved me on the palms of His hands.

Though tattoos are common, palm tattoos are not common. In fact, I have only seen one tattoo placed on the palm of a person's hand.

When I asked why he had it placed in this unusual location, he told me that tattoos positioned on the outer hand are for other people to see, but placing one on his palm was for his personal viewing. He said he wanted to be reminded of what his palm tattoo represented every time he caught sight of the inside of his hand.

Is it possible that the God of the universe wants to think of me that often? The fact that God chose to engrave me on his palms feels like such a personal, permanent, and intimate act of love. Oh, what a love He has for me!

Prayer

God, it is unfathomable that You would love me so much that You engraved me on Your palms. May I never forget the extent of Your love for me.

March 13

New Things, New Joy
By Mary Thissen
Today's Scripture: Isaiah 43:19

As my husband and I entered the medical office for the very first ultrasound of our pregnancy, my expectations for the appointment were low. After suffering three prior miscarriages and an ectopic pregnancy, I was not hopeful for good news.

Yet joy finds us when we least expect it.

As I lay on the exam table, I held my husband's hand and my breath.

And then the nurse practitioner said, "We have two babies with two heartbeats. Measuring right where you should be for this time in your pregnancy."

I grinned at my husband and felt tears spring to my eyes. Could this possibly be it? Could these babies possibly be born? After all of the heartbreak of my previous losses, would I hold these babies in my arms?

We shared our news right away with family and friends so they could surround us with prayer. Still, being pregnant was scary, and with it came a scary pandemic. Just days after the ultrasound, the first COVID lockdown happened. Curiously, as frightening as the world was, I felt a protective love wrapped around me, as if God was saying, "I know everything is scary right now. Will you trust me with this new thing?"

I progressed through pregnancy, and as the world coped with a pandemic, I walked forward on the journey with newfound confidence and excitement to see what God would do. Scared, yes, but onward on the journey with the Lord. Instead of looking to the future with fear, let us look forward with happiness and confidence, knowing that the Lord will do something new in our lives.

Prayer

Lord God, you know the terrors of this world. When we are asked to do something new, it may terrify us. Please remind us of your ever-present help and companionship on the journey, and may we follow where you lead with great joy.

March 14

Beholding Glimmers of Hope
By Kelly Hill
Today's Scripture: Romans 15:13

When dread creeps in and hopelessness whispers that I don't have the strength for another day, fear grows like weeds, choking out peace. My thoughts can become louder than God's voice, and emotions overtake the soil of my heart. On such days, it feels as though the light is dim, and joy is just out of reach.

But when I meet with God first—when I open His living Word and sit quietly in His presence—I discover where true hope is planted. In stillness, I pray, "Lord, what do You want me to know today? Will You speak into this?" As I wait, His voice waters my weary soul. My heart steadies, my mind clears, and His light begins to pierce the shadows.

I then ask, What thoughts are lovely, pure, and excellent? Slowly, hope begins to bloom. One of my morning rituals is naming the things I'm grateful for: the soft warmth of the sun, a child's laughter, the whisper of wind through the trees. Gratitude is like sunshine—strengthening what God has planted and helping hope take deeper root.

To behold hope in God's Word, His voice, and His presence is to step into His garden sanctuary. It is Eden restored in glimpses, where beauty blossoms and the soul is refreshed. Even amid trials, God cultivates life in unexpected places. Choosing to notice, we see hope breaking through the cracks, tender and resilient—a reminder of His constant faithfulness.

Prayer

Jesus, will you quiet the noise and help me rest in the symphony of your love? I want my heart to be set on the hope of your promises—knowing you will never leave or forsake me.

March 15

The Time of God's Favor
By Ms. Jewel
Today's Scripture: Psalm 69:13

The challenges of life can threaten to diminish our faith. They may even attempt to steal our peace and joy. But we, as believers, have a friend who sticks closer than a brother. (Prov 18:24) Even when we think we can't go on, Jesus makes Himself evident to us, oftentimes through a scripture like this one.

Some of us have been waiting for that favor and breakthrough for a long time. We may even question if it will ever come. We've held on to our marriages that have unraveled like the string of a kite caught in a hurricane. We've tithed from empty bank accounts, while our car runs on fumes. We've sent up so many prayers that seem to burst like bubbles as they reach the ceiling. "But I keep praying to You, Lord, hoping this time You will show me favor".

My husband used to be trapped in alcoholism. One day, during prayer, I heard the Holy Spirit tell me my husband wouldn't drink forever. For 12 years, I held onto that promise, believing it would come to pass. Through 5 rehabs and countless other relapses, doubt tried to creep in. Circumstances and the voices of well-meaning friends tried to convince me I had heard wrong. But I held on, hoping, "this time…"

In 2017, the wait ended. My husband has been sober and following God for 8 years now! God is faithful! He wants to prove it to you, too. He is still making and keeping vows today. What promise are you awaiting? Maybe this is the day you will see His favor.

Prayer

Father, I know anything worth having is worth waiting for. I trust that you have my best interest at heart, but I'm weary. By Your strength, I will endure until the moment I announce, "Today is the day of God's favor" and give You all the glory! Thank You that my future is in Your hands and it is good!

March 16

A Quiet Legacy of Faith
By Angie Vallejo
Today's Scripture: Joshua 24:15

While packing books during a move, I came across an old book of devotions that my mom gave me many years ago. The cover reads simply: *Inspirations: A Book of Devotions for Each Day of the Year*. Originally published in 1965, each message was written by a different pastor from across the country.

But it's the entry on March 16 that makes the book so meaningful to me.

The devotion that day was written by my grandpa, who, before he retired, pastored a small country church. He passed away when I was just seven years old, so my memories of him are few. However, reading his heartfelt words today gives me a glimpse of his devotion to the Lord.

The verse he reflected on was Joshua 24:15: "As for me and my house, we will serve the Lord." These words from Joshua are a declaration that a legacy of faith is to be passed from one generation to the next. My grandpa faithfully lived out that verse with unwavering conviction, and his example is the reason I follow Jesus today.

Legacy doesn't have to be loud or noticeable. We don't need fame to leave something meaningful behind. Instead, it can be handwritten notes in a well-used Bible, consistent prayers, or simply living a quiet life of obedience to God. These are the small, silent seeds of faith that can continue to grow long after we're gone.

You might not realize how your faith is influencing someone else's story—but God does. What you live today could be someone's reason to believe tomorrow. And that kind of legacy is worth everything.

Prayer

Lord, thank You for the faithful obedience of those who came before us. Help me to live in a way that honors You and plants seeds of faith into the next generation. May my daily choices reflect a heart that treasures You above all else. Use my life to bring glory to Your name.

March 17

Speak Clearly
By Jane H.DeLong
Today's Scripture: 1 Corinthians 14:9

In the spring of 2021, COVID was still an issue. When my daughter called to tell me they were heading to the hospital for the birth of their second child, I was informed that there was no need for me to rush the two hours to their home. She and her husband were the only ones allowed in the delivery room. We waited at home until we received the news: their son, affectionately known as JJ, had been born on St. Patrick's Day.

St. Patrick is known for helping to bring Christianity to Ireland, a place where he had formerly been a slave. Legend states that he used the shamrock to explain the Gospel. He used an ordinary object and spoke clearly so the people could understand.

When JJ started talking, it was evident that he needed help. He spent a couple of years in speech therapy to learn the correct way to form and say words. We sometimes still need to remind him to speak clearly.

Words are powerful. They can heal or hurt, build up or tear down. In 1 Corinthians 14:9, Paul reminds us that our words should be clear and meaningful, especially when we speak in the name of Christ. It's not about sounding impressive - it's about being understood. If no one can grasp what we're saying, how can they be encouraged, challenged, or comforted?

This applies not only to public teaching but also to our daily conversations. Are we speaking words that others can receive? Are our words filled with grace, truth, and clarity? Or are we just filling the air?

As followers of Christ, we're called to communicate in a way that reflects His heart. Today, speak so others can understand. Pray for wisdom to say what needs to be said - and say it in love.

Prayer

Father God,
Thank You for the ability to speak. Empower me to speak clearly to others today. Give me boldness to speak Your truth, and may my words be seasoned with the salt of Your love. Bless me with clarity, compassion, and courage to communicate well so others may be drawn closer to You.

March 18

One Date, Then a Wedding
By Kay Ashley
Today's Scripture: Proverbs 19:12

He knew for three years that God had told him I was his wife. But with our histories and the ministry community we were part of, we did not rush. We had both been married before. He was not eager to step into more church gossip. And I was not on board at all.

I was happily single. Healing. Whole. In my lane. The idea of marrying him felt unnecessary. I respected him deeply, but romantically, there was no spark. No flutters. Nothing.

Until one day, God opened my eyes. Literally. I saw him and I saw him. He suddenly became attractive in a way I cannot explain. I realized I want to spend my life with this man.

We went on one date. A few days later, we were married.

It was not impulsive. It was obedience. It was not messy. It was miraculous. Peace overshadowed every what-if.

Friend, sometimes God interrupts your plans with His purpose. Sometimes, He reveals the thing you were not even looking for. And when He does, your yes might look wild to others, but it will be rooted in peace.

Prayer

Father, You don't always move in ways that make sense to others—or even to me. But when You reveal, help me recognize. When You lead, help me follow. Thank You for knowing what I need even when I don't. I trust You with the timing, the story, and the yes.

March 19

A Fine-Tuned Life
By Sarah Fry
Today's Scripture: Philippians 3:14

I sit here mesmerized, baby on lap, watching Heifetz play a Bach Chaconne.

What a combination – the power of Bach through an all-time master. The thought pressing in as I listen - is control. Every note is perfectly balanced. Double stops punctuate, spiccato passages are crisp and brilliant, yet the melody soars above the technical brilliance.

And still, Heifetz plays with wild abandon – a heart and soul that lifts the Chaconne beyond cold perfection into the Divine.

Such mastery reflects unspeakable dedication: years of posture, precision, bow weight, perfected again and again, until the music breathes through him. One imperceptible breath, and it begins.

It is one thing to hear such beauty; another to feel it in your fingers, earned through aching hours. There were days I chafed under the discipline, wishing for freedom. Yet commitment drew me back, and the practice room became my friend.

I have felt the same spiritually, discouraged at how hard the walk can be. Losing hope that I could ever grow up in grace. But muscle memory comes from practice. As we lean into His goodness and grace, He grows us up into Himself.

The holy life requires discipline – bringing ourselves into the framework of His loving Word so we may be fine-tuned to brilliance. Daily testing brings patience and spiritual muscle. But we could never, ever earn His grace or become good on our own.

Wild abandon alone will not suffice. My one-year-old has abandon without discipline, and his cardboard violin proves it. But the abandonment of worship, joined with daily surrender, lets us soar. With practice comes freedom—His music alive in us.

The more we learn, the more we see our need. And we practice on, that His song may sing through us more beautifully.

Prayer

Abba, fine-tune my life. Train my hearing to discern what is truly beautiful. Discipline my fingers so that clumsiness does not hinder Your song. Bring me again to the place of practice, that I may know the freedom of being fully under Your control. Let Your Music sing through me.

March 20

In the Quiet of the Wildflowers
By Susanne Moore
Luke 12:27-28

The first day of spring started with Happy Birthday. Mama was born today in 1937 and lost her last tomorrow in the dead heat of a Texas summer, August 2016.

From day one until she met Jesus, she was a wild one. Free, marching to her own drum, clothed like the grass of the field. She never cared what others thought about her; she quietly accepted who she was and was determined to be an eclectic, educated, colorful wildflower.

Consider how wildflowers grow and how much more God provides for you. Spring is a season of joy, as new life sprouts up through the cracks, rain falls to water the roots, buds open, and bees pollinate to spread the joy of life, silent and constant.

Mama was an attentive Gardner. She watered and pruned her garden and loved feeding her squirrels and mockingbirds. Imagine God attending to you in such a quiet, considerate way.

You do not need to labor or spin. You do not need to fit in or worry about provision. You can click the button that says "pause" and trust that God clothes you. God is in the silence, God is constant. God is in the quiet of the wildflowers and in the quiet of your life. You can trust and hope in him.

When a bee lands on a flower, I think of my mama, redeemed by the blood of the lamb, and I remember the lessons she taught me about quietly accepting who I am in Jesus and trusting the clothing he has provided for me.

Do you labor or spin? Do you feel like you are constantly toiling over fitting in or making it in this life? Is your effort on the fast cycle in the washing machine of life?

Prayer

Lord, Help us to consider the wildflowers and rest in the quiet stillness of you. I pray that every reader may spring forth like the dawn and embrace your hopefulness this year. Thank you, Jesus. We praise you, for we are fearfully and wonderfully made.'

March 21

Not Even a Dark Night Can Destroy Hope
By Nora Tatina
Today's Scripture: Psalm 30:5

I'll never forget the day my world stood still. I was sitting in a dark, cold room, waiting for the worst news imaginable, desperately holding on to hope. Wrapped in a blanket, cursing the unbearable pain that felt like a volcano ready to erupt, I begged God for a better ending. But, no matter how I felt at that moment, I knew the next words would change everything. "I'm so sorry, but there is no heartbeat." Hearing those words shattered my heart into a million pieces, and my body shook uncontrollably as the volcano within me erupted.

Questions flooded my mind. What should have been a simple check-up became one of the worst days of my life. I could no longer tell my loved ones the secret I'd been waiting to share. I wouldn't need that stroller I had been eyeing or attend the newborn sale I'd planned. All my hopes and dreams of welcoming our precious baby faded away. Hope was snatched from me that day, leaving my heart broken and my future uncertain.

Sometimes life feels like a dark sky without a glimmer of hope. When pain feels overwhelming, it can seem like God has abandoned us, making us wonder if we will ever smile again. But even in our deepest pain, there is hope. The pain we feel now won't last forever. Even Jesus showed us this truth—the cross preceded His greatest victory.

It might feel like the pain you're facing will never end, but be reassured of this - darkness can never destroy hope! Let the tears fall, yell as loud as you need to, and seek counseling. But please, whatever you do, don't walk away from Jesus. Hold tightly to His unchanging hand. Even on our darkest night, with the Lord there is always hope!

Prayer

When life feels dark and the pain we're facing feels unbearable, strengthen our hearts, Jesus. Remind us of the hope we have in you. May we never give in to despair; instead, may we choose to trust you even in the dark. When our hearts do fail because they will, may you always be our portion.

March 22

You Are Able
By Richard Dubay, Jr.
Today's Scripture: Philippians 4:13

When you read today's verse, what does it do in your heart?

Here's what it does in mine:

"All things? Really? I can do all things? Come on, that can't really be true. I can't do all things."

For instance, I can't dunk a basketball. I also can't run a mile in one minute. And no matter what I do, I can't seem to stop it from being 100 degrees here in South Carolina during the summer.

There are a number of things that I cannot physically do. Yet Paul tells us in this verse that we can do all things. What gives?

For starters, I don't think that Paul was talking about all "physical" things.

The trick here is context. When we take verses out of their context and try to attach meaning to them on their own, we often put our own spin on things in accordance with our current circumstances. If we want to know the truth behind a verse, we need to put the verse in context. So let's do that here.

In the surrounding verses, Paul talks about how he has learned to be happy with little or with much. He's learned to be okay whether he has an abundance or is in need. Paul knows that, with Jesus, he can get through anything.

And so can we! We can trust that, in Christ, we are capable of handling all things. Easy, difficult, or somewhere in between. It's because of Jesus and His great love for us that, no matter what we face, we can get through anything.

That's really great news.

Prayer

Father, Thank You for Your grace to help us through anything and everything. Thank You that in You, we can do everything You've called us to do, walk through any circumstances, and come out the other side with love and joy.

March 23

Ashes to Arising: From Grief into God's Peace
By Kylie Harris McKenzie
Today's Scripture: Colossians 3:13

On this day in 2024, my world fell apart. My husband, Kevin, was killed in an accident, and in that instant, everything I knew and loved vanished.

Grief hit me like a tidal wave. I tried to numb the pain with alcohol and bitterness, but nothing could fill the emptiness. I felt abandoned by friends, misunderstood by family, and left drowning in sorrow.

Yet God meets us even in the deepest pits. When I finally cried out to Him in desperation, He didn't turn away. He lifted me from the mire and began softening my heart in ways I never imagined.

Forgiveness was the hardest step. For months, I carried anger toward the man responsible for the accident. But God reminded me of His own forgiveness toward me.

Slowly, He gave me the strength to release the weight of resentment and see him as someone hurting too. Forgiveness didn't erase my pain, but it unlocked the prison of bitterness. With each act of forgiveness, healing flowed–not just for Kevin's loss, but for old wounds I had carried for years.

God's redemption didn't stop there. He placed people in my life who prayed with me, carried me, and loved me in my brokenness. In time, He even brought my now-husband, Philip–someone who honors Kevin's memory, loves our children as his own, and walks with us in God's grace.

If you are carrying anger or grief, take a step today to release it to God– start small, and let Him guide your heart toward forgiveness. Forgiveness has been the doorway to freedom. No matter how deep the loss, God's love can turn your ashes into a rising, and He promises a future filled with hope, peace, and restoration.

Prayer

Lord, I lift up every heart bound by grief or bitterness. Help them lay down the pain that weighs heavily and choose forgiveness, even when it feels impossible. Replace anger with grace, sorrow with hope, and brokenness with Your healing presence. Remind them that You are present in every moment, and Your grace is bigger than any pain they carry.

March 24

God Understands
By Laura Lee Pettit
Today's Scripture: Psalm 91:1-2

It was pitch black as my husband and I drove in complete silence, each surrounded by our own penetrating thoughts. Just the sound of the road beneath our wheels, random streetlights, and infrequent headlights from cars on the other side of the highway.

Denial...Unwilling to fully acknowledge the swirling emotions. It was like sitting in a kiddie pool, water touching you yet not covering you.

Abruptly, my phone rang. Holding my breath as if I were going underwater, I answered the call.

Tiny shreds of hope rose as I heard my 87-year-old mom's agitated, unsteady, and frantic voice asking where I was because she thought I was missing. My emotions shifted from relief that she was still alive to concern upon hearing her delusional, fearful, and confused state of mind. I reassured her we were nearly at the hospital and would see her soon.

I read Psalm 91 at her bedside, reassuring her she was safe, and God was holding her close.

Unbeknownst to me, those were her final few days on earth. Within 24 hours after hearing Psalm 91, she slipped peacefully away. Several weeks later, I sat at my kitchen counter, reading Psalm 91 and reflecting on the past. The emotions started small, deep in my chest, until I felt as though I was being crushed by a tidal wave. God's peace washed over me as I pondered her last days.

God understood both my and my mom's fears, thoughts, and emotions. When we are sitting in fear, anxiety, sorrow, grief, and loss, God understands and holds space with us. I don't know what emotions you hold, but God understands. Sit in discomfort as He covers you with His outstretched arms.

Lean in and breathe. He understands.

Prayer

Lord Jesus, You are the One who understands our thoughts and feelings, covering us with perfect peace. In Your presence, we can dwell in the shelter of the Most High. You are our refuge and fortress, rescuer and deliverer, covering us with love and mercy. Thank You, Father God, for Your faithfulness, for comforting us in grief and loss.

March 25

Comfort in Affliction
By Mary Thissen
Today's Scripture: Matthew 5:4

As a child and teenager, I loved hanging out with my paternal grandmother. So much so that I asked her to join me on my junior class trip to Chicago. Most of the other chaperones at my all-girls' school were moms, but I was excited to hang out and explore Chicago with my grandma. A few other friends signed up for my grandma to be their main chaperone, and I was excited to hang out with them, too.

While visiting a museum, tragedy struck for our class. A classmate fell over a balcony and died. We were all gutted to lose a classmate, especially on something that was meant to be a fun bonding experience.

After this, our teachers and chaperones took on the role of ministering to us grieving girls. Many tears and hugs were exchanged in the following weeks as we tried to make sense of my classmate's death.

My grandma received many thank you notes from my classmates. The contents of the thank you notes were overwhelmingly about comfort for having a grandmother present on the trip. Grandma gave comfort to me and to my grieving classmates in a way that our moms could not.

And when I think of the life she lived, this story encompasses all that she was: a steady, comforting, faithful presence in both the good times and bad times. She had her share of difficulties, but her faith in God never wavered. As I seek to carry on all that she was, I pray that I might be that steady comfort in dark times that others need.

Prayer

Lord, Thank You for the gift of other people. Thank You for the opportunity to give comfort to those in pain. May we, as your followers, always be a place of comfort and rest to those in this weary world. Let us radiate Your love to those who hurt.

March 26

Steadfast Anchor in Life's Storms
By Josh Parker
Today's Scripture: Hebrews 6:19-20

When I read about Abraham being "fully convinced that God was able to do what he had promised" in Romans 4:21, I'm struck by the strength of that phrase. Fully convinced. Not partially hopeful or cautiously optimistic—fully convinced.

The writer of Hebrews doubles down on this certainty, calling our hope a "sure and steadfast anchor." These aren't gentle, whispered assurances. They're steel-reinforced promises designed to hold when everything else gives way.

Not too long ago, severe storms rolled through our Midwest town. Racing home from the office late that evening, I was trying to beat the approaching chaos to the safety of our house. Dark clouds churned overhead, and I could feel the atmospheric pressure dropping. The weather service was tracking a 75 mph wind front that had already produced a tornado a few miles before reaching us.

I had no control over what was happening around me—only over my response to those potentially catastrophic events. As my family and I hunkered down in our basement, listening to the roar of wind above, I realized we'd found refuge in something unmovable. Even if the house upstairs got wrecked, the basement wasn't going anywhere. It was our steadfast anchor.

In that moment, we gained perspective on what truly mattered. There was clarity in our actions despite the chaos. The foundation beneath us couldn't be shaken, no matter how fierce the storm raged above.

God's promises work exactly the same way. They don't eliminate life's storms, but they provide unshakeable refuge in the midst of them. When circumstances spiral beyond our control, His anchor holds. When everything visible seems threatened, His foundation remains unmovable. That's the unchangeable nature of our God—a sure and steadfast anchor for our souls.

Prayer

Father, When life's storms rage and human solutions fail, help me remember that Your promises are my anchor. Thank You for being steadfast when I am not, and for providing refuge in the chaos. Let my hope rest fully in You.

March 27

The Author of Life
By Elizabeth Clark
Today's Scripture: Acts 3:15

We often see Jesus as a healer, but this passage from Acts reveals a more profound truth: He is the Author, the very source of life itself. The Greek word 'archegos' gives us a helpful understanding that life is not just a gift from Him, but an emanation of who He is. This shifts our focus from seeking a temporary solution to connecting with the eternal source.

This truth is a fountain of hope. Our Father has made His Son the source of an all-conquering life. This promise applies to every area of our lives. When we are weak in faith, joy, or purpose, it is because we are weak in life. But we have a constant connection to the Author of life. This gives us hope that no matter what we face, we have a life within us that is more powerful than any sickness, despair, or death.

I used to get so fixated on my physical health and emotional well-being. I would pray for healing and peace, but I was treating them as separate gifts from God. I was looking at Him as a problem-solver, not as the source of my very being. When I began to focus on receiving more of Him as life, my anxieties lessened, and a new strength filled me.

Don't be discouraged by your weaknesses, whether they are physical, emotional, or spiritual. Jesus Christ is not just the healer of your body; He is the very source of your life. Turn to Him, receive Him, and be filled with Him. As you become strong in His divine life, you will experience His power to swallow up death in every situation. Your life is not about getting better; it's about being filled with Him.

How does the understanding that Christ is the "Author of life" change the way you pray for healing, strength, or peace?

Prayer

Lord Jesus, We thank You for being the Author of life. We confess our tendency to seek from You only healing and comfort. We now open ourselves to receive You as our very life. Fill us, Lord, with Your life that we may be strong and overcome all that we face.

March 28

The Gift of Absence
By Bri Davidson
Today's Scripture: Luke 24:30-31

Our culture is addicted to the rush—bigger lights, louder songs, stronger feelings. We long to feel the Spirit with intensity, to be swept into worship that stirs us, and to leave inspired and alive. Our senses grow conditioned to the highs of intensity and excellence. But what happens when the wonder begins to fade? When presence feels like absence, when adoration slips into apathy?

I have walked through that disheartening silence. After a season of awe, I entered years of quiet and hiddenness, holding more questions than answers about God's presence and purpose in my life. Yet it was there, in the silence, that my heart was being shaped into His likeness. In those days, His mercy and love didn't look like nearness or emotional highs. They looked like choosing faith over sight, trust over feeling, hope over despair.

In Luke 24, the disciples realized their hearts were burning only after Jesus disappeared from their sight. In the same way, when worship feels flat, when the message no longer motivates, when God seems silent, it may be in that very absence that His presence draws near. Slowly, I learned that silence was not His abandonment but His invitation. My longing deepened. My gratitude grew stronger. My faith shifted from chasing sensation to becoming steadfast. In the quiet, I was being formed into the likeness of the Jesus revealed in the Scriptures—gracious, patient, steadfast, and true.

In the ache of absence, God may be drawing nearer than we ever dared to believe.

Prayer

Lord, When you feel silent, remind me that you are near. Draw me into your quiet invitation to know you more deeply. Teach me to trust when feelings fade, even when trust feels risky or frightening. Lord, in the places of void, fill me with your presence so that I may be shaped into your likeness.

March 29

His Strength is Perfect
By Shelley Groves
Today's Scripture: 2 Corinthians 12:9

The phone rang. It was Dad. When I first answered the call, I knew that something wasn't right. He tried to tell me in his jovial way that he just had a spot that the doctors wanted to check further, but I knew from his voice that he was scared. Mother was going downhill with what we suspected was Alzheimer's. We knew that disease too well after the long road we had walked with my grandmother. Dad didn't want – no, he knew - he could not be sick on top of Mom's impending issues.

When I hung up the phone, I wanted to cry. Since last summer, things just kept piling up on top of us. Our older daughter went away to college for the first time. Our younger daughter had to have unexpected surgery. We lived in a rented house and battled to rebuild ours, which had caught fire after a lightning strike. After just starting to settle back into our home, surely there wasn't more bad news. But, there was. Dad did have cancer, and Mom's Alzheimer's diagnosis followed within a month.

I wish I could say that I handled that whole year like a saint; that I persevered through trials just like the Book of James says we should. Instead, I struggled. It was hard. At times, I didn't want to keep going.

However, I continued to turn to God's word. On the days I was overwhelmed and felt that I couldn't take another step, His word was the voice in my spirit that kept me going. "My grace is sufficient." So, most days I did my best. Despite my weakness, God was true to His word and proved to me that His power is made perfect in my weakness.

Prayer

Dear Lord, please help me remember to turn to you on the hard days and remember the faithfulness of your word. Give me the strength to trust your grace and the wisdom to receive the promises you have for me.

March 30

Spilled Coffee Spilled Words
By Teresa Montalvo
Today's Scripture:

Let it happen.
Don't try to stop the spills.
Watch them splashing, running,
moving, crawling, dripping.
Watch the freedom the spills find.

Love, Love, Love.
Let these words infiltrate, penetrate the crevices, the dry areas, the crusty areas of your heart!
Let His words splash over you, drench you, until you find your freedom and your hope, restored!

Spilled Blood, Spilled Silence.
Because of you, because of me, it happened.
We, together with our small army, could not stop what happened that day.
See it running, moving, downwards, crawling to the ground.
The battleground where the greatest battle was fought. It slowly descends and begins to drip, drip, drip to the ground, the dry, cracked, crusty ground.

AND, as the last drop falls, a small, unnoticed puff of dust arises to its final anthem of groaning with all of creation and slowly descends, in silence, sprinkling itself upon that last drop.

And Silence Filled the Air.
In the silence we taste the bitter.
In the silence we are moved.
In the silence we hear.
In the silence, we smell death.
In the silence, we are changed.

Spilled Groans. Spilled Rains.

Groaning in the stillness of silence, The universe is stunned and can hardly breathe.
The rolls of thunder gather their momentum and rumble across the vast open skies.
AND on cue, by its director, it brings all to notice.
His gradual crescendo exhales a loud, crashing, clap, and vibration is felt throughout all of creation.

And slowly, ever so slowly, fades back into silence.
Let His blood cover you, drench you,
you will find freedom and your hope restored.

Rain, Rain, Rain.
Let the rain infiltrate, penetrate the crevices, the dry areas, the crusty areas of your heart!

Prayer

Let His spring rains pour, splatter, fall into streams until you overflow, until you can no longer contain it.
Refreshed. Drenched.

You, dear child, are loved with an everlasting love.
Don't let anyone stop you!

Jesus, I ask that you meet each reader in the center of what they are walking through! Thank you for paying a price we could not.

March 31

Only One Thing Is Needed
By Maryellen Greene
Today's Scripture:

When you are worried and troubled, do you get stuck looping in the overwhelm of it all? I know that can easily happen to me. Luke 10:38-42 shows us two different responses to worry & trouble. Martha was distracted and started to complain that she was left to do the work by herself. How often have I complained in this way? I'm not proud to say that I know this verse by heart...and scripture memory is not one of my strengths.

Recently, I was very troubled by a severe illness that left our youngest child stuck in bed for six months. It was scary and heartbreaking - nothing brought relief from the pain. I spent hours contacting doctors, looking for answers. I emailed a doctor that I was certain could help. His email reply kindly explained that he wasn't licensed to treat pediatric patients. Devastated, we felt all alone in our suffering again.

But at the bottom of this doctor's email was an incredible reminder of hope...I sobbed as I read the verse in his signature line. "You are anxious and troubled about many things" (Luke 10:41). I nodded yes, as tears rolled down my face and I sat looping in despair..." but one thing is necessary. Mary has chosen the good portion, which will not be taken away from her" (Luke 10:42).

The heaviness lifted. My perspective shifted from "stuck all by myself" to "safe & secure with Jesus" - from overwhelm to Jesus, our living hope in the most dire situations.

What worries and troubles do you need to surrender at the feet of Jesus? Take time today for the one thing that is needed and be transformed as you sit with Him. Anchor your soul to His living hope - no matter what you face, this can never be taken from you.

Prayer

God of all hope, nothing is impossible for You. Forgive us for complaining instead of worshipping You. Thank you for Jesus, our living hope, who sits with us in our despair and forever changes everything. Please help us desire You above all and open our eyes to see each day with Your eternal and ever-hopeful perspective

April

hope ✱ books
collections

April 1

When Love Permits Pain
By Sandi Banks
Today's Scripture: Ephesians 3:18-19

Nothing had prepared my mama-heart for the tragic rain-soaked April morning.

It was 1976, and the drizzly greys outside the hospital window matched my emotions. I held vigil at the bedside of my precious three-year-old daughter. So tiny. So fragile.

It happened fast: a freak accident, an early-morning race to the hospital, emergency surgery, followed by agonizing hours of waiting, praying, bargaining with God—desperately hoping the surgeon would emerge and tell us our little girl would be okay.

He did emerge but offered no promises. And so, we waited and prayed some more.

I watched her sleep, dreading the moment she would awaken and feel the pain. It came. She began tearing at the bandage, moaning.

"Mommy, pleeeease! Take this off. It hurts me."
I was helpless to remove her pain. All I could do was hold her, sing to her, love on her.

In her three-year-old world, she couldn't possibly comprehend
...that the pain was deep inside.
...that the bandage was helping, not hurting.
...that our seemingly cruel withholding of food and water was temporary and for her good.

As parents, we knew healing sometimes requires painful cutting; so, we permitted, even welcomed, this surgery. We love her. We understand that sometimes love permits pain.

Suddenly, I got it: a clear picture of our loving heavenly Father, hovering over us in our hurt.

"I'm here for you, Beloved."

Prayer

Oh Father, You do love us! You allow hardship and heartache in our lives for reasons we may never comprehend. But You want us to trust You in the midst of it. You comfort us through the healing process, then encourage us to rest in Your powerful promise: Beyond our momentary pain is Your greater purpose.

April 2

The Hope We Hold
By Linda Lowe Erley
Today's Scripture: Ephesians 1:17-21

When cleaning out my childhood home, I found a piece of paper taped to the inside of my father's bathroom cabinet mirror—something he opened each day. The tape was old and dried, the paper browned and tattered from decades in that spot. The handwritten words read, "There would be no Easter without Good Friday."

As I read Paul's passage above, I believe the eyes of my dad's heart were enlightened each morning to know the hope to which he was called – that incomparably great resurrection power that raised Christ from the dead –was at work in him. My dad suffered trials throughout his life. Jesus suffered on the cross. We suffer through the crosses we must bear in our own lives.

No matter how dark it seems, there is always God's light—filled with His radiant hope and power that rose out of the grave on Resurrection Day. God is always doing something new in our lives, even in the midst of our deepest pain. Don't miss it. Don't flee from it. That power that raised Jesus from the dead is at work in us as believers! Imagine that!

What pain do you need to lay down before Jesus today? Feel it. Grieve it. Lament it. He knows what you are going through—He carried your sorrows to the cross, bearing both your sin and pain. Resist the urge to stuff it down in fear, because beyond this pain is a glorious invitation just for you, your name beautifully handwritten in gold on the envelope. Jesus invites you to open the eyes of your heart to His unending hope.

I invite you today to carry on my dad's legacy of remembering: "There would be no Easter without Good Friday."

Prayer

God of our Lord Jesus Christ, the glorious Father, I ask that whatever crosses I am called to bear, the eyes of my heart would be enlightened. May I know the hope to which You have called me, the riches of Your glorious inheritance in the saints, and Your incomparably great power for us who believe.

April 3

The Ministry of Double-Dutch
By Kendra Vantrice
Today's Scripture: Isaiah 55:12

Before there were pews, there were playgrounds.
Before we memorized verses, we made rhythms.
Before someone told us we weren't holy, we already were.

In this season of spring—of rising, re-rooting, and return—I remember:
We've always had a ministry.
Not in pulpits wrapped in robes, but in Double-Dutch ropes.
Not in stained glass, but in cracked sidewalks.
Not in Sunday choirs, but in the beatbox and boom-bap that raised us.

Hip hop was our choir. The cipher was our sanctuary.
The claps, stomps, and rhymes were sacred. We praised with breath and body, in rhythm and resistance.

The Games Black Girls Play by Kyra D. Gaunt reminded me:
Double-Dutch wasn't a game—it was a formation.
It was training in timing, in risk, in joy.
You stood on the edge, heart pounding, waiting for your moment.
And when you jumped, the circle welcomed you.
When you jumped, you belonged.

That's ministry.
That's praise.
That's theology.

We didn't need permission to be filled.
We drank from the sacred well of our own breath.
The rhythm was already in us.
The ministry was already ours.

The world may still try to convince us we're outsiders to the sacred—
that our movement, our music, our memories are too loud, too Black, too girl to be holy.
But God met us in the circle.
God danced with us in the rope.
God wrote the gospel into our games.

Even the trees clap their hands.

Even the hills burst into song.
And so did we. So do we.

This is for the Black girls who jumped in—and for those still learning: we were always in the circle. We were always the sermon.

Prayer

God of rhythm and resurrection,
Thank You for the ministry of movement,
for the theology of play,
for the gospel that lives in our breath and beats.
Help me to unlearn the lies of unworthiness
and reclaim the rhythm You wrote into me from the beginning.

April 4

Stronger Than Your Secret Fears
By Lesley Swanson
Today's Scripture: Isaiah 41:10

Fear has a way of tightening its grip, doesn't it? Forty years ago, on this very date, fear convinced me to cover up my choices and hide my sin. I was terrified of being found out, so I made a decision that left a scar I carried for decades. Believing the Christian college I attended would expel me—and my future husband as well—I chose to abort the child I was carrying. In the days and years that followed, fear whispered I was beyond forgiveness. Fear told me God could never use me again.

Maybe you've felt a similar kind of fear—the kind that keeps you silent, ashamed, or convinced you're disqualified. It's the fear of secrets. And it's heavy.

But here's the truth I've learned: God is stronger than our secret fears. Isaiah 41:10 says, "fear not, for I am with you." Fear isolates, but God draws near. Fear weakens, but He strengthens. Fear shames, but His grace redeems.

I never imagined the place I once hid in shame would become the very place God would pour out His hope and healing. Once I surrendered my secret to Him to use, He wove it into His bigger story of redemption. The scar that fear told me to keep hidden is now a testimony of His grace.

Friend, whatever your secret fear may be, you don't have to stay stuck there. God is with you. His righteous right hand is not only strong enough to hold you—it's gentle enough to lift you out of the shadows. It's never too late to turn back to Him.

Prayer

Jesus, You know the fears I keep tucked away. Thank You for reminding me that You're stronger than any one of them. Help me to lift my eyes to see Your strength holding me. Turn what I've hidden in shame into hope, and let my scars tell the story of Your grace.

April 5

Will You Take My Hand?
By Abigail Ruth Miller
Today's Scripture: Isaiah 41:10

Giving one's hand in marriage is synonymous with giving one's heart and right to living independently. Marriage is a picture of our relationship with Christ. Here, our Beloved shares incredibly encouraging and intimate words of comfort.

He knows that we are often tempted to fear, but HIS PRESENCE is the reason He tells us not to fear. Now, when we first marry our spouse, we think we know them but the longer we are married the more we learn about who they really are. When we know God better, we know how wonderful, amazing and loving He is. We will never find any fault in Him.

He also tells us not to be dismayed. Once I was serving as a missionary in the Amazon jungle and came home from a two week trip to a remote community. When I opened the door to my home, an awful stench hit me. I found that the refrigerator had lost power and was never turned back on. The stench was enough to put me in a tailspin. But in that moment, God gave me the grace to WORSHIP at the top of my voice. In that moment, God took me by the hand, reminded me who my God was and helped me not to be dismayed at the HUGE, nasty mess.

Jesus promises huge benefits here. HE is going to strengthen and help YOU. You might think that you are not important, but the Creator of the universe takes your hand and promises to strengthen, help and uphold you. I challenge you to write this verse on a card and share this truth with someone you see today.

Prayer

Father God, You are so very kind to us! You gave us Jesus, who takes our hand, reminds us not to fear or be dismayed and promises to strengthen us and help us. You did not leave us alone here on the earth. We praise You for Your grace and kindness to us. We love you and trust you! Amen

April 6

Fill in the Blank
By Richard Dubay, Jr.
Today's Scripture: Psalm 66:16

Have you ever wondered why you're here or what you're meant to do with your life?

I've always been a computer guy. Since the day my parents got our first computer when I was a child, I've been writing code to make those computers do things. So it came as no surprise to me that when I asked God what I should do with my life, He said, "Use technology to reach people for Jesus."

God has given me talents and made me proficient in a few areas, so I can use those gifts for Him in whatever way He sees fit. The same is true for you. But how do you figure out what you're called to do? I've found a few helpful ways.

First, what are you good at? Where are your talents? Look to the ways the Lord has gifted you for clues.

Then, consider what burdens you. What things have captured your heart? Is there an opportunity where your talents and burdens meet? That's a good sign.

Finally, and most importantly, what has God said you should do with your life? Have you asked Him? I believe you can find your purpose by asking God to help you complete this sentence: "To use _blank_ to reach people for Jesus."

Everyone's calling is different, but they all lead to the same end. Whether you're a preacher, a plumber, a mechanic, a mom, or anything in between, use what you've got and let your life "tell what He has done" for you. You'd be amazed at how evangelistic a good life can be.

Prayer

God, we praise You for creating us with purpose and calling us into a story much bigger than ourselves. Help us to know our purpose and "fill in the blank" for us, so that we can use that purpose to make You famous.

April 7

Following His Path
By Kathy Gustafsson
Today's Scripture: Proverbs 3:5-6

I'm sitting at my kitchen table, in our partially renovated house, in the Upper Peninsula of Michigan. My view is of the pine and birch trees on our property, the ground covered with ferns that grow thick and high during the summer. Leaves flutter and shake in the breeze. Chipmunks dart and weave through the flora. The beauty and serenity of the U.P. are unrivaled, but sometimes I look around and wonder how I got here.

Our move to the U.P. started with a feeling. A sense that God was up to something and change was on the way. Then, a job change for my husband. Then the passing of my mom. Then a prayer that set our feet on a course where we couldn't - and still can't - see the finish line.

"Lord, make our next step so obvious that it would be disobedient not to follow."

A bold prayer is a dangerous one. His answer may keep you right where you are and offer new possibilities to know and serve Him. Or His answer may take you 900 miles away from home, into a new community and culture, into a new church and job, and to new people to whom you can minister.

It is exciting and equally terrifying to pick up and move to a place you've only visited a few times. But when you're walking in the path God has laid out for you, there is comfort and provision. When you're obedient to His call, there is blessing. When you pray big, bold prayers, there is assurance that God has heard your prayer, and He will show you which path to take.

Prayer

Lord, Thank You for the privilege of prayer. Thank You for being the infallible center of my trust. You know the big thing which is heavy on my heart today - move in Your power, move in Your truth, move in Your provision. I am ready and willing to walk the path You will show me.

April 8

Stay Rooted, Reflect Christ
By D'Toya Dove
Today's Scripture: Colossians 2:6–7

There's something powerful about being deeply rooted. When your roots are firm, storms may shake you, but they won't break you.

In Colossians 2:6-7, Paul reminds us to stay rooted in Christ, not just believing in Him, but walking with Him daily, reflecting His character in what we say and do. That kind of faith isn't surface-level. It takes time, intention, and consistency. But it's how we grow strong enough to stand steady when life feels chaotic.

The start of a new season always brings a mix of peace and pressure. Smooth days and unexpected disruptions. We can't control what comes our way, but we can control how we respond. And the more we're rooted in God's Word, the more our responses reflect Him and not frustration or fear.

Being rooted also means setting boundaries. It means prioritizing rest, protecting your peace, and fueling your spirit with truth. When we're spiritually dry, it's easy to react in the flesh. But when we're spiritually full, we can show up with love, patience, and wisdom even in hard moments.

So here's a heart check: What's been spilling out of you lately? If it's not reflecting Christ, don't shame yourself. Just pause, re-center, and get rooted again. His grace meets you there.

Let this be the time you grow deeper in God. You don't have to go through life alone – just stay rooted in the One who holds you steady. He will never leave your side.

Prayer

Heavenly Father, Thank You for Your Word. As I stay rooted in You, help me grow stronger in faith and respond with grace. I declare I won't be shaken or overtaken because I am grounded in You. Continue to build me up as I follow Your lead.

April 9

Hope Rides Steady
By Katrina Mintz
Today's Scripture: Psalm 23:5

In the saddle, posture is everything. One inch off can throw your balance, distort your cues, and confuse your horse. Tension builds. Communication breaks down. And joy? It gets lost in the struggle.

The same is true in our spiritual lives. When we lose focus—when we give the enemy even an inch in our thoughts, our relationships, or our calling—we drift. We brace. We forget the rhythm of grace.

Riding instructors often say, "Soft hands. Eyes up. Focus on the horizon." It's not just about technique—it's about trust. You can't lead with clenched fists or a downward gaze. You must ride with intention, surrender, and vision.

Scripture echoes this wisdom. Philippians 4:8 calls us to fix our minds on what is true, noble, and lovely. Galatians 6:9 reminds us not to grow weary in doing good. And Psalm 23:5 offers a stunning promise: God prepares a table for us—even in the presence of our enemies.

But we must stay seated. We must not let fear, shame, comparison, or distraction pull us out of alignment. Because where your eyes go, your body—and your spirit—will follow.

So today, check your seat. Loosen your grip. Lift your gaze. And ride with the kind of focus that honors the One who invited you to the table.

Prayer

Lord, Help us pause and consider our spiritual gait— whether bold or steady. Give us courage to claim every inch of our saddle with Your power and grace. Teach us submission, renew our focus, and steady our seat when the ride gets rough. Let joy rise in the rhythm, the learning, and the partnership with You.

April 10

Waiting On The Lord
By Tara L. Banks
Today's Scripture: Psalm 130:5

I don't know about you, but I don't love to wait. However, it is important to note that waiting on the Lord is not the same thing as waiting for your child to find their missing shoe. Waiting on the Lord is about learning to actively trust the plans He has for us and placing our hope in Him, regardless of the outcome. Sometimes, you may be filled with joyful expectation, as if you cannot wait to see what He's up to. At other times, you may be on the "edge of your seat" waiting, frustrated because you can't figure out why He's not on the edge of His. These are the moments when His timing seems off, and maybe, if you're honest, unkind.

Both kinds of waiting can be good and can draw us closer to Him if we allow ourselves to trust Him in the process. When we start talking about "waiting on the Lord," it's good to know how to do it well. I've found the best way to wait is by opening the pages of the Word of God. He speaks to us there and offers us direction. Trusting Jesus in the waiting is not about having all the answers and skipping along unaffected. Waiting on Him is a reminder that His word is true and can be trusted—not because we know the plan and the path ahead—but because we don't.

Before we know it, if we're waiting and putting our hope in His word and the clarity He can bring us, we'll realize that He was with us in every bit of the waiting, the exciting, and the excruciating. Then, on the other side of that time, His word will have made its way into our hearts and brought the hope that only He can provide.

Prayer

Lord, help me to wait well. Help me to lean on the strength of your word when I'm tempted to get ahead of your plans in excitement or when I don't understand your timing. Thank you for the hope that you bring us when we put our complete trust in you and in the words that you say.

April 11

Find Your Sense of Granny Gratitude
By Odessa Glover
Today's Scripture: 1 Thessalonians 5:18

Think for a second about your grandparents. As a kid, did their stories just seem to drag on like a road trip? What about as you got older? At some point, you learn to stop and truly listen. You might even find the little details laughable. If you can relate, you've got the key to appreciating life as it comes. I call it having a sense of granny gratitude.

My great-grandma is 97 years old today. She sets the utmost example for me on how to rejoice in the life God blessed us with. How so? Well, let me first point out that Granny has certainly faced her share of challenges over the years, including multiple losses of her own flesh and blood. Even after some devastating setbacks, it remains clear the Granny never takes anything for granted. An unexpected health concern? She is brave throughout the diagnosis and laughs it off when an easy remedy triumphs after all. A simple bottle opener? She finds it to be the handiest little thing. Our family reunion? Of course, she cherishes the time spent with her sister during that annual road trip!

Now, what about times in life that can leave you feeling defeated? Such times might seem to drag on like your grandparents' stories, too. Acknowledge the unwanted feelings that arise, but refuse to dwell on them. Otherwise, you lose all hope for what good still awaits you. God has the map to guide you out of that ditch of defeat, over the hills of harsh truths, and back onto the road of resilience. Never forget the stories, the lessons, passed down to you. Learn from them. Rather than asking God, "Am I there yet?", tap into your sense of granny gratitude along the unpredictable path to Purpose Palace.

Prayer

Heavenly Father, Thank You for the gift of life and ongoing blessings. In times of uncertainty, I look to You with hope in Your promises. Fill my heart with peace and guide my steps with love. Please help me remain grateful, trusting that Your plans for me are always good.

April 12

Recharge With Purpose
By D'Toya Dove
Today's Scripture: Philippians 2:13

Before we pour out, we must first plug in. That's the reminder I needed not just to prep naturally for what's ahead, but to pause, seek God, worship, pray, and recharge with purpose daily.

Recharging with purpose means recharging God's way, not in our own strength, but by abiding in Him and allowing His Spirit to renew us from the inside out.

God is not asking you to go through life empty. His Word in Philippians 2:13 reminds us that it's not our strength, it's His. He's the One working in us, energizing us, giving us both the desire and the ability to walk in His purpose. You don't have to force it. You just have to plug in and do what He says.

When we pause to honor God, to pray, and to worship, we create space to be filled again. That's where clarity comes. That's where peace flows in.

So today, I want to encourage you (just like I had to encourage myself): Stop striving in your own strength. Lay down the pressure to figure it all out or carry it all alone. Instead, receive His strength, let Him empower and energize you for this day and the days to come.

God has already gone before you. As you stay connected to His truth, He will fill you, guide you, and sustain you from the inside out.

Prayer

Heavenly Father, Thank You for working through me, for strengthening me, energizing me, and giving me both the desire and the ability to fulfill Your purpose. I don't want to live in my own strength. Recharge me with Your purpose today, for Your glory and good pleasure.

April 13

Don't Let the Weeds Win
By Dr. Shelley Kemp, Ed.D., SHRM-SCP
Today's Scripture: Luke 8:14

In Luke 8, Jesus tells a story about seeds—and one part has stayed with me: the seeds that fall among thorns. They take root, but the thorns grow up right alongside them and choke the life out of what was meant to thrive.

That feels all too familiar.
Because worry? It's a weed.
Distraction? A weed.

That constant striving for approval, the chase for the next opportunity, the next dollar, the next "like"?
Weeds, all of them.

And the thing about weeds is—they don't need an invitation. They show up unannounced and grow fast. Quietly. Subtly. Until one day, your mind is too crowded and your spirit too tangled to hear God clearly.

As a mindfulness coach, I've reminded so many women: When your inner world is cluttered, God's voice can get drowned out in the noise. Not because He's stopped speaking—but because we've stopped noticing.

So today, let me remind you:
Check your soil.
Uproot the weeds.
Tend to your heart.
Create space for stillness. For peace. For God.

Because you weren't created to live in survival mode. You were created to bear fruit that lasts. The kind that grows from good soil—nourished, intentional, and uncluttered.

Don't let the weeds win.

Prayer

Lord, help me tend the soil of my heart. Uproot the weeds—distractions, worries, and pursuits that don't reflect You. I don't want to miss Your voice. Make space in me for peace, presence, and purpose. Teach me to pause, notice, and nurture the fruit You're growing. I trust You to make it flourish.

April 14

He Delights In You
By Laurie Ostby Kehler
Today's Scripture: 1 Thessalonians 1:4

Today is National Gardening Day, and believe me, all of us gardeners have plants we delight in!

My favorites are fluffy peonies I can bury my nose into, old-fashioned double hollyhocks, and antique roses. My sister likes growing vintage apple trees and heirloom tomatoes (they make excellent sauces).

While we all have favorites in the garden, would it surprise you to know there are people in the Bible that God delights in as well?

God spoke with Moses in a close and intimate way, "Thus the Lord used to speak to Moses face to face, as a man speaks to his friend" (Exodus 33:11). God said about King David, "I have found in David the son of Jesse a man after my heart, who will do all my will" (Acts 13:22). And this favoritism wasn't about perfect performance. Both Moses and David failed tremendously in their lives—a fact God knew ahead of time!

When the angel Gabriel approached the virgin Mary, he told her, "Do not be afraid, Mary, for you have found favor with God" (Luke 1:30). Imagine that, to know you are one of God's favored ones!

But in fact, because of what Jesus did on the cross, we too, have become those in whom God delights.

He has bestowed upon us tender titles, such as children of God (Romans 8:16), friends of Christ (John 15:15), and loved and chosen by God (1 Thessalonians 1:4), to name just a few. Even more to the point, in Romans 8:15, we are told that we can call the Creator of the universe, God Almighty, Abba, which means Daddy.

It's a myth that your past mistakes, the addictions you struggle to shake, and your tendency to wander off the path disqualify you for God's favor. In his garden, you are one that God delights in, and he's very fond of you!

Prayer

Heavenly Father, what a delight to know that I'm one of your favored ones. So much of my thought life revolves around the idea that I'm falling short. Thank you for Your Word, which reminds me that I'm a new creation in Christ. Help me remember and walk in the confidence that I am called a child of God, your friend, and that you want to be close to me—like a Daddy.

April 15

Hope in Every Season
By Brenda Kaker
Today's Scripture: Romans 15:13

Living in Colorado, I'm reminded every spring just how unpredictable the seasons can be. Even when we know a season is coming, we can't always predict what it will hold. Some springs are unusually warm and pleasant, luring us into the hope of summer, while others are filled with snow and howling winds that remind us winter isn't finished yet. And then there are springs that tease us—one day offering sunshine and warmth, the next sending us back to scarves, gloves, and the snow shovel.

In the same way, life is full of seasons—some filled with joy, others with sorrow—and sometimes both arriving at once. Certain seasons we can anticipate: children starting school or graduating, weddings, or retirement. Yet even then, the details often surprise us. Sometimes they're brighter than we imagined; other times, stormier. Then there are the seasons we never see coming—the sudden loss of a loved one, an unexpected diagnosis, or a job loss.

The reassuring truth is that we can always choose how we respond and walk through change. We can resist it and exhaust ourselves, or we can lean into God's steadfastness, knowing He is never surprised by what each season holds. We can trust that He is already at work in ways we cannot see. Every season invites us to embrace a deeper faith and even deeper knowledge of Him.

Today, I want to encourage you—whether you're in a season you've dreaded, one you've longed for, or one you never expected—God's got this. He's got you. Lean into Him with open hands and an open heart. Look for where He's at work, and follow Him there. No matter what your season looks like, He is still writing a story of hope and redemption in your life.

Prayer

Lord, Thank You that You are with me through every season of life. When things feel uncertain, remind me that You already know what's ahead. Give me the courage to lean into Your leading and notice the ways You're at work around me. Teach me to walk with faith, hope, and a heart that's open to You.

April 16

Renew And Re-Awaken Season
By Veronica Bobo Morris
Today's Scripture: 1 Corinthians 15:3-4

Have you ever wondered about the significance of the day you were born? I'm just one of those who do and decided to find out some of the significance of my birthdate and month.

April is the 4th month of the year, marking the arrival of spring when nature starts to reawaken, renew, and rebirth itself after the winter season. The flowers and trees start to bloom with vibrant colors, and overall, nature is turning green again.

Not only is April synonymous with spring, but it is also one of my two favorite seasons. A season for all things new, beautiful, and refreshing. Just as God's word is a refresher to the soul, so is the Springtime.
Spiritually, April is a month of resurrection, hope, and positive change.

April is the month that Easter is most often observed (when Jesus arose from the dead, declaring all power, giving believers hope that is real and lasting). Occasionally, Easter falls on April 16th, for which I feel honored. Other Christian holidays in April include Mardi Gras, Shrove Tuesday, AKA Fat Tuesday, Ash Wednesday, and Lent.

In reference to the Bible, the number sixteen is a representation of Love and Loving. And in 1 Corinthians 13-4-8, there are 16 references to God's love in being patient, kind, non-envious, non-boastful, not being proud, and not to dishonor others, not to be evil-doing or being easily angered or self-seeking, non-provoking, but bearing all things and believing, hoping, and enduring all things.

Surrender to God in
Prayer to
Renew and
Inspire
New
Growth

Prayer

God, it is through Your way of showing us love and how to be love, from the death of Your Son, Jesus, on the cross to save us from our sins, that I have Faith and hope. I pray always to show gratitude to You and Your son, Jesus, for Your love, never having to imagine life without Your love.

April 17

Valuable Temple
By Erica Lewis
Today's Scripture: 1 Corinthians 6:19-20

Second Chronicles dedicates six chapters to the original temple's construction and dedication. The care and thought that went into it were immense, not just at its creation, but also how the priests continued their duties within it. Paul declared that we are the living and breathing temples of the Holy Spirit, meaning we had even more care put into us when God made us.

That same care should continue throughout our lives. I know in my life there have been several times when I let other people's opinions or actions cause me to believe that I was valueless and didn't deserve to look nice or care for myself spiritually. In those moments, I forgot my value as not just a child of God, but as a dwelling place of His presence.

Caring about yourself physically is important; however, spiritual care is where your true value is solidified. Spending time in Scripture, prayer, and godly companionship allows you the opportunity to become closer to God and learn about Him and who He says you are. It's much harder to care for a house (or temple) that doesn't belong to you if you don't get to know the owner (God).

Today, I encourage you to intentionally choose a time to spend getting to know God. This time should include reading the Bible and prayer, but it should also include times of silence. God wants to help you see your value as the temple, and He wants to teach you how to care for yourself, which is why we need to allow time to hear Him speak. Once you make this a lifestyle, it will be easier to remind yourself of your value as God's child and temple and become confident in who He says you are.

Prayer

Lord, Thank You that I am valuable and that You've chosen to allow the Holy Spirit to dwell within me. Remind me daily of my worth and help me to make time to spend with You. Teach me more about You and help me to live as the valuable creation I am.

April 18

Look Up: Turning to God for Strength
By Deb Schroeder
Today's Scripture: Psalm 28:7

Praising God and declaring His glory is not easy when faced with loss and heartache. In fact, in these moments, our voice often quiets as we draw inward to find the strength to endure, rather than looking to God. Our faith can waver when we feel broken. Yet, God's love is with us always, in every season. Looking up, instead of inward, can change how we experience both pain and God in our lives.

I learned this lesson first-hand throughout my dad's cancer battle. Whenever asked how he was, he responded with "Fantastic!" Some might say that he wasn't being truthful, but for him, these were the most honest words because he had placed his love and trust entirely in God long before cancer entered his world. Throughout life, he chose to counter hardships with his love for God, and facing cancer was no different.

I watched my dad sing the Lord's praises regardless of his physical pain as cancer ravaged his body. I saw my dad proclaim all the blessings from God despite cancer returning a second time to eventually capture his life. In every moment, I witnessed my dad look up and look to God because he knew that it was from Him that strength would come.

As we face struggles in our lives, we will have the choice to look up or look inward to find strength. The truth is, when we turn to God, rather than ourselves, we invite Him into our pain and allow Him to help carry those burdens. We acknowledge our own limits and glorify God's power and love for us. We open ourselves up to feeling God's presence as we navigate life's struggles. We are placing our trust in God, and that is truly a fantastic place to be.

Prayer

Heavenly Father, when I am in a season of struggle, remind me that You are always present and always with me. Help me to remember to look to You, to seek Your face, and to rejoice even in my pain because I can trust how much You love me and can trust that You will strengthen me.

April 19

Hope Rising
By Maria Burnett-Carroll
Today's Scripture: Psalm 42:11

A true confession: sometimes I interview my soul. It starts with pen and paper as I draw a simple stick figure of myself. Then I write my troubles, each a word or short phrase, creating an umbrella of stress and sadness.

Engaging in a similar exercise, the author of Psalm 42 wrote, "Why are you cast down, O my soul, and why are you in turmoil within me? Hope in God; for I shall again praise him, my salvation and my God." (Psalm 42:11).

Transferring my swirling, dark angst onto paper makes me breathe a little easier; my shoulders come down. Naming my weights and worries helps me identify what is really bothering me. It is the beginning of my journey to surrender my burdens to God. Honesty with myself and with Him brings sweet release and relief.

The truth is that we can confidently name our cares and cast them on God (1 Peter 5:7). He is the safest place for our truth-telling because He knows everything that we're carrying and loves us right in the midst of them. Jesus invites us to come to him with our weariness and burdens (Matthew 11:28-30). He exchanges them all for rest.

God's Word gives us hope that, despite how things look or feel, He can write His story of redemption over it all (Romans 8:28). The hard things in our lives don't get the final word. His goodness is always one step ahead of us, even into eternity. With Him, hope is rising.

Prayer

Heavenly Father, help me be honest about why my soul is feeling discouraged and weary. Help me name the things that are burdening me, so that I can surrender them to You. I trust in Your compassion for me that never fails (Lamentations 3:22-23). Help me turn to Your Word to fuel my hope when it is fading.

April 20

Get In The Boat
By Ada Bontrager
Today's Scripture: Genesis 7:1

Noah was a man of faith and obedience! He trusted the voice of God. He obeyed. He endured years of mockery, judgment, and ridicule. What was he thinking, building a boat of that size? After all, it hadn't rained in a long time! There appeared to be no need for an ark. The people had no idea what was about to come. We can learn from Noah that even if we can't see the end, it's important to trust and obey. It could be life-saving!

Noah wasn't just a man of faith and obedience. He was a surrendered man. He understood that the will and plan of God was way more important than his own. Noah was willing to lay down his own life to fulfill God's purpose. When he, his family, and all the animals were secure on the boat, it was God who shut them in! God sealed the ark for Noah and his family. God provided a place of protection for His children during a violent storm. Do you trust God like that?

When we are willing to lay down our own plans, agendas, desires, and even our own lives, it opens up a whole new world of possibilities! We get to partner with God and what He wants to do on this earth through us. What a powerful revelation that we have a larger purpose on this earth than to just live.

Surrender is rooted in faith and trust. It's about acknowledging God as the ultimate authority. Are you willing to get in the boat and let God take you where He wants you?

Prayer

Heavenly Father, I surrender my life to You. Increase my faith and strengthen my trust in you. I'm willing to do what you ask, go where You send me, speak what You tell me. My life is Yours. I want to be used by You for Your kingdom's sake.

April 21

The Aspiration of a Heart for God
By Elizabeth Clark
Today's Scripture: Romans 12:1

God's work on earth requires human cooperation. He is searching for a willing vessel, and the salvation of many depends on our willingness to be for Him. This helps us understand that our role is not passive; it is a vital part of God's plan. Our lives are meant to be living sacrifices, available for His use, not just for our own interests.

This is an incredibly optimistic message. God deeply treasures our aspiration for Him. He doesn't need perfect people, but those with a heart that longs to be used by Him. The stories of Moses and Hannah's mother show that God does not forget our desire to be for Him. We can be confident that God sees our hearts and will use them in His perfect timing.

For a long time, I felt like my life was too small to be used by God. I was busy with daily responsibilities and felt that my aspirations to serve Him were a distant dream. I would hear stories of missionaries and feel my life couldn't measure up. But this verse helped me see that God isn't looking for grand accomplishments; He's looking for a heart that aspires to be for Him. God treasures my simple prayer to be a willing vessel.

Do not let the anxieties of life distract you from God's purpose. Remember, you are an integral part of His plan. Your aspiration for Him is a precious treasure, and He will not forget it. Whether you are young or old, your heart for Him is what matters most. Present your body as a living sacrifice today—it is your reasonable service, and your Heavenly Father is looking for a willing partner to accomplish His will.

What are the things in your life that are occupying your time and energy? How can you re-prioritize your heart to aspire more to be for God and His purpose?

Prayer

Lord, We present our bodies to You as a living sacrifice, holy and well-pleasing. We confess our tendency to be occupied with our own affairs. Give us a heart that aspires to be for You and for Your work. We trust that You will honor our desire and use us to accomplish Your will on earth.

April 22

The Earth is the Lord's
By Laurie Ostby Kehler
Today's Scripture: Romans 1:20

Today is Earth Day. For the Christian, it's an opportunity to celebrate the world God has made—a world alive with color, movement, and wonder. All of creation—from peregrine falcons hurtling through the heavens to otters holding hands while they sleep, from neon-hued tropical fish to the quiet rustle of autumn's golden leaves—every corner of creation whispers of God's creativity and delight.

You don't have to travel far to witness this beauty. Step outside your door. Listen for the birds. Notice how the wind moves through the trees. Watch the dew on the daffodils or the insects investigating your garden. God is there, speaking through every detail, inviting you to pause and delight in his handiwork.

Spending time in nature restores more than our minds; it refreshes our souls and bodies. Science shows that even a brief walk among trees or by water calms the mind, lowers blood pressure, and lifts the spirit. Imagine that—God's design not only amazes us but also heals us.

When we notice His creation, we begin to see his heart. When David marveled at the sparkling night sky, he wrote, "What is man that you are mindful of him?" (Psalm 8:4). Each star in the night sky, each bloom in the spring, speaks of God's creativity and care for us.

This Earth Day and every day, take a moment to get outside. Breathe deeply. Look closely—delight in the small and the magnificent alike. Let nature remind you of God's unending creativity and his tender care. In noticing his creation, we discover hope: even in a chaotic world, the Creator's love is all around us, steady and true.

Prayer

Heavenly Father,
Thank you so much for this world that is saturated with your creativity and care. It is truly a wondrous thing to behold roses unfurling their petals, puppies bouncing in the grass, and amber leaves fluttering from stately oaks. Thank you for getting to witness this on a daily basis. Forgive me for taking it all for granted. Remind me to notice your artistry every day.

April 23

It's Always Sunny Above the Clouds
By Amy Leigh Hughes
Today's Scripture: 2 Corinthians 4:17-18

I will never forget the first time I flew in an airplane, when I was about 15 years old. It was a cloudy, rainy day. Soon after the excitement of take-off, the plane was fully inside those clouds, and there was white all around us. I held my breath.

The moment the plane burst out through the clouds into a completely blue sky and bright sunshine, I was awestruck. It had never really occurred to me that the sky was always blue, even when all you see on the ground is the clouds. From so high up, those clouds looked like little spots compared with the vastness around them. Though the sun was as bright as ever, the people on the ground were still experiencing the rain.

Something about seeing the world from such a zoomed-out perspective made the stormy problems of life seem much less permanent. It's easy to be consumed by the storms when they come because you are experiencing them with all your senses, fully embodied. Even when our whole being feels the pain and darkness, we have an anchor of truth, knowing what lies just beyond it.

The radiant sunshine streaming through the plane's windows felt like a call to hope. It was a reminder that no matter how gloomy things look, that's not all there is. The goodness of God doesn't disappear when the cloudy days come. It's always there, a permanent fixture from horizon to horizon.

Even more glorious than the sunshine is God's glory. How deeply we will rejoice to see his glory, having emerged from the dark storms of this life!

Prayer

God, even in the midst of the storms, please remind me that these afflictions are only temporary. Help me to trust that right above my pain, your glory stretches out eternally, unchanging. Thank You for Your goodness, and the strong hope of eternal bliss that is mine to claim in Christ.

April 24

How Long Til Morning?
By Diane Ward
Today's Scripture: Psalm 30:5

My eyes opened to a new morning, and for a split second, all seemed well until the overwhelming grief came pouring in once again, gripping my lungs to near suffocation. Yesterday had indeed really happened.

At 33 weeks pregnant, I went in for an ultrasound to check on my baby, and there was no heartbeat. I was in a state of shock. Was this really happening? How would I ever be able to endure the delivery of my baby into the world?

What do you depend on in seemingly impossible situations? My faith in God was what I clung to. I searched His Word for His promises and prayed like I had never prayed before. I asked God to help me so I would not be afraid when I delivered my son. And do you know what? He did. He gave me courage and amazing help. He brought a Christian labor/delivery nurse to my bedside who prayed with me before my induction, and He brought a waiting room full of fellow believers to pray for me while I gave birth.

The darkness of grief was real that day as my doctor placed my precious, lifeless son in my arms, but the undeniable peace and comfort I felt was also very real. Can grief and peace co-exist? I believe they can. It happened to me. As grief pierced my heart, a peculiar peace was also present. In that moment, I absolutely knew Jesus was the One comforting me in ways I never thought possible.

My faith grew to a new level during that time. Even though the sorrow lingered morning upon morning and the darkness of grief was real, I had the beautiful assurance engraved on my heart from Psalm 30:5 that joy would come again one day. And it did.

Prayer

Dear God, Thank You for Your immense love and for knowing each of us intimately well. I pray for those who are grieving the loss of a loved one today. Please draw close to them and fill them with Your perfect peace and the blessed assurance that joy will once again be theirs – one beautiful morning.

April 25

Broken Places Need a Healer
By Jennifer Niemann
Today's Scripture: Psalm 51:8

Today was my daughter's due date. Sure enough, labor began early that morning. Despite the epidural, I heard and felt a SNAP deep inside as I labored and pushed.

"What was that?!?" I gasped in alarm.

I fought to maintain composure and counter anxiety. My body was petite, my bones small. While delivering my son, I had experienced a broken tailbone and a painful year. I desperately wanted to avoid that situation again! My new doctor assured me she could prevent it.

A few more pushes, and my daughter arrived. The doctor proclaimed my tailbone untouched, and I relaxed, thankful for that particular mercy.

The next morning, as I unwrapped my newborn, I noticed something awry. When she cried, only her right arm flailed up and around. The left arm remained still at her side. Oh, no! Dear Lord, could she have the broken bone?!? I felt awful. X-rays confirmed a broken collarbone. Thankfully, newborn bones are like green sticks, and she would heal within a month. We needed only to be careful with her.

Broken bones require patience in physical healing. But often, we need patience in healing broken spirits and emotions as well. Heartbreak, trauma, grief, sin, and shame all require a gentle healer. Jehovah Rapha, God our Healer, invites us to bring these things to him in trust. He is the only one who carefully heals us in all of these ways.

Broken bones often mend stronger than before. Similarly, God can take any brokenness in us and restore us to a greater wholeness. And our scars tell stories of grace about how God, our Healer, mends us back together.

What broken places of your life is God at work healing today? Brokenness encourages us to wait on Him.

Prayer

Heavenly Father, You are Jehovah Rapha, God our Healer. Grant us patience while You bring healing to our broken places. Carry our pain and mend us back to complete wholeness, stronger from Your gentle care and grace. Thank You, Lord.

April 26

Hang On
By Hannah Louise Cox
Today's Scripture: Galatians 6:9

When things get hard, I want to quit, and honestly, in some situations, I have quit. Several years back, I was diagnosed with a birth defect that required major surgery, and I pulled out of on-campus college life for the second time within a year. I was ashamed, defeated, tired, and in physical pain. I wanted to quit college and write it off, saying I tried it, but it's not for me. I was tired of trying to make "normal" college work for me. I was done. But, while I was recovering, my mom challenged me to stick with it, not to make a rash decision based on challenging circumstances.

Life is hard and sometimes incredibly painful, but pain and suffering don't get the final word in our stories. Love does, and when we hang on to Jesus, we will be given the strength to persevere when life doesn't look like we thought it would. My life has been a series of pivots and taking the wild backroads to find a greater adventure with Jesus than the path walked by the people I wanted to be like.

This is your journey, and God's faithfulness has marked it, but it's also your choice to keep going one step at a time when it doesn't make sense. I hope you keep walking forward when you want to quit and aren't afraid of the pivots, as crazy as they seem, sometimes they lead to your wildest dreams. I graduated from college. It was an eight-year journey that led me to become an author writing to you. Cling to Jesus and His promises to you, and you will journey through the hard with a persevering spirit.

Prayer

God, Thank You for always keeping Your promises and never leaving me or forsaking me in any circumstance. Help me understand that perseverance is for both the staying and leaving seasons. Give me the wisdom to know when to stay and when to move on. Your love is carrying me through.

April 27

The God of Peace Is with You
By Sasha Abele Katz
Today's Scripture: Phillipians 4:9

Every night, after a few hours of sleep, my mind would wake, followed by a shooting pain down my chest. I have been here before. I know the feeling of anxiety and panic. Typically, my daily life moves forward without worry. However, once I am settled into sleep, my mind jolts awake, and my body alarms me, letting me know all is not right in my world.

For the last three years, we've sent two kids to college, and expenses have been adding up. To be candid, the debt had added up. Until I sat down and calculated, I didn't realize the total balance. The seasons were moving so fast that I lost track of paying off expenses on time. I had let the speed of life distract me.

From a wise friend, I learned about prioritizing types of debt and budgeting for every season. After wholeheartedly putting her advice into practice, the night anxiety should have stopped, but it didn't. The enemy sought to magnify what the peace of God had already carried me through. Once I recognized that I was holding the hand of God, who was leading me to the other side of the circumstance, I began to sleep peacefully again.

Even after we make a necessary shift in our lives, the enemy desires to keep our minds in chaos. However, the Apostle Paul teaches us that when we learn, receive instruction, and put wisdom into practice, the peace of God will be with us. The enemy can't have a hold on us when we clearly know that God is with us, for us, and helping us. We can live in godly confidence as we put wisdom into practice. We can sleep peacefully because the peace of God is with us.

Prayer

Jesus, help us to recognize our mistakes, learn from them, and receive wise counsel. Guide us as we put into practice what we learn. Lead us to the truth of the scriptures so that we can recognize where the enemy seeks to disturb our hearts and minds. Allow us to have peace as we put our trust in you.

April 28

Nothing Lost...Nothing Gained
By Elizabeth M. Anderson
Today's Scripture: Romans 5:3-4

Thirteen years ago, I said goodbye to a job I'd held for sixteen years. Chronic illness stripped away not just my career, but my apartment, my car, and my sense of stability. Questions were all I had left—and a haunting thought: should I end it all? At the time, I couldn't imagine another way forward. Hope felt lost.

Then I heard a still, small voice whisper: "Listen to a sermon by Bishop T.D. Jakes." The first message I saw was titled "Nothing You've Been Through Will Be Wasted." That sermon saved my life.

God didn't just see my tears, heartbreak, and despair like a spectator at a sporting event. He felt everything I felt because it was His pain, too.

That sermon marked the start of my life-changing faith journey. I began learning who I am in Him, what He believes about me, and how deeply He longs to restore what's been broken.

Did you know God has experienced loss, too? He lost the perfect world He created (Genesis 3). He lost the children He lovingly formed (Genesis 3). He lost His only Son to a vicious cross (Matthew 27:33-56).

Being stripped of what I thought I couldn't live without stretched my faith in ways I never imagined.

Thirteen years later, I see the purpose in my wilderness season: to prepare me to help others who feel lost, fearful, and hopeless. There is always a purpose in the pain.

This journey hasn't been easy, but it's been necessary.

Don't lose hope if you've felt loss, brokenness, or loneliness. Know this: God has a plan for your life. I never imagined I'd become an author—but here I am, a living testament to His plan. And I look forward to seeing what God has in store for you.

Prayer

Dear Heavenly Father,
You never promised a life without trouble, but You did promise Your presence. When life shifts unexpectedly, You remain our rock. Nothing surprises You. In Your sovereignty, we find peace; in Your foresight, hope. Thank You for being our protector, provider, and calm in every storm. Help us to trust You completely.

April 29

He Still Speaks Today
By Ms. Jewel
Today's Scripture: Jeremiah 33:3

How do you feel when you hear the words, "God told me"? I've witnessed a couple of responses. Either the listeners' eyes light up, they lean in close and eagerly await the words to follow, or they become uncomfortable and look for ways to redirect the conversation.

Do you find it hard to believe that God still speaks today? Our Old Testament verse for the day serves as proof that the Holy Spirit loves to reveal Himself to His own. I will even go as far as to say that He adores the heart of a true seeker.

Many are familiar with Jeremiah 29:11, but have you ever read past verse 11 to an even greater treasure? Jeremiah 29:12 says, "Then you will call upon me and come and pray to me, and I will hear you." He listens to us! Oh, but there is more. Verses 13 and 14 say, "You will seek me and find me, when you seek me with all your heart. I will be found by you, declares the Lord, and I will restore your fortunes and gather you from all the nations and all the places where I have driven you, declares the Lord, and I will bring you back to the place from which I sent you into exile."

Our captivity can take many forms. Mine was depression. My husband had alcoholism. At different points in our lives, the Holy Spirit has illuminated this same passage of Scripture as each of us has sought Him wholeheartedly. Then He led each of us to Jeremiah 33:3 " Call to me and I will answer you, and will tell you great and hidden things that you have not known."

The Lord wants to be found. He desires a relationship with us, and in a relationship, we converse with one another. It all begins by becoming a seeker. Then He will make Himself known to us, even speaking to us in ways we never thought possible!

Prayer

Father God, Sometimes I find it hard to believe that You would care to speak to me. Your Word assures me that if I seek You, You will reveal Yourself to me and speak to me. Oh, Lord, how I long to hear Your voice. Thank You for this promise. Today I wait expectantly to hear from You!

April 30

A Book About Me
By T.L.Hoff
Today's Scripture: Psalm 139:13-18

I am praying for you, My beloved child. Before I formed you in the womb, I knew you. I know every breath you've taken, every tear you have cried, every hair on your head. Even the places you have wandered. I know everything about you and love you with an everlasting love. On your best day, on your worst day, I love you the same. I created you for a purpose, with plans to prosper you.

Spend time with Me in My Word. I AM your Heavenly Father, full of mercy and grace. My beloved Son, Jesus Christ, gave His life for yours. Even if you don't know how to start, your Helper, the Holy Spirit, will guide you. It's always been about a purposeful relationship together, not man-made rules of religion.

Step towards me, and I will run to you. My arms are always open to you. My plans and purposes remain unchanged by your choices. Don't let the deception and distractions of this world destroy your eternal inheritance through Christ Jesus. Let go of the past. In times of weakness, fear, and exhaustion, take My hand in yours, and through Jesus, you can do all things.

My beloved child, I love you always and forever.

Prayer

Dear Lord,
Thank You for the marvelous works of Your hands, creating me so uniquely complex. I'm not a mistake and have a true purpose that You wrote about me before I was born. Thank You, I am washed clean through the blood of my Savior, Jesus Christ. Help me receive and believe Your truths about me and who I am in Your Son, Christ Jesus. Show me the way ahead and give me the courage to walk in Your integrity and wisdom. When it seems hopeless, guide me in Your Word, show me the way, and reveal who You are for me as my Heavenly Father. I will obey Your truth and leave the results to You alone. With a surrendered and loving heart to You, my Lord,
Your beloved Child

May

hope✱books
collections

May 1

Hope in the Valley
By Brooke B. Stark
Today's Scripture: Romans 8:28

One week before my due date with our second daughter, my life changed in an instant. A vehicle crossed into our lane and hit us head-on. By God's mercy, both my baby and I survived. My recovery took time, but my sweet daughter was left with a traumatic brain injury. After four tender years, the Lord brought her home to Heaven, fully healed.

Those years in the valley of suffering were some of the hardest I have ever walked. Yet, they became seasons of the deepest growth in Christ. Questions, grief, and tears were many, but in the midst of it all, the Lily of the Valley was present—His fragrance sweeter than the sorrow.

Trials press on our hearts and make us question God's character. "Why this, Lord? Why now?" Yet even when we cannot see, we can trust that nothing touches us without passing through His hands. Sometimes He shows His work in the lives of others. Sometimes it is in our own hearts where we see His refining. And sometimes, we are asked to wait in mystery, resting in the truth that He knows what we do not.

We are not abandoned in our pain. God is never cruel, and He never wastes a trial. In His time, when His purposes are fulfilled, the trial will end. Until then, we cling to the eternal hope in Christ—the promise that one day every sorrow will be swallowed up in joy.

So whatever trial you face today, remember this: God is in control. He is faithful. And He will never leave or forsake you.

Prayer

Dear Heavenly Father,
Help me to find joy in today's circumstances and grant me rest for my soul right where you have me. Thank You for being my everlasting consolation. Your character is good, and I trust You completely.

May 2

True Health Starts with Fear of the Lord
By Jenna Le Hamilton
Today's Scripture: Proverbs 3:7-8

From the very beginning, sin has been tied to our desire for independence from God- leaning on our own understanding instead of His. In the Garden of Eden, Eve fell for the lie that gaining her own wisdom by eating the forbidden fruit would bring her even greater life. Sadly, it only brought death and separation from God. That's the pattern: when I lean on my own wisdom apart from God, I wither. But when I lean into His wisdom, I find life.

The promise of Proverbs 3:8 is strikingly physical: "healing to your flesh and refreshment[b] to your bones.." The Hebrew word for "health" here is rooted in the verb rapha, which means to heal, restore, or make whole. This term is used throughout Scripture for God's healing power—both physical and spiritual. In Proverbs 3:8, "health" isn't just absence of sickness—it's wholeness, refreshment, restoration. God knows the ache in my body as much as the ache in my heart. His wisdom brings peace that seeps into every layer of who I am.

One way I yield to the Lord's wisdom is trusting the way God designed my body—to honor its signals, to rest instead of striving, to believe He didn't make a mistake in the way He knit me together. The boundary lines God set for me exist so that I may flourish. This hope in God that leads to healing also points me forward to the full restoration of my body that will come when Jesus returns.

So today I remember: my own wisdom ends in death, but God's wisdom leads to life. Life that is full, whole, and healthy in Christ—now and forever.

Prayer

Heavenly Father,
Thank You for reminding me that I don't have to rely on my own limited wisdom. Teach me to trust You fully, to turn away from what pulls me from Your presence, and to rest in Your guidance. Bring healing to my body, peace to my mind, and nourishment to my soul as I walk with You. Fill me with awe for who You are, and help me find hope and renewal in Your wisdom today.

May 3

When God Whispers a New Beginning
By Lesley Swanson
Today's Scripture: Psalm 138:8a

On May 3, 1999, I came home from a conference for Christian authors, speakers, and leaders with something stirring in my heart. At the end of those three days of teaching and training, the Lord whispered to me that I would write a book–and it would be called Secret Scars. It would be based on one of the hardest decisions of my life–the abortion I had kept hidden for years.

That night, I sat with my dad and told him what God had placed on my heart. He was weak and near the end of his life, but I still believe he heard me. After years of smoking, my dad was battling cancer. I used to pester him about quitting, sometimes a little too bluntly. He eventually did, but not soon enough. Even so, that evening, as I shared about the book, I felt hope over what God was just beginning–mingled with grief over the impending loss of my dad.

Looking back now, I see how God often plants new beginnings right in the middle of endings. Loss doesn't cancel His plans. In fact, it can deepen them. That night reminded me that even when life feels fragile, God's promises are strong and His purposes endure. As Psalm 138:8 says, "The Lord will fulfill his purpose for me; your steadfast love, O Lord, endures forever. Do not forsake the work of your hands."

Friend, maybe you're in a season where something precious feels like it's slipping away. Don't miss the gentle whisper of God's new beginning in your story. His steadfast love will never let you go.

Prayer

Lord, thank You that Your steadfast love endures forever. Even in seasons of loss, Your whispers of new beginnings are not silenced. When my heart feels fragile, remind me that Your promises remain strong and You will fulfill Your purpose for me. Grow what You plant in me into something that honors You and brings hope to others.

May 4

Faith in the Small Things
By Jessica Haberman
Today's Scripture: Proverbs 16:9

Before I ever met my husband, he was already making choices that would shape the life we share today. While many of his age were quick to spend, he saved. While others sought the next best thing, he invested wisely. He even went without basic comforts, like keeping the heat off in the winter, because he was determined to build a steady future. He learned to live with less, not knowing that one day those decisions would make room for more.

At the time, I doubt he could have seen how those small, daily choices would have such a lasting legacy. But now, as I sit in the cozy home we've built together and watch our children grow up on our farm, I see the fruit of his faithfulness. His discipline made our dreams for our family possible. My husband's wisdom and diligence made it possible for us to obtain the farm we longed to raise our kids on.

It humbles me to remember that God was preparing our story long before our paths crossed. What looked like a sacrifice was also an investment. What felt like a delay was a foundation under construction.

Nothing is wasted with God. The unseen choices we make today, like acts of discipline, sacrifices of comfort, even long stretches of patience, are never meaningless. They are the very things God can use to prepare us, and those we love, for blessings we cannot yet imagine.

What faithful choices, big or small, might God be asking of you today to prepare for tomorrow?

Prayer

Lord, Thank You for the ways You use ordinary choices to prepare extraordinary blessings. Help me be faithful in the small things today, trusting that You are writing a story bigger than I can see. Please guide me to make choices today that honor You and prepare the way for the future You're building.

May 5

Streams in the Desert
By Karen Kay Smith
Today's Scripture: Isaiah 43:19

Today marks the day I stood at the altar and said "yes" to love again. It was not the journey I expected my life to take. Loss had written itself into my story, and loneliness had often sat heavy on my heart. Even as I walked into this new chapter, I carried both joy and sorrow.

What surprised me most in that season was not the joy of finding love again, but the loneliness that came with it. The people I hoped would celebrate with me did not. Instead of support, I felt the sting of disappointment and the weight of being misunderstood. Their response stirred insecurity and even shame in my heart—shadows I didn't expect to carry into such a hopeful day. Yet, in the quiet, God reminded me: You are never alone. I am your steady presence, your constant companion, your greatest support.

God has a way of bringing new life out of barren places. Just as a spring bubbles up in the desert, or roots stretch down to find hidden streams, He gives us strength to stand and courage to begin again. Sometimes His greatest gifts come wrapped in unexpected beginnings—chapters we never thought we'd write, but ones He lovingly authors. When others cannot or will not cheer for us, God Himself is our steady applause. Loneliness may visit, but abandonment never will.

If you are walking through a season that feels uncertain, or if you find yourself craving support that others cannot give, take heart. God is already making a way for you. What feels like wilderness can bloom with beauty when His hand is on it.

Prayer

Lord, You are the God of new beginnings. You bring streams to our deserts and strength to our roots when life feels dry. When others are absent, let us feel Your nearness. When joy feels fragile, breathe peace into our hearts. Help us receive Your gifts with gratitude and walk forward as witnesses to the fact that You make all things new.

May 6

Hope Abounds in Trials
By Sasha Abele Katz
Today's Scripture: Romans 15:13

Of the three Christian virtues, Faith, Hope, and Love, I was the least acquainted with hope. My skin-deep friendship with hope was not because I didn't know its definition. In fact, I had used the word many meaningful times in my life. I just didn't know hope's value. Hope is like most virtues or truths; we must meet them face to face before they become intertwined in our hearts.

During my daughter's senior year of high school, just ten days before the college dance audition season began, she seriously injured her back. In some instances, we praise God's timing and, in others, we question it. After thirteen years of dancing without serious injury, I was baffled and crushed for my daughter. What was God doing through this injury in this unreasonable timing?

In times of disappointment, hope is easily shaken. When rocked, we have the opportunity to be wide open to the growth of hope in our souls. God is not only the God of Love and Giver of Faith, He is also the God of Hope, who promises to fill us with Joy and Peace, in believing.

What do we believe in our circumstances? Sisters, we have the privilege to believe that God will work out our circumstances for our good and to His glory. This is the meaning of Hope. But it's not in our own strength, it is by the power of Holy Spirit that we will abound in Hope.

My daughter is now a sophomore in college, and she is thriving. As a mama and a sister in faith, I am now well acquainted with hope. Hope has a deep place in my heart. I just needed to meet the God of Hope, face to face.

Prayer

Jesus, Meet my sister in her questions about your timing in her life. Help her to be open to hope when life does not make sense. Give her the faith to believe that you will work out her life for her good and your glory. Overcome the obstacles in her life as she sees you as the God of Hope.

May 7

Teach Us to Pray
By Laurie Ostby Kehler
Today's Scripture: Luke 11:1-4

Today is the National Day of Prayer. For many of us, prayer can be frustrating or, at the very least, very mysterious.

We don't see immediate answers to our prayers. Is it because we are not praying correctly? Do others have more "pull" with God? What should we say? Is there a formula that will work?

Perhaps we're frustrated because we start with the wrong focus. When Jesus taught what we call The Lord's Prayer, he announced a new king and a new kingdom, coming to earth.

When we pray, rather than focusing on merely "my" needs, perhaps we should focus on inviting the Kingdom of God to earth.
Begin by acknowledging who God is—his power, authority, and position.
Remind yourself that his name is holy and not to be used lightly.
Invite the Kingdom into your state, city, or home.
Surrender your wishes and desires. Keep an open hand, not a closed fist. It's not my will be done, it's thy will be done.
Now we get to the asking part. Ask not just for your needs today. Ask bigger.
Don't forget that you need forgiveness, all of us do. And He grants it as we forgive those who have sinned against us.
God knows we struggle, so ask for his help to be immune to temptation and be delivered from evil.
Sum up with a reminder of who you're talking to, and gratitude for His ability and authority to make things right.

While you might feel he doesn't want to hear from you, or he's too busy in the Middle East right now, scripture assures us that this is not so. 1 Peter 5:7 says, "casting all your anxieties on him, because he cares for you."

Prayer

Heavenly Father, Thank You for so thoughtfully teaching us how to pray. I admit that I often forget to think about or speak of your majesty and authority. How incredible that the God who split the Red Sea and set the planets spinning wants to hear from me. Thank You for this honor and privilege to be a part of Your kingdom come and Your will be done!

May 8

Trust the Pace
By Reverend Dr. Juana Jordan
Today's Scripture: Proverbs 16:9

I was on vacation with my best friend. We took a walk one morning, and she left me in the dust. She's a fast walker. At one point during the walk, she turns around and yells, "Hey, J., are you okay back there? I'm sorry I walk so fast." I told her there was no need to apologize or wait on me or slow down, because we all have our own pace.

I was supposed to graduate with my doctoral degree in 2023, but I moved to a new city, took on a new job, and was unable to finish. I wouldn't be able to graduate at what I perceived to be "on time." And I was devastated. In my mind, this pushed me back. I would be on the sidelines instead of graduating with my cohort.

This was not the plan.

I called a friend who was also in my program, and to my surprise, she wasn't graduating either. So, "we can walk together," she said.

The Proverbs writer reminds us, "The heart of man plans his way, but the Lord establishes his steps." Although we have agency, we must also live with flexibility. God can change and shift our life plan and pace at any time. I had a plan – to graduate at a certain time – but God "directed my steps" in a different way. My journey would just be different.

Two days before this day, on May 6, 2024, I graduated with my Doctoral degree. And along with it, a deeper faith and trust that God's way robs us of nothing.

As the old saying goes, "delay does not mean denial." It just means God's timing and pacing are better than our own.

Prayer

Lord, Thank You for being the director of our steps. Forgive us for striving to stay on our own timeline instead of trusting Yours. Help us to find peace at your perfect pace and to see every detour not as a setback, but as a path forward to the More you have for us.

May 9

Hidden in Plain Sight
By Alana Deutschmann
Today's Scripture: Isaiah 43:19

I do not have a green thumb. Anything I know about plants comes from my dad. He came to visit one afternoon and checked on how my small tabletop palm tree was doing. I told him it was dying, so I'll be throwing it away. "But there are new shoots growing, didn't you see?" After he casually said this, I was shocked, embarrassed even, because I had definitely not seen them yet.

Hours later, I was still pondering our simple interaction when I realized that while it was my earthly father who pointed this out to me, it was reflective of our Heavenly Father. My dad didn't chide me for not taking better care of the plant or make any peckish comments about the new shoots being right there. What was evident to him was a blind spot for me. My focus had only been on the bigger palm fronds, which were clearly withering. I had completely missed the new shoots growing. In the same way, God does not berate or shame me as His child for failing to notice what should have been obvious.

This plant was a vivid reminder that I can spend so much time fixating on or ruminating over seemingly lifeless areas and then miss where God is actually tending to new growth. Maybe I'm assuming or expecting Him to move in a certain way, and He is doing something completely different. Sometimes, I just need others to speak hope into the dreary, dormant places of my life.

What about you? Can you believe afresh today that it's possible for Him to make a way where there seems to be no way? Or is there someone who needs your words of life and blessing spoken over them or to their situation?

Prayer

Good Shepherd, you are gracious and patient, but I confess that it often feels easier to believe this for others than it does for myself. Give me eyes to see you and what you're doing. I offer the hopeless places in my soul and circumstances to you as I rest in your faithfulness.

May 10

More Than You Can Imagine
By Reverend Dr. Juana Jordan
Today's Scripture: Ephesians 3:20

If my late college President, Dr. Robert Albright, could see me now, he might be wearing that coy smile of his and saying, "I told you so!" On the eve of my college graduation, I was adamant: There would be no master's degree in my future. I didn't need it. "I'm going to be a journalist, Dr. Albright, and that is on-the-job training."

He was smiling then.

Wouldn't you know it, 18 years, post-grad on May 9, Mother's Day, and the day before my mother's birthday, I was among those at Candler School of Theology at Emory University in the Class of 2011, walking across the stage with a Master of Divinity degree. Heading into the world to be a pastor, no less. I was graduating from the same university where my grandmother and aunt took me on a sightseeing tour during Thanksgiving break, my first year in college.

It's all mind-blowing.

God is always actively working to show us that there is more and that our biggest dreams are still small to God. Paul speaks to it here: "Now to him who is able to do far more abundantly than all that we ask or think, according to the power at work within us..." (Ephesians 3:20).

I never asked for a master's degree or a life as a pastor; it was beyond my imagination. And that trip my grandmother and aunt took me on was not a random sightseeing tour; it was God's subtle way of preparing me for a place I didn't even know I was destined for.

So, just think about what God has in store for you. What if the detour in your life or the unexpected change in plans is God leading you to what you can't yet imagine?

After all, God is full of surprises.

Prayer

Box-shattering God, thank You for your surprising plans that are so much bigger than our own. Forgive us for limiting You with our small imaginations and our own timelines and goals. Help us to trust that your detours are divine appointments, leading us to a future more abundant than we could ever ask or imagine.

May 11

Never Walking Alone
By June Wilkerson
Today's Scripture: Romans 12:2

I had felt a tugging at my heart for some time now, but I was afraid to take the leap. I was terrified, in fact. What if I wasn't good enough, or what if I was a complete disaster?

This year, I chose to return to the classroom to teach middle school students. It was, of course, terrifying, but I knew I was meant for more. I knew I was exactly where I was meant to be. I had the opportunity to change lives for the better and support students with disabilities in helping them become better individuals.

Letting go of all of the noise, all of the trauma, all of the nonsense in this world, has allowed me to just simply sit and pause and reflect on my why, my who. Even on the darkest days, the lord has been my light. Eventually, I grew into the light for others.

I see my students for who the lord intended them to be. The lord always provides what you need to get the job done. That can be your coworkers, your family, your friends, and, oftentimes, those you least expect - your students. Even when we stray from the path of the lord, no matter how long or how far, he is always waiting to meet us where we are.

No matter how low we may feel, or how much distance is between us, he never leaves our side. Wherever our mind may take us, God is always with us.

Prayer

Heavenly Father, Thank You for your many blessings, and Your will to provide for us. May You continue to meet us where we are and provide the heavy lifting for those who need to be lifted up on this day.

May 12

The Beauty In The Battle
By Brittany Pennel
Today's Scripture: Ecclesiastes 3:11

Eleven years ago, I said yes to a man I loved, and to the covenant of for better or worse. I just didn't know how much "worse" would come before the better. We both brought brokenness, two children each, and wounds from being battered, bruised, and abandoned.

I didn't believe people stayed. He had a guarded heart and deep struggles with trust. We were fighting invisible battles—and didn't have a honeymoon phase.

Our parenting styles clashed. The silence was louder than apologies. The pain felt too familiar, and I wanted out. This was not what I signed up for. I cried out to God, but every time, His answer was the same: Stay.

Staying wasn't easier—but God was doing something deeper. He was teaching me obedience. Obedience that said yes to the promise, even when emotions lied. Obedience that believed God could do the impossible and that chose love. Loving through pain, forgiving when it hurt—that's the kind of obedience that pushes back darkness. And somewhere in the ashes, beauty began to rise.

Forgiveness softened hardened hearts. Our love grew deep roots. Our children became best friends. What was once his, mine, and ours became our family. Obedience doesn't feel brave—but it is.

Choosing to love through pain, to forgive, to hope—it is a holy act of war against everything the enemy tries to steal from us.

Jesus did what only He can. He healed the broken parts, taught us how to trust, and taught us how to fight for one another instead of against each other.

Today, I have a marriage that I fight for in prayer. A miracle full of laughter, deep friendship, prayer, and a love that's been tested and made stronger. What was broken has bloomed—because I stayed, because God is faithful, and because obedience leads to healing.

Prayer

I believe you are in every battle. Remind me of who you say I am when I feel weary, unseen, or unsure. Be my strength when I am weak. Bring healing, hope, and restoration. Give me eyes to see my spouse the way you see him. Make my marriage a place of refuge, laughter, and friendship. Let your grace cover every gap.

May 13

Friendship and Joy
By Dr. Katrina Hunter Mintz
Today's Scripture: Micah 6:8

In a world that feels like it's unraveling, friendship, woven with love, kindness, and humility, becomes a quiet resistance. It reminds us that love is a practice, not a posture. In that practice, anger softens, and joy has room to breathe. Even when the air is thick with grief and noise, lightness can be found in shared stories, laughter, and simple presence.

We hear plenty about what people are against. But opposition without vision rings hollow. What we stand for shapes our leadership, our choices, and our relationships. When we fixate on what we oppose, we risk being defined by resistance instead of being moved by compassion.

We were made to walk with God—doing justice, loving kindness, and choosing humility—not to live in perpetual opposition.

Joy can feel hard when anger feels justified. Yet joy is not denial or the opposite of righteous anger; it is love in motion. It slips through the cracks when we choose connection over isolation, presence over fixation, and gentleness over reaction. Find the place where the heart steadies, and gratitude is thick. That is where joy arrives unforced. It's the shared laugh with family, a calm hand, the friend who volunteers just to be there. Joy turns ordinary tasks into sacred ground.

I want to be known for that kind of joy. The kind that makes space for trembling bodies and tired hearts. The type that steadies, listens, and keeps showing up with love, patience, and time. When we push away anger and make room for joy, even when it's inconvenient, we're not merely reacting to what's wrong; we're choosing what is right and resilient.

Prayer

God of Light,
In the heaviness of this world, help us choose joy. Let friendship be our quiet resistance, and compassion our loudest voice. Fill our hearts with soul-rooted joy that heals, connects, and strengthens. May we show up with courage, live with purpose, and spread Your hope wherever we go.

May 14

Child of Promise
By Dava R. Caballero
Today's Scripture: Isaiah 43:1

When God gives a promise, you can bet the enemy will try to steal it away from you. Such was the case with our third child, Alex. After a difficult pregnancy, he burst into life full throttle! Alex radiated joy and never met a stranger. A few months before his 4th birthday, we almost lost him.

My sister and I took our toddlers to a salon. I watched as Alex and his cousin played with some toys on the floor. My sister was finishing up with her cut when a vehicle came crashing through the storefront wall. Dazed, we all emerged mostly unscathed from the site, except for Alex.

The details are now a blur; all I remember is him eventually lying in my arms, falling in and out of consciousness, blood dripping from his mouth. My sister and I sat on the curb with our babies. As we waited for the ambulance, the Holy Spirit waited with us. We prayed in the spirit, and supernatural calm enveloped the scene.

When a pastor friend came to pray with us during the two-week hospital stay, he commented that we just don't know why these things happen. I confidently replied, "I know why! Because God has a plan for his life that the enemy is trying to derail."

Of course, we shed many tears and logged hours of personal and community prayers for our little guy. He pulled through with precious scars that remind him of God's faithfulness to this day. Different and heightened petitions went up during his teen years as we saw our son of promise wander and stray off course. Yet again, God came through! Alex is now in full-time ministry, sharing the love and miracle-working power of our awesome God with everyone he meets.

Prayer

Thank You, great Jehovah, for comforting us in times of distress. You are our ever-present help in times of need. You make the way before us, and You lead us through the fire. Help us to see through Your eyes. We trust You. We trust Your plan.

May 15

Dolphins, Monarchs, and Milkweed
By Janet Armitstead
Today's Scripture: 2 Timothy 1:7

I had felt afraid and alone, unmoored, like a ship without a safe harbor. Ironically, going out into open waters, spending a star-filled night under the cover of only a simple tent, with the silence of an island blanketing me, again showed me how God restores me through the natural world.

The ocean always renews me, and on the crossing to Santa Cruz Island, aboard the Island Packers ferry, I breathed in draughts of sea air, and my panic abated. Feeling the powerful swells beneath me, seeing the endless expanse of blue, I felt soothed. We were met with a pod of playful bottlenose dolphins. As I leaned over the railing, one of these large animals leapt from the water, like an aquatic ballet dancer, splashing me and causing me to burst with delight. I squealed and grinned like a child. Another dolphin expelled air through its blowhole–and the mist kissed my face. My heart and mind felt whole.

On the island, I learned about the resilience of this wounded place, which experienced the devastation of anthropogenic stressors. The island is still recovering, but there is reason for hope. The number of endemic island foxes is now stable. The milkweed, which has existed there for thousands of years, is flourishing. The monarch butterflies are preparing to overwinter. Bees are pollinating the plants, as they have always done. I realized I am resilient, too, and that God takes delight in restoring me. I am inspired not just to embrace nature's recovery, but also my own.

I look forward to returning to Santa Cruz Island to further aid in research and preservation efforts, as the island continues to heal. I have faith that I will find perennial wholeness in God by turning my anxious thoughts over to Him for His regeneration.

Prayer

Untamed God,
Thank You for reforming us into courageous people who embrace the wildness of life. May your power live in us, allowing us to experience both sound and hopeful judgment, and may all our fears vanish like sea spray in the summer sunlight of your gaze.

May 16

God's Love...Agape Love
By Dawn Reselle Fowler
Today's Scripture: 1 Peter 4:8

There are storms of life that can bring about chaos, anger, hopelessness, and confusion, but once everything comes to a complete halt in our lives, things begin to change. The problem or situation that seemed so difficult and unbearable at first becomes a place of love, peace, and hope. Gratitude shows us how to navigate imperfect situations,, and God's unconditional love demonstrates His acceptance. It creates an opportunity for you to see God's unending, everlasting, and never-ending love through His eyes. His love and compassion are overflowing, and they carry grace, mercy, hope, gentleness, and forgiveness. Therefore, if you have found God's love and gratefulness, you have found everything; you have found agape love.

When we take the time to reflect on God's love, it is like finding a treasure. It is filled with so many wonderful things and experiences that exploring the treasures of God can exceed a lifetime. I know that for many of us God used various examples of unconditional love: family, friend, event, etc. Ultimately, finding God's unconditional agape love slowly, gradually, and purposefully begins to unfold and radiate through different parts of our lives as we let it. Eventually, it should not be hard to express or give love because it changes your life. The amazing thing about God's love is that it not only changes you, but it also affects others around you. It gives you a sense of peace and comfort like never before. You begin to truly feel good on the inside and outside, and you gain a new perspective on life. Remember that the beauty and power of God's love and learning to be grateful through life's imperfect situations bring about acceptance and more love in your life.

Make a list of ways you have experienced God's unconditional love.

Prayer

Jesus,
Thank You for all you did for us in Your race here on earth, keeping Your eyes on the prize of joy. Lord, would You help us keep our eyes fixed on the joy set before us—the glorious moment when we will be fully and completely united with You? We love You and long to be with You.

May 17

Not Counting the Minutes
By Kati von Schmitten
Today's Scripture: Ecclesiastes 3:1-8

Last Sunday, I was happy. I smiled through Mass. I flitted from room to room, crossing off small tasks. I snuggled with my husband. I took time to read. I was sunshine. There was no real reason for my joy. It just was.

This Sunday, I struggled to get out of bed. My limbs felt heavy. I wanted to be alone. Nothing seemed to bring me into the present moment. The fog wouldn't lift. There was no real reason for my depression. It just was.

Both days are valid. Both are days I will experience again, often without warning. I used to get bogged down in guilt when I was having a great day, ruining it with anxiety about how long it would last.

But Ecclesiastes reminds me to rest in peace. There is a time for a good day. There is a time for a hard one. Neither will last forever, and that's okay. Their impermanence makes both worth acknowledging, appreciating, and accepting.

And somehow, knowing this makes the bad days a little less heavy, and the good days shine just a little brighter.

Prayer

Lord,
Thank You for being with me on every kind of day. Thank You for understanding that Your creation will experience both, and for letting us know it's okay. Let Your steady love be my constant, when everything else rises and falls.
May I trust that You are present in both the bright and the dim, and that in all things, somehow, all shall be well.

May 18

Silent Prayers, Faithful Answers
By Annette Stanly
Today's Scripture: Psalms 37:4

In India, arranged marriages are part of our culture, but as a young girl, the thought of marrying someone I barely knew felt overwhelming. I was encouraged to pray for my life partner while still in high school, and I did so faithfully.

One prayer was especially dear to me: I asked God for a full year to get to know my husband before marriage. I never told my parents. It seemed too unusual to even suggest. But I whispered it often to God, trusting He understood my heart's longing.

During those waiting years, my mother would periodically bring me a bio and photos of potential matches, asking for a decision by the end of the day. The pressure was overwhelming. But God guided me through family members who would voice concerns, and I began adding to my prayer: "When it's my man, everyone would say yes."

Years later, through a mutual friend, my mother heard of a good family searching for a groom for their daughter, who also had a son. My mom casually suggested that if both families liked each other, we could arrange marriages for both children. When she brought my future husband's bio, her first words were exactly what I had prayed: "Everyone says yes." Both families agreed, and my engagement was set before I even met him.

Since my brother's wedding also needed to be arranged, the timing worked out perfectly. We were married exactly one year from our engagement, on May 18th. God had answered the prayer I had carried silently in my heart for so long.

Friend, God hears the silent prayers you dare not speak aloud. He knows your heart's deepest desires even before you voice them. Trust Him with those whispered longings. He cares about every detail that matters to you.

Prayer

Lord, Thank You for hearing even the quietest prayers of my heart and for guiding me through every closed door. Help me trust You more deeply, knowing You care about every detail of my life and protect me in ways I cannot see. Teach me to delight in You daily, and wait patiently for Your perfect timing.

May 19

Clothed with Strength, Compassion, and Dignity
By Michelle Barringer
Today's Scripture: Proverbs 31:25

Does anyone help you choose your clothes? With four older sisters, I had plenty of help. But one day, someone clothed me with something unexpected.

My dad's birthday was May 19. (God rest his soul!) In his mid-thirties, he became ill. Tragically, Multiple Sclerosis (MS) invaded his body. I was one year old at the time.

The father I grew up with was not the man my older siblings experienced. Dad built them furniture, fixed broken machinery, and danced with them. I witnessed him lose his bodily functions. Before I was a teenager, I assisted with his care, helping him walk and eat.

One day, Dad's spastic arm caused him to spill hot coffee on his lap. Someone else cared for him during the day, so we didn't learn of it until evening when he started to go into shock after wetting himself.

While waiting for the ambulance, I held his hand as Mom removed his wet clothing. That's when she discovered third-degree burns. I saw my dad cry for the first time in my life. Having experienced a third-degree burn myself just a couple of years prior, I knew this excruciating pain.

As mom laid a clean sheet over his lower body to hide his nakedness, I felt something being wrapped around my teenage heart. Just like my mom draped a sheet over my dad, Jesus draped compassion and dignity over my heart. Jesus revealed that just because Dad was disabled and couldn't take care of himself didn't mean he wasn't worthy of honor and respect.

Jesus clothed my heart with compassion and dignity. And guess what? Those match anything we choose to wear on the outside.

Every day we can choose what we wear, but there's only One who can drape us with strength, compassion, and dignity.

Prayer

Father in heaven, clothe us this day with your strength, compassion, and dignity so that we can value, respect, and honor others. Every person deserves to be treated with dignity. Help us to remember that. Drape us in Your clothing so that we give You honor and glory in how we treat others.

May 20

Keeping Your Heart Focused on Christ
By James Hatcher
Today's Scripture: Proverbs 4:23

Each day we stand at the crossroads of so many choices: friendships, dreams, and challenges. The world will say, life is wide open, but as a believer, this thinking can bring our hearts under fire. The world will pull on it, tempt it, distract it, and even try to shape its desires. This is why the verse in Proverbs is so powerful.

Solomon knew all of these temptations would pressure us, and so he tells us we can't guard our hearts, once in a while, or if we get time. At all times, we must make Jesus our top priority.
We guard our hearts because "from it flow the springs of life" (Proverbs 4:23).

The person we become is the culmination of our habits, choices, and, more definitively, our focus.
The heart that focuses on comparison will live chained to insecurity.
The heart that focuses on affirmation will crave being liked more than being genuine.
However, the heart that focuses on Jesus and His truth, His love, His correction, that heart will grow to desire the things that please the Lord.

Solomon challenges us to consider what's taking most of my attention and lay those things at the throne of Christ. Are the things my heart is focused on making my walk with Jesus stronger or weaker? Do my habits have me spending more time looking at a screen... or turning to the One who made me?

Prayer

Jesus, help me guard my heart. There are so many things trying to pull me away from Your goodness. Help me keep my focus locked on who You are. Give me wisdom and the strength to say no to what pulls me down, and passion to chase after Your heart.

May 21

A Holy Interruption
By Rose McCombs Jordan
Today's Scripture: Psalm 116:7

By the time 2020 ended, most of us felt worn thin. It was a year heavy with loss, change, and uncertainty for the entire world. For my family, that heaviness carried an even more personal weight. After two years of remodeling our home, we sold it in September. The day before we signed the closing papers—while loading the last of our belongings into storage—my mother-in-law passed away. My job had already stretched me beyond my limits, demanding more than I could give. By the time the sale was complete, I was drained—physically, mentally, and spiritually.

We moved in with my father-in-law to help him through the transition of losing his wife. While we searched for a new home, months slipped by without success. Then, an unexpected door opened: the chance to serve as park hosts at our favorite state park. We bought an RV, and on May 21, 2021, we pulled into our campsite and began a new season of life.

It wasn't just a change of address—it was a holy interruption. The rush and noise that had defined my days gave way to the steady rhythms of creation. At first, the stillness felt unfamiliar—like stepping off a moving train and finding the world strangely quiet. But in the kayak, with water lapping gently against the hull, or in my hammock beneath the whisper of leaves, God began to restore me. I discovered that stillness is not the absence of purpose, but the presence of peace. When we set aside the noise, we enter sacred space—where God meets us with His gentle voice, His healing touch, and His renewing presence.

Prayer

Lord, Calm my restless thoughts and quiet my striving. Teach my soul to rest in Your goodness and trust Your timing. Help me turn down the noise and receive the peace only You can give.

May 22

God's Love
By Francesca Follone-Montgomery, OFS
Today's Scripture: Matthew 22:37

Relationships are wonderful opportunities to share God's love, even if they may not always be easy. They often require a forgiving heart, a compassionate soul, and an open mind towards compromise and sacrifice. Imagine someone who would sacrifice their life for you. Someone capable of such selfless love is quite rare, yet when you feel a very special connection to someone, you start to believe in the possibility of that sacrificial, endless love.

I felt that when I met my husband in 1996 in my home country, Italy.

Three years later, we got married on this date. Thinking about it made me realize the sacrifices we both made to adjust to our different cultures and blend them to create our own unique one. It was not easy, and it still feels challenging at times; yet, I think about a metal cross someone gave us as a gift: it has two wedding bands replacing the body of Christ. It bothered me at first, then I realized that it symbolizes both spouses' sacrifices to achieve Eternal love.

Jesus Christ made that sacrifice by dying on the cross to show us all His unconditional love and to keep God's Eternal promise. I dare not compare a marriage to a crucifixion, but I do think that the Matthew 22:37 quote reflects the matrimonial vows.

Your spouse is not God, of course, but your love for God could be part of your love for your spouse. By inviting God in your marriage and asking the Holy Spirit to help you seek Christ in your spouse, soon enough you will feel that special connection amplified as you will be able to see God's Love in your spouse's eyes.

Prayer

Eternal God,
Thank You for your merciful, eternal love.
Please fill our hearts with unconditional love for our dear ones,
send Your Holy Spirit to be our companion through life, and
help us always to see Christ in others.

May 23

When Temptation Calls, Faith Whispers Strength
By Margaret Ellis
Today's Scripture: Galatians 6:9

I remember it vividly. I was the "good girl" on a high school graduation trip to Cancun. I never drank alcohol, smoked, or crossed physical boundaries in relationships. Sure, I was tempted at times, but I was deeply rooted in my church youth group and had little desire to chase the typical teenage rebellion.

But Cancun brought a whole new environment—no parents, no curfews, and a legal drinking age of 18. Surrounded by more than 20 friends, the pressure was real. I stuck to drinking Coke, though my friends occasionally tried to spike it. I was also the only girl in our room of four who was actually sleeping in my assigned room each night. My faith in Jesus gave me the strength I needed to withstand temptation.

There's something especially hard about waiting when temptation whispers, "You could have it now." Whether it's a desire for attention, success, intimacy, or escape, the urge to take a shortcut can be strong – especially when doing the right thing feels slow and unrewarded.

Then came college – an even greater test. Parties, boyfriends, and a culture that glorified recklessness. The temptation to blend in was constant. During that season, I stumbled upon Galatians 6:9. It became my anchor.

Choosing to rely on my faith in Jesus to help me with self-control wasn't always easy. I wasn't perfect, but I aimed to please Jesus.

Looking back, I realize what God was showing me: self-control is a form of strength. It isn't about restriction; it's about walking in the Spirit with purpose. In a world pushing indulgence, discipline becomes your quiet superpower.

What's one area where you can show self-control today? Trust me: God sees your perseverance. And He will reward it.

Prayer

Dear God,
Strengthen us to resist the temptations that promise quick satisfaction but lead us away from You. Help us stay faithful when the waiting feels long. Teach us to trust Your timing and believe that the reward You have promised is worth every moment of obedience.

May 24

Fishes and Loaves
By Amanda Wise
Today's Scripture: John 6:1-13

Long ago, nestled among a multitude of hungry people, a young boy surrendered his supper. Those fishes and loaves were meant to sustain him for the day. We don't know much about this unnamed boy, but we do know that he gave all he had—and that he didn't go hungry. In fact, he was more than satisfied. In his willingness to surrender what seemed so small into the hands of Jesus, he was filled. Yet not just him—thousands of others were also fed and satisfied, with twelve baskets left over as a display of abundance. This young man's simple gift, offered from what he had, sparked a ripple effect that Jesus used to bless many.

No matter our past—whether lovely or tainted, no matter our skills—whether many or few, no matter our level of mastery—from simply willing to try to seasoned professional, no matter the labels given to us by ourselves or others, no matter our past victories or failures—when we surrender to the kingdom of God, whatever loaves and fishes we carry become an offering acceptable and pleasing in His sight.

The spotlight shifts from our limited view of life to possibilities we never thought imaginable. We move from clutching tightly for ourselves to participating in the multiplication of the kingdom of God. When we give what we have for His glory, we will not lack. Instead, our deposit—our willingness (no matter how small our offering may seem)—becomes like a pebble dropped into water. It cannot help but create a ripple effect of blessing for others, perhaps even a multitude.

Prayer

Dear Lord, Thank You that all I have comes from You. Thank You that You can redeem and multiply whatever I place in Your hands. Show me the areas of my life that I have not yet surrendered to You, and give me a heart like that of the young boy who trusted You with all he had. May You be glorified, and may Your kingdom be advanced through my fishes and loaves.

May 25

The End is Better than the Beginning
By Sasha Abele Katz
Today's Scripture: Ecclesiastes 7:8

Twenty-five years ago, I walked down the aisle in the month of May. The procession was conducted through a beautiful garden pathway to a gazebo with a view of the New River, which flows through downtown Fort Lauderdale. Although my in-laws claimed it would rain, it was a perfectly mild, sunny day. I had both my mom and dad on either side of me, and I moved with confidence that the Lord was present in this lifelong commitment between two twenty-somethings.

Twenty-four years ago, life got hard. We had babies right away - met with equal joy and exhaustion. My dad was diagnosed with cancer that didn't have a cure. My in-laws disagreed with a lot of our life choices and pressed in hard. The economy crashed along with our little mortgage business. That was a lot for a young and inexperienced couple.

Leading up to our wedding date, I purchased a vintage placard featuring the most famous verse about love. It said, "True love bears all things, believes all things, hopes all things, and endures all things. Love never ends." My twenty-something self didn't know what all of that actually meant. However, my fifty-something self has some of those qualities written on my heart.

Dear friends, especially you newly married sisters, life comes in seasons. Some seasons are gut-wrenching. Difficulties can stretch your marriage and cause you to question the godly confidence you once had on your wedding day. There will be a handful of times where it appears that obstacles can't be overcome, and perhaps you are better off parting ways. I am here to tell you that there is value in staying until the end of a matter. The end may very well be better than the beginning.

Prayer

Lord Jesus, Help us to remain steadfast in love in our marriages. Teach us to embody love in every season, even through obstacles that seem impossible to reconcile. Help us stay the course with hope and optimism. Give us the faith to embrace the wisdom that, oftentimes, the end of a matter is better than its beginning.

May 26

Putting Our Plans In His Hands
By Alana P. McIntyre
Today's Scripture: Proverbs 19:21

I can still picture the bright-blue binder I carried with me daily during the six months I planned my wedding. And I can still remember the excitement I felt as I tucked in magazine clippings of decor, dresses, and decadent desserts. Planning that special day gave me such joy. From music selections to the minute-by-minute itinerary I distributed to absolutely anyone involved in our nuptials, I thought I had every detail completely figured out. I was as prepared as I could possibly be.

And then came the day of our wedding. Thunderstorms raged in the morning, my soon-to-be husband's face was sunburned from a last-minute golf trip the day before (how would that look in the pictures?), and the caterer dropped our cake on the way in (that would definitely not look great in the pictures!). One by one, my perfectly laid plans were tainted by the harsh reality of life. But I still married the love of my life; I still got to celebrate with family and friends from near and far. I still made memories that I carry with me to this day. And I still laugh when I lug out my photo album and show my kids our lopsided wedding cake.

As time went by, and our family expanded, my plans became even more intricate, with multi-state summer road trips and a nearly impossible weekly schedule of four kids involved in after-school activities. The truth is this: more often than not, my original vision never came to pass. And yet, each week we overcame obstacles and learned to savor the surprisingly simple moments. Slowly but surely, I'm learning that plans will come and go, but even when things don't go exactly as we expect, God has His hand in the outcome. And some things turn out even better than we imagine!

Prayer

Dear God,
Thank you for being the ultimate Creator, the great Designer, the detailed Planner. We are made in Your image, and I am grateful for that innate desire to plan. But more than that, I am grateful that I can entrust all my plans to Your care and trust You with the outcome. Because Your plan for each of us is good! May we rest in that truth.

May 27

The Frazzle Free Formula: Your Path to Peace
By Tasha Spears
Today's Scripture: John 15:5

I plopped down in my chair as thoughts swirled in my mind. I mentally reviewed the list of things I needed to do and the places I needed to be over the next few days. The more I thought about it, the more overwhelmed I felt. I knew I had prayed over each opportunity and received God's peace, committing to each one. So, why was I feeling so overwhelmed?

I know that God's plans for me do not include feeling frazzled. So, how do I go about my day without feeling anxious and frazzled?

I must remember that God's original plan for His people is to dwell with them. God dwelt with Adam and Eve in the Garden, and later, God's presence dwelt in the tabernacle. Jesus came to dwell with mankind on earth and encouraged His followers to abide (or remain) in Him. After Jesus died on the cross and rose from the dead, He ascended to heaven. God then sent the Holy Spirit to be our Helper, Counselor, and Defender. The Holy Spirit indwells every person who has accepted Christ as their Savior. His presence is with us every moment of every day.

Abiding in Christ means we have an ongoing relationship with Him. We read the Bible, talk to Him, obey Him, and depend on Him. As we participate in this relationship, He will guide our decision-making, be our rest and comfort, bear our burdens, and be our strength. Abiding in Him is a choice we make.

How can you intentionally choose to abide in His presence today? How does the awareness of being in God's presence transform your perspective today?

Prayer

Lord, Too often I feel overwhelmed and frazzled. Help me to reframe my thinking about my day to "Jesus and me". Everywhere I go and everything I do, it is "Jesus and me". Today I choose to abide in You.

May 28

Letting Go and Letting God
By Tyann Beenken
Today's Scripture: Psalm 46:10

I was struggling to stay afloat, juggling the needs of a growing family, homeschooling, and the demands of running my own physical therapy practice. I began to sense God whispering in my soul, "It's time to let it go." The "it" was my business. Only I did not want to let it go. Instead, I tried everything I could think of to keep it going. Then one day, I had my own "road to Damascus" experience. While out for a walk, I heard God ask, "Why are you fighting so hard to keep a door open that I intend to close? Stop fighting against Me and start trusting in Me."

At first glance, Psalm 46:10 may seem to call us to a quiet, contemplative life, but, in context, it is given as more of a rebuke. The Hebrew root word for "be still" is "rapha," and it means to cease striving. It carries the image of someone giving up a fight, letting go, and surrendering. In this passage, the command is to stop fighting against God and to acknowledge His power, sovereignty, and control over all things. He alone will have the final say.

That day on the road, God spoke to my heart. He had more for me, but His more required that I stop resisting His voice, obey, and let go. In the surrender, I found the joy, peace, and rest that I did not even know I was missing. How about you? Is there something that God is leading you to do, but you find yourself struggling to obey? Are you holding on to something He wants you to let go of? Cease striving and trust the I AM who can do more than you could ever imagine, even in the letting go.

Prayer

Abba Father,
I confess my desire to control things and have my own way. I acknowledge that Your ways are not always my ways, but they are always for my good. Help me to trust You, and give me the courage to obey, even when it means letting go.

May 29

Grounded in Faith, Growing in Love
By Kia Simmons
Today's Scripture: Ecclesiastes 4:12

Today, Ken and I are so blessed to celebrate 21 years of marriage and 25 years of friendship.

It's been a beautiful journey filled with highs, lows, and plenty of unexpected twists and turns. Through it all, we've learned that the key to staying strong and committed to each other isn't just love or communication—it's our shared faith.

Over the years, we've discovered many lessons, but here are three that mean the most to us:

1. Read Scripture and Worship Together
When you invite God into your relationship, you create space for healing, growth, and clarity. In times of hardship, verses like Ecclesiastes 4:12 – "a threefold cord is not quickly broken" – remind us that there is strength in unity and that we can face challenges together.

2. Marriage Isn't About Being Perfect
We've made mistakes and had our share of disagreements, but what matters most is learning to forgive. Colossians 3:13 says, "bearing with one another and, if one has a complaint against another, forgiving each other; as the Lord has forgiven you, so you also must forgive." Choosing grace, patience, and forgiveness has carried us through the rough patches.

3. God Has a Plan for Your Union
As we grow, both individually and together, we hold on to the promise of Jeremiah 29:11: "For I know the plans I have for you, declares the Lord, plans for welfare and not for evil, to give you a future and a hope." Keeping our hearts anchored in His promises gives us hope for tomorrow, instead of fear.

Prayer

Lord,
Thank You for being at the center of our marriage. Continue to strengthen our bond, guide our hearts, and let our love shine as a reflection of You.

May 30

The Strength of Deep Relationships
By Liz Caffman
Today's Scripture: Ecclesiastes 4:9-10

I remember lying on the floor watching the Daytona 500 in 2001. I was fresh out of high school, in my first year of college, and most weekends I returned home for the comfort of the familiar. College was stretching me academically, but even more so relationally, and I longed for the people who knew me best.

That Sunday, around twenty of us gathered at my "aunt and uncle's" house. Not one of them was related to me by blood, yet every voice in that room was one I had known since childhood. I felt no awkwardness, no distance—only the warmth of belonging. Then came the crash. My dad's eyes stayed fixed on the screen as Dale Earnhardt Sr., his favorite driver, collided with the wall. The gasp in the room was unforgettable, as was the stunned silence that followed.

But when I look back, it's not the tragedy on the television that stands out most clearly. It's the people. These chosen family members had shaped me in countless ways—through their hospitality, honesty, and a willingness to speak the truth, even when it was hard. They taught me how to honor others, how to love deeply, and how to walk through both joy and pain with open hands and hearts.

That was the first time I ever watched tragedy unfold in real time. Today, such moments are all too common. Yet, I still carry the lesson of that afternoon: the weight of sorrow is bearable when you are surrounded by people who know you and love you. Deep, meaningful relationships can anchor us when life crashes unexpectedly. They give us room to breathe when grief threatens to suffocate and remind us that we are not alone.

We were never meant to do life in isolation. God designed us for connection—relationships that don't shy away from hard conversations, but instead open the door to hope, healing, and possibility. When tragedy strikes, it is the presence of others who truly know us that helps us see light breaking through the tunnel.

Because in the end, it's not just the events we remember. It's who we were with, and how their love carried us through.

Prayer

Father, thank You for surrounding me with people who love, encourage, and strengthen me. Teach me to treasure deep relationships and to be a source of love and truth in the lives of those around me. When life feels heavy, remind me that I was never meant to walk alone. Place me in a community that reflects Your heart, and help me to do the same for others. In Jesus' name, Amen.

May 31

Significance
By Sarah Fry
Today's Scripture: John 15:4

We live in a day when everyone seems to be an expert, with a platform to prove it. It's easy to feel hopeless or confused about what it means to be significant. God has been reshaping my understanding of significance, and here are a few things He's teaching me.

Our desire for significance isn't sinful—we were made in God's image to reflect His glory. But that desire must be understood, educated, and ultimately released. What makes us feel significant often stems from the very gifts He has given us. Yet when we try to fill the God-shaped space within us with our own significance, it becomes counterfeit and leaves us unsatisfied. True significance shines when our gifts flow from His life within us (Ephesians 2:10).

But what about anonymity—feeling invisible? The longing to be recognized can disguise itself as striving, false humility, or people-pleasing. Yet Jesus reminds us that making a "big difference" is not the goal. His short ministry was marked by solitude, surrender, and communion with the Father, yet it changed eternity.

What about the constant push to "hustle harder"? Nowhere in Scripture are we told to hustle. Dreams aren't wrong, but the way of Christ is steady obedience. Fruit comes not from hurry, but from daily cultivating the right conditions and leaving the results to Him.

So how do we know where to be significant? Frederick Buechner said, "The place God calls you to is the place where your deep gladness and the world's deep hunger meet." Paying attention to what drains us versus what gives life can bring clarity.

Ultimately, significance is not found in achievement, recognition, or comparison. It is found in being fully known and loved by God. From this deep abiding, true fruit grows.

Prayer

Jesus,
I want to learn from the example of Your life. Sometimes I feel like I am hopelessly hidden. But then I see the powerful example You gave me... walking in step with the Father, impacting a few in a deep way. Please help me to lean into the things that give me deep joy and reflect Your glory!

June

hope✱books
collections

June 1

His Sheep Know His Voice
By Kay Ashley
Today's Scripture: John 10:27

I didn't grow up in church, which is wild when you consider that my father was one of twenty children. His parents had even built their own church with their hands out of an old army barracks. That's how deep the legacy ran.

But instead of continuing that heritage, my father ran in the opposite direction—far from Jesus, far from the church, and far from the gospel his parents held dear.

He gave my sisters and me names with African, Arabic, or even Muslim roots. No Bibles in the house. No prayer over food. No "Jesus loves you" lullabies.

And yet... Jesus still came for me. Not through tradition. Not through religious routine. But through His voice. Gentle. Personal. Life-changing.

I've now been walking with the Lord for over 25 years. This was not because my father passed down the faith, but because Jesus doesn't need a paved road to find His sheep. He will call you out of darkness, into light, and onto a path that makes no sense without Him.

Maybe you're praying for someone who seems far gone—someone who was raised better or never raised to know Him at all. Don't lose heart. Jesus has never lost one that the Father gave Him. His voice breaks through lineage, rebellion, and unbelief.

Prayer

Jesus, You don't need a perfect family tree to do a perfect work. You find Your sheep even when they don't know they're lost. Thank You for calling me by name. I trust You with the names I'm praying for. Speak, Lord. They'll hear You. They'll follow. You're faithful, and I believe.

June 2

As I Follow
By Jane H. DeLong
Today's Scripture: 1 Corinthians 11:1

"I love God!" My two-year-old grandson declared to his parents. As they walked along, Ethan continued to talk. "Ethan going to get baptized." "What does it mean to be baptized?" His mama asked. "I follow God."

The Sunday before this conversation took place, Ethan had watched and listened intently as his mama and thirteen other people shared their testimony and were baptized. Some may say two is too young to understand such a complex spiritual concept. But God tells us to "train up a child in the way he should go..." (Proverbs 22:6) and that God's righteous acts will be told to children not yet born (Psalm 22:31).

We do this through our prayers and by faithfully living a Christ-like life before our children and grandchildren. Ethan's understanding of baptism began because he saw his mama's baptism, and she and our son talked to him about what it meant.

Children mirror what is modeled.

We must be intentional to model Christ before them. We don't have a "do as I say, not as I do" attitude toward parenting; we say as Paul, "Be imitators of me, as I am of Christ" (1 Corinthians 11:1).

Michael and Kelly are walking out what their words are saying, and Ethan's young heart is being shaped by what they are living in front of him.

What child in your life needs to see Jesus modeled by you? Today, remember: Young hearts are shaped by what you live out. Follow Jesus while they follow you.

Prayer

Father God,
Thank you for blessing us with children in our lives. Empower us to live Christ-like lives before them. May we reflect Jesus so that they become like Him. Let our lives become their lessons.

June 3

That Can't Be God... Or Can It?
By Kay Ashley
Today's Scripture: Isaiah 55:8

At home, he was perfect.

My son obeyed without attitude, cleaned as well as I did, and said "Yes ma'am" like he meant it. But at school? He was terrorizing his teachers. The same child who honored me at home became unrecognizable in the classroom. I didn't know what to do.

Then I heard God say, 'Call his dad.'

It didn't make sense. We weren't close. I felt like a single mom even when we were married. I didn't even know if his father was truly rooted in the Lord. But God wouldn't let it go.

I obeyed.

And then I heard Him whisper: I'll take care of him.
My son went to live with his father, and they never looked back.

Today, he's thriving in Washington, D.C., serving in the honor guard. He's one of the most respectful, focused, responsible, and level-headed young men I know. He has a strong bond with his father, a great bonus mom, and a restored relationship with me. He still honors his dad's words as an adult.

That obedience, the one that made me question everything, turned out to be one of the holiest yeses I have ever given God.

Maybe He's asking you to release something... or someone. It feels unnatural. Unsafe. Illogical. But hear me: when God says go, let go. He sees the end while we're still wrestling in the middle.

Prayer

Lord, Thank You for being trustworthy even when Your instructions feel risky. Give me the courage to obey without all the answers. Help me trust that what feels like a loss might become the greatest blessing. Remind me that surrender is never wasted. You are faithful to finish what You start.

June 4

The Faithfulness of God
By Gwen Christeson
Today's Scripture: Matthew 17:20

If you are facing a problem that seems as big and immovable as a mountain, turn your eyes from the mountain and look to Christ for more faith. It is the power of God, not our faith, that moves mountains.

Today is my grandson's birthday, and I will always remember seeing God's perfect love. Despite my grandson's diagnosis and having to spend sixty days in the NICU, we saw them turn to God during this hard time. My son and daughter-in-law waited patiently. They never gave up.

My grandson's birth was filled with so much joy and so much pain. But God promises to carry us when we are unable to walk beside Him. All they could do for their newborn son was to love him fiercely.

I saw it in how they showed up every day. They were even living in an RV in the hospital parking lot so they could be there for their son. All we could do as a family was to pray and trust God with the outcome.

When we are discouraged, we must remember God's faithfulness. My son and daughter-in-law showed us how to persevere, even on days we didn't think we could go another day waiting for him to come home.

My grandson is a testimony of God's faithfulness. We thank God for the precious gift of this beautiful boy. The journey ahead may look different from what we expected, but we trust God. God has blessed them with strength, courage, and love.

Prayer

We praise You, Lord, for loving each one of us with your everlasting love. Help us live lives overflowing with purpose. We pray our loved ones never forget how much we love You and how much we love them. Thank You for being with us during hard times and for moving mountains to show others they can be moved.

June 5

Hope Deferred But Not Denied
By Robin Pobiak
Today's Scripture: Proverbs 13:12

Several years ago, I was leaving work when a sudden wave of dizziness struck, followed by numbness on the right side of my body. My heart pounded as I debated whether to drive home or head to the ER. For months, I had experienced similar episodes–along with unexplainable fatigue–and chalked them up to stress from work and my master's program. Was this another panic attack, or something worse–a stroke?

I chose the ER. Soon, I was undergoing CT scans, bloodwork, and being hooked to heart monitors. After an overnight stay, doctors ruled out anything heart-related but referred me to a neurologist. That visit marked the beginning of a long and exhausting journey.

Months of tests eventually led to a diagnosis of multiple sclerosis. My heart sank. At the time, my husband and I had just helped launch our church's first family ministry program. Then, almost overnight, I had to step away to focus on my health. The anchor of hope I had been holding onto seemed to slip away.

Perhaps you, too, have faced an unexpected challenge that made you question God's promises. You're not alone. Even John the Baptist–who had baptized Jesus and declared, "Behold, the Lamb of God, who takes away the sin of the world!" (John 1:29)–later, in prison, sent messengers to ask if Jesus truly was the Messiah. Pain and uncertainty can shake even the strongest faith.

But hope deferred is not hope denied. Remembering God's faithfulness in past struggles renewed my hope. Though my health journey continues, I've learned that God often uses our hardest battles to produce the greatest fruit. For me, that fruit has been a deeper trust in His presence and a peace that blossoms even in uncertainty. This growth has become a tree of life in my walk with Him.

Prayer

Lord, When health challenges threaten to steal my hope, remind me of Your faithfulness. In moments when my heart grows sick with waiting, strengthen my faith in Your promises. Help me trust that Your perfect timing brings healing–physically, emotionally, and spiritually. Thank You for being my anchor of hope.

June 6

His Dwelling Place
By Karen Kay Smith
Today's Scripture: Psalm 26:8

I was born "cute as a button." My parents saw me as beautiful, loved, and treasured. But somewhere along the way, I stopped seeing myself that way. I'm not sure exactly when it happened. Maybe it was the whispers of culture, maybe comparisons with others, or maybe lies I told myself. My thoughts about my body were critical. Body shame took root, and eventually, I stopped eating. What began as a desire to be accepted and loved landed me in a treatment program for an eating disorder.

Body shaming is a struggle many women face. We are bombarded with messages that say we must look a certain way to be worthy. But when I came home from treatment, still fragile, God's Word spoke directly to my heart. Psalm 26:8 reminded me that my body is His dwelling place—the home of His Spirit. If His Spirit dwells in you, how can you despise what He has chosen as His dwelling place?

That truth began to heal me in ways treatment alone could not. God doesn't just restore health—He restores perspective. He shifted my eyes from what I hated about my body to the One who calls my body His home.

Friend, maybe you, too, have looked in the mirror and only seen flaws. Perhaps you've believed you are "too much" or "not enough." But here's the truth: you are already loved, already chosen, already His.

Today, pause and thank God for making you His beautiful dwelling place. Walk in that hope.

Prayer

Father,
Thank You for loving me just as I am. When I am tempted to see my body with shame, remind me that I am Your beloved dwelling place. Wrap me in Your Spirit, restore my perspective with grace, and help me rest in the beauty of being Yours.

June 7

Breaking Free From Fear's Prison
By Jennifer Hope Longenecker
Today's Scripture: 2 Timothy 1:7

Sometimes the prisons we inhabit aren't made of bars and concrete, but of fear and familiar walls. As I've gotten older, I've become more aware of my anxiety—something I suspect I've carried my entire life without truly recognizing it until my neuropsychologist diagnosed me with Generalized Anxiety Disorder in 2023.

My anxiety doesn't manifest as panic attacks; instead, it often presents as an overwhelming urge to stay home, rooted in fear that can trap me inside if I don't make deliberate choices to venture out and confront it.
This realization was both liberating and unsettling—finally having a name for the invisible force that had shaped so many decisions.

During my recent trip to California with my husband, I experienced this acutely. On our first day, despite having complete freedom to explore, I felt an overwhelming sense of being trapped. The irony wasn't lost on me—here I was in a beautiful place with endless possibilities, yet anxiety had erected walls around me more confining than any physical barrier. As I sat quietly reflecting, I realized I was allowing fear to confine me within my anxiety.

Scripture reminds us that "God gave us a spirit not of fear but of power and love and self-control." (2 Timothy 1:7). Fear whispers that safety lies in avoidance, but God calls us to trust Him beyond our comfort zones. Like the disciples who left their boats to follow Jesus, sometimes courage means stepping into the unknown, even when our minds resist.

The beautiful truth is that God meets me in my anxiety, not with condemnation, but with compassion. He doesn't minimize my struggles or demand instant healing. Instead, He walks alongside me as I make deliberate choices to move forward, despite my fears, and celebrates each small victory.

Prayer

Father,
When anxiety builds walls around my heart, help me recognize the cage. Give me the courage to make deliberate choices that honor You over fear. Walk beside me as I step beyond the boundaries of my comfort, trusting Your strength when mine feels insufficient. Grant me Your spirit of power, love, and sound mind.

June 8

The Extra E
By Terrie Stevens
Today's Scripture: Isaiah 43:1

When I was born, my mother was tasked with naming me. She chose the name Terrie. But as she looked at the letters – T-E-R-R-I – it didn't feel complete to her. So, she added an "E" to the end.

Throughout my life, people have spelled my name Teri, Terri, and Terry. Occasionally, a new version pops up on junk mail or spam emails, and it always makes me laugh.

Today, in a letter from my veterinarian, it was Tarry. That one's new.

Over the years, this extra "E" has been both a blessing and a curse.

As a child, it was popular to attach little state license plate replicas to the backs of our bikes – each one stamped with our name. Mike, James, and Jenny all had theirs flapping proudly behind them. I longed to be included. But with my "odd" spelling, I had to settle for T-E-R-R-I, or go without.

As I grew up, that unique spelling started to feel like a gift. It made me feel different – maybe even a little special. I took pride in it.

Names hold a special place in the Bible. God often changed people's names to reflect their purpose or transformation. Simon became Peter. Abram became Abraham. Jacob became Israel. Their names told a story – not just of who they were, but of who they were to God.

I still tease my mom about the spelling (something she's grown tired of), but it doesn't really matter.

I love my extra E. And I know that God knows my name – spelled perfectly, spoken lovingly. It may not come before Terri or Terry in His book, but I know it's there. And that's all that matters.

Prayer

Dear Jesus,
Thank You for knowing my name.
Thank You for being the Good Shepherd who calls each of His sheep by name.
When You speak my name, it sounds like music – and I want to dance.
Your love and faithfulness will carry me through all the days of my life.

June 9

It Wasn't the Devil. It Was Destiny!
By Kay Ashley
Today's Scripture: Amos 3:7

It was June 2009, and I was driving my school bus when I saw it.

An open vision—me, standing in a white robe, preaching and singing boldly. In front of people. Full voice. Full fire. And off to the side, I saw my husband—my husband at the time—walk to the altar with a short woman I instinctively referred to as his wife. I dismissed the vision as demonic.

Because surely God wouldn't show me preaching and singing, I was terrified to do both. And certainly not alone on a platform, while my husband—my husband at the time—walked to the altar with another woman I instinctively referred to as his beautiful wife.

In the vision, I called him my ex-husband, although we had never even discussed divorce. We'd been together for ten years. Everything felt fine. There was no way this vision could have been from God... right?

But it was.

By 2017, every detail had come to pass. Down to my ex-husband remarrying a woman significantly shorter than he is—just like I saw in the vision. And me? I was stepping into the very calling I once feared: preaching and singing without shame. Bold. Free. Anointed.
What I thought was the enemy was actually God showing me my future—way before I could believe it.

Friend, maybe you're questioning something God showed you because it doesn't fit your present. Don't panic. Don't throw it away. If it is from Him, it will unfold. He's not confused. You're just early.

Prayer

Father, Thank You for revealing glimpses of Your plan, even when I don't understand it. Help me not to dismiss what feels too big, too bold, or too soon. Give me discernment to recognize Your voice and courage to trust Your timing. You don't show visions to tease me—but to prepare me.

June 10

Bus Stop Gardening
By Sandi Banks
Today's Scripture: 1 Corinthians 3:6

Every June, my sister's garden was a masterpiece. Mine? Not even close.

So, when I read in the Bible about planting seeds of faith, I responded somewhat like Moses: 'Here am I, Lord, send my sister.'

Thankfully, instead, He sent me on a "planting" mission while stationed in northern Italy. Every Tuesday and Thursday, I arrived at the bus stop with my Italian New Testament, a smile, and a prayer. Often, I sensed God leading me to one person.

"Mi scuzi, Signora, puo aiutarmi, per piacere?"
(Excuse me ... could you help me, please?)

"Si, Signora," they usually replied as they took the Italian New Testament from my hand, eager to help me learn their language.

I'd have it open to John 14:6, and begin in Italian.

The English translation:

"Jesus said to him, 'I am the way, and the truth, and the life. No one comes to the Father except through me.'"

A simple sentence to memorize. But a powerful, life-changing message to behold.

"Brava, Signora!"

Some had perhaps never held a Bible in their hands and seemed curious, even captivated, as they thoughtfully leafed through its pages. Some embraced it as if it were a treasure—which it is!

Some asked further questions. Our conversations often continued as we boarded and rode the bus together. My destination was Casa Biblica, the evangelical Christian bookstore downtown, where I volunteered on translation projects twice a week.

I'd offer the bookstore's ministry card and depart with a "Ciao" and a silent prayer.

Prayer

Thank You, Lord, for divinely orchestrating opportunities to sow seeds of faith, and for making them grow. Please help us be faithful to plant where you lead us to plant, then use our words for Your glory. May we keep alert to every opportunity you give us.

June 11

He's Working in the Waiting
By Hope H. Dover
Today's Scripture: Psalm 27:13-14

Throughout my life, I have had my fair share of waiting. Sometimes it was waiting for the right job to come along. Other times I waited for clarity on the next steps I should take. The longest, most heart-wrenching waiting period I experienced was waiting to mother living children.

Waiting seasons have a way of stretching us thin. Whether it's waiting for healing, direction, or a door to open, our hearts can grow weary in the in-between. Even though we know God is faithful, sometimes His timing feels like silence.

In all of my waiting seasons I did all the "right" things. I prayed, journaled, and sought counsel. Despite my efforts, God still felt quiet. As time passed with no clear answers, I began to question Him.

In one particular waiting season, something began to shift. God wasn't withholding answers; He was inviting me into deeper trust. I began to notice His presence in small, ordinary ways. I noticed it in the sunrise peeking through the blinds. His presence showed up in the peace that met me during worship. I felt it in the quiet strength that helped me take one more faithful step when I didn't know the way forward. Noticing God's presence gave me a quiet assurance that He was working even when I couldn't see it.

Waiting isn't wasted when we surrender it to Him. Waiting can be the space where our faith grows deeper. It can be where we learn that His goodness isn't something we wait *for*. It's something we wait *in*.

Prayer:

Lord, teach me to trust You in the waiting. Help me rest in who You are when I can't see what's ahead. Grow my faith to believe that Your timing is perfect and that Your goodness is already here. Amen.

June 12

A Gentle Unraveling
By Katrina Mintz
Today's Scripture: Isaiah 43:19

At Equine Paths, retired racehorses often become mirrors for the veterans we serve, especially Stone Crazy, a warhorse with 84 races behind him. His body remembers the track. His spirit resists the change. And yet, in the round pen, toe to toe with veterans navigating their own transitions, Stone invites connection. His story echoes theirs: the ache of identity shift, the courage to begin again.

One sound ties them together: the bugle call "First Call." Used initially to summon military buglers before Reveille, it still echoes across bases and racetracks alike. When I played it in the barn, every retired racehorse stopped eating. Heads raised. Ears perked. Feet moved. Their bodies remembered.

So do ours.

For veterans, sounds and smells can trigger trauma or longing. For horses, it's instinct. For all of us, it's a reminder: God knows our triggers. He knows our breath, our anxiety, our need to feel safe.

Transition isn't about erasing the past. It's about honoring it while stepping into something new. The bugle may stir old memories, but it also signals a new day. A new rhythm. A new purpose.

You are not broken. You are becoming.

Prayer

Lord, help me honor the slightest try. Let the transition be tender. When the bugle sounds, let me rise with courage, Step forward in grace, And trust that You are doing a new thing. Even in me.

June 13

Don't Cheat the Butterfly
By Ada Bontrager
Today's Scripture: Romans 12:2

The metamorphosis process for a caterpillar to a butterfly is a short one, approximately 2-4 weeks. The caterpillar literally changes form. During this transformation process, the caterpillar's skin hardens to form the chrysalis, which provides protection for the forming butterfly inside. While in the chrysalis, the butterfly strengthens its wings. When the wings are strong enough, the butterfly will use its wings to break open the chrysalis. It is then free to fly away! If the butterfly is freed from the chrysalis prematurely, the wings are not strong enough to sustain life. It will die! The process of transformation must be completed for life to exist outside of its protective shell.

We can be transformed from the inside out. The transformation process begins with a renewal of our minds. When we renew our minds and think like Christ would think, we emerge as a new person with a new character and a new heart. Changing our thoughts eventually leads us to changing our hearts! When we can see the world through the eyes, mind, and heart of God, our perspective shifts. We can see people through the lens of our Creator and begin to relate to them in a Christ-like way.

I once let people's opinion of me consume me. It meant more to me than what God thought of me. It was suffocating! I had to start changing the way I think about myself! All of my sins, mistakes, and difficulties were part of the spiritual growth process. I now have confidence in who I am because I know Who I belong to! I'm no longer a shy, timid person. I am strong, confident, and I trust my God to make me more like Him.

Begin your transformation process today by thinking about what you're thinking about!

Prayer

Heavenly Father, I thank You for the transformation process! I submit my mind, thoughts, will, and emotions to You. I pray that the Holy Spirit would guide them into truth and transform me into Your image.

June 14

Pull the Power Chord
By Susanne Moore
Today's Scripture: Psalm 18:28

Did you know that darkness does not exist? Darkness is the absence of light. Who is light? God is light. This is profound. If you sit in darkness long enough, your eyes will adjust to the light. God is always present.

On this day in 1994, I found meth in the towel bars of my bathroom, while my husband was strung out, wielding a shotgun, and hallucinating that the law was coming for him. Our daughters were screaming as our neighbor busted through the door and knocked my husband out cold. He loaded him in his car and took him to a halfway house.

As I sat alone in the darkness, holding my crying children in my arms, I began to pray, "Jesus, please help me". The guiding light of Jesus came on, and I collided with myself. I needed redemption and freedom. The truth of Christ's gift of salvation finally penetrated my walls, and I understood the sinfulness of my own heart. I had to figure out how to face myself, my choices, and to live a new life in Christ.

Some moments break you, so God can penetrate the darkness with His presence and turn the light on.

Light illuminates the precipice, uncovers the struggle, and guides you forward to safety. God's gracious exposition of our hearts and circumstances is a gift that pulls us into His arms and away from the dangers we face in this world.

Every year, as this day rolls around, I reflect on my journey. I remember how powerless I felt, and how God has never stopped lighting my lamp. Our darkness is merely an absence of God, an invitation to pull the power chord; let God shine brightly in the shadows.

Prayer

Lord, May we remember to reach out for you, to know you are present even in our darkest moments, illuminating the truth. Even if our circumstances are beyond our control, you bring hope into those difficult places and spaces. You enlighten our souls to see you and help us to seek change in our own hearts. Thank you for your light, may we find refuge in the shadows of your wings.

June 15

Our Faithful Father
By Dava R. Caballero
Today's Scripture: Lamentations 3:22-24

I call it our "Job" period – when everything went haywire. It began with a devastating illness that tried to take me out. With God's help, my health stabilized somewhat, just in time to jump into a massive pot of hot water with our finances. My husband lost his job, and his mind was occupied with trying to help his parents out. Savings quickly disappeared along with our joy. My Stepfather died suddenly at my brother's wedding reception. To say the least, life was strained. With health, family, and finances all in disarray, I got pregnant. Not the best timing!

Even still, God was there. I felt a profound sense of peace and hope amidst the chaos. Miraculously, my health improved. Emotionally, however, my head barely stayed above water. I'll never forget one night, overwhelmed with tears of sorrow and despair, God revealed himself in an extraordinary way. Crying out to Jesus, I laid a hand on my pregnant belly, praying for the future of the gift inside. The unborn babe responded to the touch and began to trace the outline of my hand – not just once, but meticulously over and over. Tears of lament turned into tears of joy. It was as if God was saying – "I formed you; I've formed this child; lay it all in my caring, capable hands."

He arrived right after midnight – the birth of a new day. We named him Joaquin Javier – "God will establish a new house."

We continued wading through the waters of affliction for some time, but our son gave us purpose and hope for the future. Now, in times when I cannot see a way in the darkness, I remember the small hand and the still small voice of the Savior. All shall be well.

Prayer

Heavenly Father, You are our ever-present help in times of need. Thank you for the grace and mercy You give us each day. Thank You, Holy Spirit, for drawing us close and comforting us with Your peace, and for bringing us great joy.

June 16

God Never Fails
By Laura Lee Pettit
Today's Scripture: Psalm 30:5b

The sound of the telephone jolted me awake.

My husband's youngest brother was speaking, his voice full of emotion. He was saying, "Nicole is dead, she killed herself." My brain simply could not connect with his words. I could not comprehend. Was he really telling me my 28-year-old niece died by suicide? What could have happened to bring her to such a decision? To leave behind twin toddler girls? I was in shock and disbelief.

When Nicole was a teenager, lies and insecurity tortured her. She strived to be productive, to make good choices, to practice healthy coping methods, and still, life remained extraordinarily challenging. There were glimpses of vulnerability when she was open to the guidance and support of family, friends, and counseling.

Life appeared brighter when she became a mom, yet the internal battles continued. When it became overwhelming, she lost hope.

Mental illness makes life difficult, like a road full of construction and potholes. Without guidance, navigation can seem impossible.

Losing a loved one to suicide leaves so many unanswered questions.

God met me in my confusion. He reminded me Nicole was not alone, not abandoned, and He did not fail her. As waves of emotions flooded my soul, I was overwhelmed with peace.

God is greater than our feelings, and He knows everything. (1 John 3:20b)

Each of us experiences grief in our own unique way. Jesus responded with emotion and sorrow, weeping (John 11:35) when his friend Lazarus died, even though He knew He would raise him from the dead.

Do you feel alone or hopeless? Or are you grieving from a loss? Invite Him to be your deliverer in the midst of pain.

Weeping may last through the night, but joy comes with the morning. (Psalm 30:5b)

Even when all hope is gone, He never fails.

Prayer

Almighty God, You hold and know the future, You are in the details for Your good plan and purpose, even when we don't understand. Jehovah Shammah, You are everywhere, watching everything that concerns us. God of all hope, Your love never ends, Your mercies never cease, great is Your faithfulness. You never fail, and joy will come in the morning.

June 17

The Gift with Heavenly Lessons
By Janis Van Keuren
Today's Scripture: Psalm 112:1

Butterflies swirled in my stomach as I anticipated Tom's arrival home from work. I welcomed my husband with a kiss and a question. "Honey, did you have a chance to call the adoption agency today?" The predictable answer matched my routine question. "Project deadlines are breathing down my neck at work," he said. "I'll call tomorrow." Parenthood had eluded us for three years. Adoption was always part of our plans for a family.

One morning, as I snuggled in our comfy sofa for my prayer time, I contemplated the devotional I had just read on obedience. God's gentle spirit spoke to my heart, "You are not to mention adoption to Tom again. Wait until he brings up the subject."

"You can't really mean this, Lord?" I stammered. "You don't know Tom. He's an engineer and only focuses on his job!" My fervent pleas were met with silence. I squirmed on the sofa and wondered, could I place my deepest desire in God's hands and trust Him? Silently, my heart nodded, "Yes" to God.

Months passed, and I wondered if Tom would miss God's prompting.

As summer rolled around, we escaped to the cool mountains. One evening after prayer, Tom whispered, "Guess what the Lord told me? When we get home, we're to apply for adoption."

A year and a half later, on June 17th, Tom called me home from work. When I arrived, a baby car seat greeted me as Tom said, "Hi, Mommy. We have a baby boy." Two days later, we cuddled our son in the hospital nursery.

I remember the joy of holding him, the nurse calling me Mommy, and sitting in the nursery rocker as she answered my questions. God was faithful to answer the prayers of my heart in His time.

Prayer

Heavenly Father, Thank You for answering the prayers of my heart in Your way and time. May I always trust You and follow Your lead for my life. Your plans are for our good and give us hope and a future.

June 18

Grace in the Mayhem: A Wedding Story
By Colleen Ann Ruggieri
Today's Scripture: Romans 8:28

Early morning sunbeams spilled through my window. After a year of prayer and planning, my wedding day was here. From saying yes to a dress to preparing cookie tables for the reception, I was ready. The outdoor thermometer read 90 degrees. My wedding story was about to be written through searing heat, and it would be everything but the day of my dreams.

An electricity overload knocked out the air-conditioning; it felt like a furnace inside our church. I glanced at my bridesmaids and noticed shredded specks of tissue clinging to my sister-in-law's cheeks as she dabbed away perspiration. After the ceremony, my husband and I stepped outside to discover that the limo driver had overheated our car.

My heart nearly stopped at the reception when the DJ told us that he'd brought the wrong music and had none of the songs we'd selected—these were the days before streaming music services. Trying to remain happy, I tossed my wedding bouquet only to turn and see a stranger catching it. Later, I learned it was a wedding crasher who walked off with my flowers.

Just as today's brides seek likes on TikTok and Instagram, I planned a day to be remembered for its grandeur. In my pursuit of a flawless celebration, I learned that the quest for perfection can cause us to lose sight of a wedding's greatest gift—uniting a bride and groom in holy matrimony.

Today, as my husband and I celebrate our 32nd anniversary, we laugh at that beautifully flawed day and realize that God was weaving grace through every misstep. As the years have passed, we've forged our marriage purposefully and anchored our hearts in His eternal promise. Our plans may falter, but God's grace endures, shaping a legacy of love that no mayhem can steal.

Prayer

Heavenly Father, Thank You for weaving grace into my life's imperfect and worst moments. Even when my plans seem to unravel, your love restores and renews me. Thank you for transforming my beautiful disasters into radiant displays of your wondrous grace. I surrender my quest for perfection, trusting your enduring promise to write my story with love.

June 19

The Gift of a Grandchild
By Susan Wheeler Smith
Today's Scripture: Numbers 6:24-26

Today we were blessed with our first grandchild, a girl named Nora. Though I once thought I would not have children, this gift from a gracious God brings our family both joy and a living testimony to His grace for those who turn to Him with their whole hearts.

Our journey to this day has not been easy. From the beginning, our marriage was rocky. By our third anniversary, we were one signature away from divorce. However, today, as we celebrate the sweet gift of a grandchild, we are reminded that God's enduring love guides one generation to the next. With Nora, we now have the responsibility and joy of praying over her, modeling Christ's love in our words and actions, and being a steady presence of faith and hope, one that reaches beyond our own years.

Take time today to pray for your marriage and the legacy you wish to leave. Thank God for the miracle of your children and grandchildren, present and future. Pray for their health, wisdom, and joy. Show your love for Jesus through your words, your willingness to forgive, and your service.

The Psalmist says in Psalm 127:3 that children are a "heritage from the Lord." An eternal blessing that will last long after we are gone. Just as Timothy's faith was nurtured by his grandmother Lois (2 Timothy 1:5), so too can we plant seeds of faith that will grow in the hearts of our grandchildren.

Prayer

Father,
We thank You for children and grandchildren. We ask for Your blessings upon them, from generation to generation. Thank You for allowing us to be a part of their lives and to teach them about You. To model Christ for them. Thank You for entrusting us with precious children. Help us to be faithful encouragers and intercessors in their lives.

June 20

One Day Closer
By Becky Sims
Today's Scripture: John 14:1-3

Every day we're one day older. And if we're following the Lord, hopefully we're becoming a little wiser and more loving. We're learning to live with more intention and intensity for the Lord, knowing we're one day closer to meeting Him face to face.

All we truly have is this day, this moment. How will we make it count? It's not always about doing big things, but even small things with love and the awareness of how special and precious each opportunity is.

Each day, we can spend time in prayer and praise, using our gifts to bless others and encourage them to move closer to the Lord. We don't need to work all the time or accomplish everything. We just need to move a little closer, love a little more, and rest while connecting with Him. Hurrying won't help, but waiting until tomorrow won't work. We need to move forward every day. We must remember, "The heart of man plans his way, but the Lord establishes his steps" (Proverbs 16:9). Our Heavenly Father lovingly leads the way.

We can all do things in love–both the magnificent and the mundane; providing for people and guiding them toward heaven, completing daily tasks, or powerfully praying.

When we invest the time and talents God has given us, we can expect to hear, "Well done, good and faithful servant" (Matthew 25:23). Paul states that, " For now we see in a mirror dimly, but then face to face. Now I know in part; then I shall know fully, even as I have been fully known" (1 Corinthians 13:12).

So today, when troubles try to take you down, or tasks at hand seem too stressful, remember that at this day's end, you're one day closer to meeting Him.

Prayer

Dear Lord,
Thank You for this day. Thank You for lovingly guiding us through each day and helping us with everything we encounter. Please help us to live our time on earth with our hearts focused toward You. May our hearts be joyful knowing we'll be with You at Your appointed time.

June 21

Known and Loved
By Angie Hanson
Today's Scripture: Jeremiah 1:5

Birthdays remind us of the miracle of life. They are milestones that invite us to pause and remember the unique imprint each person leaves on the world. When someone we love is no longer here to celebrate, these days can stir both gratitude and ache. Yet God reminds us that each life is known, loved, and created with eternal purpose.

I remember the first time I held my son Garret, marveling at his tiny fingers and the miracle of his life. Even now, years later, I can still hear his laughter and picture the spark in his eyes.

It's easy to measure life by the number of years lived, but God reminds us that He has known us since before our first breath. Our value is not in how long we are here, but in the eternal significance He has given us. Garret's time on earth was far too short for my heart, but it was never insignificant in God's plan. His presence had a profound impact on everyone who knew him, and his memory continues to shape my life today.

Birthdays for someone we've lost can be tender. They hold both joy for the gift of their life and sorrow for the years we wish we had. But we can choose to let these days become a celebration – not only of who they were but of the God who created them with purpose.

When I think of Garret today, I thank God for entrusting me with his life. And I look forward to the day when I will see him again, whole and restored, in the presence of the One who knew him first.

Prayer

Father, Thank You for the precious gift of life and the eternal purpose You give each of us. Today I celebrate Garret and the joy he brought. Help me honor his life in the way I live mine, trusting Your promise that we will be reunited one day.

June 22

Prayers for a New Daddy
by Lisa Todd Wilkins
Today's Scripture: Psalm 68:5

When I was four years old, my dad died very suddenly of cancer. I was devastated. At bedtime, I began to add a simple request to my nightly prayers: "And please give me a new Daddy."

cried every night as I prayed that prayer faithfully for three years. As a child, I didn't fully understand loss or timing—I only knew my heart ached and longed for God to fill the empty space my dad had left. Each night, tears and whispered words poured from my heart, trusting God to hear even the prayers of a small, grieving child.

I had no idea who Paul was or that my mom was quietly seeing him. Their relationship was kept a secret, so when I was introduced to Paul, it was a complete surprise—he was already engaged to my mom. At that moment, I accepted Paul as my dad. I knew deep in my heart he was God's answer to my prayer. He became my Dad in June 1979.

I am reminded of God's promise in Jeremiah 29:11: "For I know the plans I have for you, declares the Lord, plans for welfare[a] and not for evil, to give you a future and a hope." Even in waiting, God had a hope-filled future prepared for me.

Sometimes God's answers take years, but they are always worth the wait. He hears every whispered prayer, cares for every longing, and works behind the scenes, arranging good gifts we cannot yet see. Our faithful God never forgets the desires of our hearts.

Prayer

Lord, Thank You for hearing the prayers of my heart. Help me trust Your timing, remain faithful in waiting, and recognize Your good gifts when they arrive.

June 23

The Gift I Didn't Know I Needed
By Karen Kay Smith
Today's Scripture: Jeremiah 29:11

I can still remember the swirl of emotions. At an age when most of my friends were moving toward teenagers and empty nests, I discovered I was pregnant. I didn't plan on this. I had already sold every bit of baby items I ever owned. I was done having children. How could this be happening? My best friend was struggling with infertility, and guilt was pressing heavily on me as I carried a child I hadn't wanted or planned.

But on this date in 2009, my daughter entered the world. The child I never dreamed of having is one of God's greatest gifts to me. I can't imagine life without her.

Looking back, I see what I couldn't at the time: God was writing a story bigger than my plans. What I received as an interruption was, in truth, an invitation to hope. God's surprises often come wrapped in ways we don't expect—sometimes even in what we resist. But His gifts are always good.

Scripture tells us, ...His plans are to prosper us, not to harm us. And while my journey began with reluctance and guilt, it blossomed into joy and gratitude. My daughter reminds me daily that God's plans are higher than mine, and His blessings are richer than I could have imagined.

Maybe you're staring at something in your life that feels unwanted or unexpected. It may not be a child—it could be a move, a diagnosis, or a shift you never asked for. What if, like me, God is planting hope in your heart through the very thing you thought you didn't want?

What feels unwanted today may one day become the very highlight of your life.

Prayer

Father,
Thank You for surprising us with gifts we never knew we needed. Forgive us when we resist Your plans or carry guilt for what You've given. Open our eyes to see unexpected blessings as treasures of Your love. Teach us to trust Your timing and receive with joy.

June 24

Live Everyday with the Hope of Eternity
By Dr. Brittany Javier
Today's Scripture: 2 Corinthians 4:17-18

Each day, we are given a new opportunity to live for Christ. Scripture says that the Lord's mercies are new each day, and we can rest assured that God follows through on His promises in Scripture. While we are given these opportunities day by day, our everyday life is not always easy. Scripture promises us that even though the challenges we may face in this life can be arduous and taxing, not a single difficulty or hardship we face compares with the glory of what we will one day experience when we stand in the presence of Christ.

One day, every hard and awful thing we have experienced on this earth will fade into the background, as we stand – or fall on our faces – before our mighty Savior. Our Savior, Jesus Christ, faced trials and tribulations, culminating with the cross. Yet, He promises us that the calamities of this world cannot compare to what we will experience being in His perfect presence one day.

I do not know what you are facing today, but I do know that we can have hope, no matter what we face, because we have a God who promises us that an eternity with Him is worth it. I encourage you to remember the hope we have in Christ today. He has already overcome the world and is preparing a place for you and me, His children. When we live in light of eternity, keeping our gaze fixed on Jesus' promises, then we can live one step at a time with unwavering hope that every hardship we face will be nothing compared to the glory of Christ in eternity.

Prayer

Abba,
I pray that you strengthen and encourage your children's hearts and remind them that You are worth it all. I thank You that we have a Savior who is familiar with trials and hardship and walks with us each step of the way, reminding us that He is our hope.

June 25

Stand Tall, Child of the King
By Trudy Bosman
Romans 8:16,17

I go to an exercise class called "The Silver Foxes" three mornings a week. They are a wonderful group of lovely, mature ladies. Recently, several members have taken turns leading the group, occasionally using videos as part of the class. Towards the end of one video, "Dave" led us in a stretching exercise. One thing he had us do to help with posture is called "The Cobra".

To do this, we slump over - head down, arms hugging the sides of the body - making us look like the head of a cobra. When I do this, I feel like I must look like the most miserable person in the world - without any hope, trying to hide from the world and everyone in it. Then we straighten up - head high, shoulders back, looking up like the most regal person in the world.

What a picture this is of my life. I think my memory holds on to times in my life when I was told or felt that I did not measure up – when I was made to feel like I was not smart enough or good enough. Sometimes I make a mess, like accidentally spilling things or mixing up dates or places. Satan pulls out those memories and shoves them in my face. I start calling myself names... "Stupid, stupid person! Look at this mess you made!" I fall into a slump. Sometimes tears flow. I know I need to get out of it.

I need to throw my shoulders back, lift up my head, and tell myself, "Stop it! Put your head up and straighten your crown! You are a child of the King! You are not worthless – you are loved and precious to God." Then, I need to take a deep breath and just clean it up and go on.

When Satan tries to make you slump, remember who you are and stand tall, straighten your crown, and rejoice that you are a beloved child of the King.

Prayer

O my Father, thank You that I am Your loved one, precious in your sight. When Satan tries to make me feel worthless, help me to never forget who I am and who I belong to. I love You.

June 26

You Will Find Me When You Seek Me
By Melissa Lindsey
Today's Scripture: Jeremiah 29:13

I walk across the grass, coffee in hand. It is a beautiful morning. A rooster crows in the distance, and the scent of peonies and lilacs fills my senses.

While I enjoy the world around me, I also have a mission. I settle down under a pine tree in a good spot to hunt and get to work. My hands move over the grass in front of me, my fingers brushing back and forth as I search for the elusive four-leaf clover.

I am confident I will find the treasure I seek. Over my lifetime, I have found hundreds of them. Sometimes, I find them easily, while other times, it takes hours of effort. But they are there, waiting to be discovered. The key is to stay focused and committed to my search.

Jeremiah 29:13 reminds us of a promise about finding God. It assures us that He is with us and that we will find Him when we seek Him with all our hearts. In today's culture, I believe our biggest challenge is focus. Instead of putting our attention on God first, we often find fulfillment in material things, such as work and cell phones. We have forgotten how to be still and quiet, which helps us hear God's voice. Seeking God isn't a casual pursuit; it is an invitation to build a relationship. It involves spending focused time in His presence and making our relationship with Him a priority.

Seek Him through prayer.

Know Him through His Word.

Follow Him with your whole heart.

Prayer

Dear Lord,
This world can feel overwhelming. Many voices surround us, creating noise – sometimes preventing us from hearing the one voice that truly matters. I pray that You quiet our hearts and help us focus on You. Guide us to prioritize time with You every day. Teach us to listen for Your voice and practice obedience in our daily lives.

June 27

Through the Valley
By Angie Hanson
Today's Scripture: Psalm 23:4

Grief anniversaries are some of the hardest days to face. They bring a flood of memories that feel both precious and painful, leaving us caught between remembering and longing. In those moments, it can feel like the valley will never end – but God's Word assures us that even here, we are not walking alone.

June 27th is the day my world changed forever – the day my son Garret left this earth. I can still recall the way the air felt, heavy and unreal, as if the world should have stopped to acknowledge the magnitude of the loss. But it didn't. The world kept spinning, even when mine felt shattered.

Psalm 23:4 has been my lifeline in the years since. It doesn't pretend that we will avoid the valley; it promises that we will never walk it alone. There's comfort in knowing God doesn't stand at the edge, calling us to hurry through. He is in step with us, guiding, protecting, and sustaining us with His presence.

On grief anniversaries, memories can wash over us with both sweetness and ache. There is the beauty of remembering, and the pain of knowing those moments won't come again in this life. Yet even here – in the shadowed valley – God's light breaks through. His comfort has shown up in ways I could never have imagined: in a friend's gentle words, in a sunrise I didn't expect to notice, in the quiet assurance that Garret is whole and safe in His presence.

If today you find yourself in your own valley, know this: you will not always feel this lost. God is walking with you, and His comfort will meet you in ways that keep you moving forward, one step at a time.

Prayer

Lord, Thank You for walking beside me in the hardest places. Help me feel Your presence when the shadows are heavy. Comfort my heart with Your peace and steady my steps with Your strength. Remind me that Your light is always with me, even in the valley.

June 28

The Day the Lord Won the War
By Lisa Todd Willkins
Today's Scripture: Exodus 14:14

Baffled, I stood with my dear friend Laura and exited the courtroom. Rage and confusion filled my mind. Trial? For what?

Quarterly custody hearings had become routine. I had exhausted every effort to reach an understanding with the girls' father. A new judge presided on this late June day.

For years, I had collected evidence of the mental, emotional, and verbal abuse "The Wilkins' Girls" endured. I had witnesses and video evidence I was ready to present—if the day ever came.

Sworn in, I endured questioning aimed to prove parental alienation on my part. I prayed continually, waiting for cross-examination. With no witnesses or evidence present, I felt unprepared to defend my daughters.

After years of not being seen or believed, at last there was an audience. Several times, the judge threatened to place him in "the box," a holding cell for those out of order.

When dismissed from the stand, I turned to the judge: "May we have a continuation? I was unaware of this trial and did not come prepared."

She replied firmly, "We're going to take care of this today."

Her words carried urgency and a knowing beyond my understanding. I stepped down in peace and began the cross-examination.

Moments later, the judge delivered her verdict: full custody to me.
God had gone before me, preparing the way. I only had to show up. He did the rest.

Prayer

Lord, Thank You for going before me. When I feel unprepared, remind me that You are my defender and strength. Help me to trust Your timing, knowing You fight battles I cannot see.

June 29

Fisherman Math
By Jessica Haberman
Today's Scripture: Luke 6:38

Our neighbor insists that the more fish he gives away, the more fish he catches.

We met one fall afternoon when he and his wife pulled into our driveway and asked if they could glean apples from our trees. We had more than we could gather before they began to drop, so we welcomed them to take what they could pick. A few days later, he returned with an apple pie, still warm from the oven.

After that, he became a regular visitor, always with fish in hand. They were cleaned, portioned, and vacuum sealed. Sometimes he brought smoked salmon. Other times, he would drop off tuna that they had canned at home. Just to be sure we understood the possibilities of canned tuna, he showed up one evening with a bubbling tuna casserole and a handwritten recipe from his wife tucked alongside.

We thank him and try to return the kindness, but we'll never be able to catch up.

When we asked about his generosity, he just smiled and said, "I love to catch fish. The more I give away, the more I catch."

And I can't help but believe he's right, that when we live with open hands, God keeps filling them. It's easy to clench your fists around what you have. Especially when the pantry feels bare, the budget is tight, or the schedule is even tighter. But God doesn't ask us to give because He needs what we have; He asks us to give because He knows what He's waiting to give us.

What's in your hands today that you could freely give? A meal, a prayer, an hour of your time? You don't need to wait until you feel like you have enough. Start with what you have. Trust God to fill the net.

Prayer

Lord, help me to give like You do, with open hands, without fear. Teach me to trust that when I sow kindness, resources, or time, You can multiply it in ways I may never see. Make me a cheerful giver, not just of things, but of myself.

June 30

A Shared Birthday – Celebrating Generational Influence
By Melissa Lindsey
Today's Scripture: Psalms 145:5

Our son is a specialized pharmacist who works closely with doctors and medical professionals to support children facing psychiatric issues. Each day brings new challenges, but it also offers new opportunities to serve. Recently, my mother, his grandmother, fought cancer. She relied on medical professionals to make crucial decisions that ultimately saved her life. Grandmother and grandson share a birthday–today, June 30th. One is just starting a career of helping others in the medical field, while the other has recently received care.

Over the past few years, I've seen the deep influence one generation has on the next. My mother embodies a strong sense of service, always finding fulfillment in caring for her family and helping others. Her unwavering work ethic and servant's heart have been passed down to her children and grandchildren. However, cancer taught her not only to give but also to accept care at times. Although it was difficult for her, watching her graciously accept help sets a positive example just as much as watching her serve. Serving others is a blessing, but being served is also a blessing.

As Psalm 145:5 beautifully states, one generation teaches the next about God's mighty works. I am grateful for the Christian parents who guided me from birth. It is our duty as parents and grandparents to love and teach our children within the framework God has designed. Through hard work, learning to serve others, being willing to be served, and most importantly, experiencing God's gracious love and the salvation through Jesus Christ, we can make a meaningful difference in the world.

Prayer

Dear Lord,
I thank You for our medical staff all around the world. Thank You for the knowledge they possess and their servant hearts. Thank You for the generational influence of Godly parents and grandparents in all our lives. Let us continue to support our young people in their growth and empower them to rise and take the torch to pass it on to the next generation.

July

hope✱books
collections

July 1

Hands Wide Open
By Rose McCombs Jordan
Today's Scripture: Today's Scripture: Psalm 16:5

When my husband and I searched for a new home after selling ours in 2020, I made a quiet decision: I would live with my heart and my hands wide open. With every house we toured, I prayed a blessing over the seller and the future owner—whether it would be us or someone else. It wasn't easy. Walking through those homes, I could picture our life unfolding inside them. Three times we made offers. Three times I felt the pull to set my heart on a dream. Yet every time, I whispered the same prayer: If this is from You, Lord, open the way. And if not, help me release it in peace.

God has been gently teaching me that living open-handed isn't about letting go after a tug-of-war with Him. It's choosing not to grip so tightly in the first place. Clenched hands are filled with fear and striving, but unclenched hands rest in trust. They are free to release and free to receive.

Psalm 16 reminds us that the Lord Himself is our portion and our security. Our hope doesn't rest in a house, a job, or even in an answered prayer. It rests in the One who holds all things together. Even the elders in Revelation lay down their crowns—the very symbols of identity and achievement—before His throne. What a picture of worship: lives fully surrendered and hearts completely yielded to Him.

There is freedom in loosening our grip. And with that freedom comes a steady hope—the assurance that God is trustworthy and good. When we live this way, our open hands become testimonies—reminding others that peace is possible, even in uncertainty. A yielded heart discovers peace that clenched fists never can.

Prayer

Lord,
Help me live with my heart and my hands wide open before You. Teach me to hold even good gifts loosely, trusting that You alone secure my portion. Quiet my fears when I'm tempted to cling, and remind me that nothing entrusted to You is ever lost. May my surrendered life point others to Your goodness and faithfulness.

July 2

Mercy Ruled
By Tracey D. Beers
Today's Scripture: Today's Scripture: Romans 9:14-18

July 2, 2003. Charleston, SC

"Where you from, Honey?" the nurse drawled. " 'Cuz you wouldn't be strollin' in here fixin' to get a CAT scan if you had a ruptured 'pendix." Neither of us expected that I would soon be surrounded by doctors, stabbed with morphine, and swiftly carted to the nearest surgical suite. Sometimes invisible diseases (whether physical or spiritual) are insidious, causing toxic distress despite our cluelessness.

Pharaoh also suffered from unseen sickness - a cancer of the heart called pride. His calloused heart refused to heed God's words. Attempting to exalt himself as a god over the Israelites, he unwittingly exalted the God of Israel over himself. It was for that very purpose, God hardened Pharaoh's heart—that He might show His power and that His name might be declared in all the earth, and God was right to do so. A holy God has only one option—administering justice. And Pharaoh deserved justice.

"But wait," you say, "Isn't God a god of mercy?"

Yes, but unlike justice, God's mercy is not merited. Mercy is a gift of restraint designed to save us from the condemnation we provoked. It was bought at a great price at the cross and offered whether we ever realize we are diseased. The justice due our wayward hearts was poured out on Christ so that God's mercy could be poured out on His children.

Christian, like a truly trounced sports team rescued by the "mercy rule", you have also been mercied. God raised you up for this very purpose, that He might show His power in you and bring glory to His name. What greater power can be shown through you than the transforming power of forgiveness and mercy offered in Jesus Christ?

Prayer

Most gracious and merciful Lord,
We humble ourselves before You. We pray and seek your face, that we may turn from the disease of our wicked ways and be healed. Hear us from heaven. Help us to proclaim as David and his son, Solomon, that the Lord is good and his mercy will endure forever.

July 3

Strength for the Journey
By Laura J. Antos
Today's Scripture: Philippians 4:13

There are seasons in life when the weight of suffering feels too heavy to carry. Sometimes these seasons arrive when a special loved one passes away, a job is lost unexpectedly, or fear of an uncertain future weighs heavily on you. Other times, it may simply be one of those weeks when you overcommit your time and nothing seems to go smoothly. It is both in the significant and the trivial moments of life that you find yourself crying out to God for help.

It is in these fragile places that Paul's words in Philippians 4:13 come alive; "I can do all things through him who strengthens me." Paul wasn't promising that life would have an easy button or that pain would be taken away. Instead, he was pointing to a deeper truth—your strength doesn't have to come from you. It comes from God. His presence fills the empty spaces when grief and fear have drained you. His power steadies you when your body or mind feels tired and frail. His hope whispers to your soul that you are not alone. He is with you always.

Think back to a moment when you felt too overwhelmed to go on, yet somehow, you did. That unseen strength was God holding you close. Whatever you are facing today, breathe deeply and welcome his presence, for he waits gently beside you.

God's replies may be in a whisper or a blessing wrapped in disguise. Rest in the certainty that his love will carry you, his strength will sustain you, and his hope will light your way forward.

Prayer

Lord Jesus,
Thank you for being my strength when I am weak, anxious, or in pain. Help me to remember that Your love and strength sustain me through every trial, no matter the size. May Your hope fill my heart today and remind me that with You, I can endure all things.

July 4

Your Body is a Temple
By D'Toya Dove
Today's Scripture: 1 Corinthians 6:19–20

As you begin your day, I want to remind you that taking care of yourself is part of honoring God. Your body is not just yours – it's a temple, a dwelling place for the Holy Spirit. And when you care for it well, you're better equipped for the work He's called you to do.

This has been real for me lately. Over the summer, I was dealing with pain. Through prayer and paying closer attention to what I was eating, I began to feel better. As the weeks passed, I slowly let some of those foods back in, and the pain started creeping back in too. Stress didn't help either.

I tried to brush it off, "It's not that bad," I thought, but the Holy Spirit checked me,
"You've got to get your flesh in check. That includes your emotions, your appetites, and your choices. The decision is yours, but remember your choices will have consequences, either good or bad."

That hit me hard. Because, in the past, food was a source of comfort. But I've been delivered from that cycle, and I don't want to go back. I was reminded that this journey isn't just about food, it's also about rest, emotional health, spiritual alignment, and walking in obedience.

Taking care of your body isn't about perfection; it's about stewardship. It's a daily act of surrender and alignment. And the beautiful thing is, the Holy Spirit will guide you... if you're willing to listen.

What's one way you can honor God with your body today, whether through food, rest, exercise, or even managing stress with His help?

Prayer

Heaven Father,
Thank You for reminding me that my body is not my own, it's Yours. Help me steward it well. Guide my choices, strengthen my will, and give me grace when I fall short. I want to honor You with how I care for this temple You've given me.

July 5

As the Bell Tolls
By Teresa Montalvo
Today's Scripture: 1 Thessalonians 5:16-18

There was one year when I realized my family and I were struggling to find a heart of gratitude. We were caught up in the busyness of life, with many things vying for our attention. Being the family history keeper, I understood the power of journal writing. Even though I wanted those that I love and care about to do the same, if it was not their cup of tea, I repeat, it's not their cup of tea!

I felt like I'd had a Holy Spirit unction, and I ran with it. Much to my surprise, my husband and all of my children–plus a few extras, including a nephew–participated in a year-long project. I sent them a message each day asking for one or two sentences about a moment of gratitude that had filled their day, and they responded. I jotted those down in a journal–treasured moments now recorded!

Years later, when my world crashed unexpectedly, I found myself starting a daily journal entry of the little things that were in my pathway. You know those unexpected moments of gratitude. And I would say to my Lord, "I have noticed and I am grateful!"

Will you hear the bell?
Will you hear the hopelessness?
Will you tend the sadness?
Will you?

My soul is downcast.
My heart is shattered.
My hope it has disappeared.
Help me.

It is not well.
It is not well with my soul.
Pause and try again.
It is well.

It is well with my soul.
Hope breathed in,
Despair expelled out.
It is well.

I let the words slip through my lips.
It was a sacrifice of gratitudes,
And in the midst a great exchange.
Mercy and grace for my doubt and unbelief!

Hope restored.

Prayer

Father God,
Would you help me to notice the small moments that delight my heart? That comfort would be found—the kind that you give me. Restore this heart of mine with a full tank of gratitude, and may hope bloom!

July 6

Forgiveness of the Unfaithful
By Terrie Stevens
Today's Scripture: Hosea 3:1

At 18 years old, I agreed to love and honor my husband—not long after, I shattered every promise I made that day. I vowed no one would control me, convinced I knew best. I saw both husbands and God as limits on what I wanted from life. I turned toward Paganism, Buddhism, and Atheism—anything to escape the God I had praised in childhood and my teen years.

Quietly, my husband prayed for me—and for us. He recruited his church family to pray on my behalf, and he never gave up.

God spoke to him: "Hold on. Be patient. I have plans." God wasn't done with me yet. Thirty years passed with no relief.

I remember it like an audible crash—the job I loved was gone. Friends drifted away. Even my family grew weary of my chaos. My life imploded. I was alone—and the worst part? I knew I deserved it.

Stuck in despair, I found the answer in my own home—when I looked into the eyes of the man I had betrayed. An aura of peace and security welcomed me, and I wanted to learn his secret. I longed to feel as I did when I was young and knew God—when the world was safe, joyful, and full of color.

One Sunday, I slipped into a church for the first time in years. Sitting in the back, my heart ached with all I had lost. An older gentleman prayed with me, and as tears streamed down my face, I found my way back home.

Just as God never gave up on Israel, neither did my husband—or my God—give up on me.
This year we celebrate 43 years of marriage—not because I was faithful, but because He was.

Prayer

Dear Jesus,
Thank You for being there for a lost soul. Thank You for opening Your arms to welcome us back, even after we've betrayed You in such terrible ways. Thank You for seeing beyond our failings and helping us grow in Your love and forgiveness.

July 7

His Heartbeat of Hope for *You*!
By Maryellen Greene
Today's Scripture: Isaiah 40:11

Do you remember what it feels like to be carried as a young child?

Most of us probably don't have memories that reach that far back to those very early days. But all of us were carried at some time in our lives. We all had to depend on someone to carry us throughout our early existence. Based on varying individual circumstances and development, we stop being carried by others as we learn how to crawl and then walk and become increasingly independent.

Has your independence or dependence on your own abilities stopped you from realizing that you are carried through each day by our careful and caring Shepherd? Maybe the troubles and pain from a health crisis, a financial hardship, or a relationship wound have caused you to resist closeness with our loving Heavenly Father? I know I have had plenty of those independent, "I can do this on my own" moments. I have also found myself too busy and distracted or too bitter to rest and draw close to the heart of Jesus.

How comforting and hopeful is this passage from Isaiah 40:11, reminding us that "He tends His flock like a Shepherd. He gathers the lambs in His arms and carries them close to His heart." No matter what we are facing, God sees us and hears us. God knows us and cares for us as a perfect protector and provider. Whatever we are going through, God is with us. His fingers are not pointed at us in disappointment, but rather, His arms are wide open with grace. He lifts us up and carries us close to His heart through every moment of every day. Do you feel God carrying you? As He holds you close, can you hear His heartbeat of love and hope for *you*?

Prayer

Father God, our loving Shepherd who carries us through each day,
Forgive us for trying to live life apart from you. Thank you for giving us Jesus and providing for us to be forever Yours. Please open our ears to hear Your heart of love and hope—may it echo into every situation and every person we encounter.

July 8

Consider the Ravens
By Janet Armitstead
Today's Scripture: Luke 12:24

I sobbed on my friend Lisa's shoulder. She said, "You need to pray–and you need joy." My time with Lisa was filled with grace, and it showed me how much I love people, especially those who are kind, in whom I see the love of God. A few weeks later, on this July day, I drove to the mountains. It was there that I experienced an inspiring connection with a Common Raven, which brought me joy, renewed my faith in God, and placed me, once more, in community.

At the Alpine Zoo, a group of us were introduced to the resident animals, including the ravens (my favorite birds!). We were encouraged to feed them in order to enhance their socialization. Tightly holding a peanut, I approached the cage. My heart was in my throat. I desperately wanted this moment, and this connection.

Holding the peanut, I experienced kinship with an animal of incomparable grace and intelligence. I spoke to the raven as he crept toward me, as I would encourage a person or a pet. "Bliki" came timidly, but purposefully, towards me, in a sort of hopeful dance, just as I had been soft-shoeing my way back to God–and others. He took the peanut swiftly. I felt a rush of air and then saw the relieved and joyous flutter of wings as the raven tucked into his prize. My heart soared. It was one of the most beautiful moments of my life.

One gentleman, James, in his attempt to feed Bliki, didn't have a good grasp of his peanut, and so it fell, unclaimed. Out of kindness, I offered James my peanut, but he urged me to keep it, and thus, I experienced the joy of connection through his compassion. We never fight any battle alone. True joy is found in God and in reaching out to others.

Prayer

Heavenly Father,
You remind us that, no matter what happens to us, everything will be all right. You are in control. You are the author of divine appointments. You send your creatures to comfort us. Signs of your love surround us, pointing us always and ever back to You–and to our human family.

July 9

The Choice to Hope
By Shelby Lung
Today's Scripture: Lamentations 3:21–23

Sometimes hope feels more like a word for a cute mug or a trendy wrist tattoo than something that actually lives in your heart. When the unexpected shows up, the "what ifs" crowd your mind, or life just feels heavy—hope doesn't feel easy. It feels hard.

When my daughter was born and we heard the words down syndrome, the "what ifs" came fast: heart problems, delays, challenges I wasn't ready for. My heart felt crushed under the weight of tomorrow. I didn't feel hopeful. I felt fear.

But in the middle of my fears, God gave me a lifeline—the choice to hope. To cling to Him and believe that, even though I couldn't see it then, I was actually receiving the biggest blessing of my life. Slowly, I realized hope doesn't silence the "what ifs," but it answers them. It says, "Even if the hard comes, God's grace will be enough."

That's exactly where Jeremiah was when he wrote Lamentations. His city had been destroyed, his people were suffering, and everything around him looked hopeless. Yet in the middle of ashes, he chose hope. He called to mind God's faithfulness, saying, "But this I call to mind, and therefore I have hope." (Lamentations 3:21)

Hope isn't always a feeling—it's a choice. It's a daily practice. It's remembering God's character and setting our minds on Him, even when the "what ifs" are loud. Some days, that looks like barely-whispered prayers. Some days, opening Scripture when scrolling would be easier. Choosing hope is stubborn trust that God will show up even when we don't see it yet.

Hope is remembering that His mercies are new every morning, and even in uncertainty, His love will not fail.

Prayer

Lord,
Remind me that Your faithfulness doesn't depend on my feelings. Help me call to mind Your promises and choose hope each day, trusting that Your mercies are new every morning.

July 10

When is Cold Season, Exactly?
By Kati von Schmitten
Today's Scripture: Isaiah 59:2

I hate getting a cold. My nose clogs, my ears feel plugged, my head pounds, and the world is off balance. Everything I do feels harder, and I'm the whiniest person. I can't see straight, hear clearly, or think clearly. You can tell I've succumbed when I opt to stuff my nostrils with tissues, leaving them hanging from my nose.

Sin has the same effect on me. My vision is blurred. My heart is clogged. I can't sense Him clearly, can't hear His guidance, and my perspective is skewed, which also makes me whiny. Just like a cold makes the familiar world feel *uuuuggghhh*, sin distorts our spiritual perception.

The remedy is similar in principle: attention, care, and intervention. We clear a cold by resting, hydrating, and treating the symptoms. There is no shortcut. We clear sin by repentance, confession, and leaning into the Holy Spirit. There is no shortcut. The Spirit works gently, unclogging our hearts, restoring clarity, and helping us perceive God's presence again.

When the congestion clears, whether from a cold or from sin, we notice the world differently. When we repent and listen, the nudges of the Holy Spirit become unmistakable. Peace, clarity, and direction return. God hasn't moved; our awareness has. His presence was there all along.

Prayer

Lord,
I know I'll never be perfect, and though I don't want to sin, I still stumble. When I do, draw my eyes back to You. Teach me to repent quickly and sincerely, and help me see that confession isn't failure, it's a step toward seeing You more clearly.

July 11

Finding Healing in the Father's Arms
By Caroline Abblitt
Today's Scripture: 2 Corinthians 1:3-4

Do you feel broken? Does your heart hurt? Do you long to be held in loving arms that will bring true comfort and relief?

I remember feeling like that. I remember longing for love that would satisfy the ache and soothe the pain in my heart. I cried out to the Lord, again and again, and He took me on a beautiful journey that began with the simple step of surrendering it all to Him.

He met me, taking me on a path that was more thorough than I'd expected, but more amazing, too. He poured in His love. He led me on a gradual journey that has brought, and is still bringing, deep heart healing. Looking back, I struggle to remember what it felt like to be where I was then.

He guided me through a beautiful process, lovingly revealing things I needed to see. I needed to let go of things I clung to instead of Him. I needed to turn from the wrong ways and receive His forgiveness. I needed to forgive. I needed to release the tears in His presence. I needed to let Him speak His truth into the lies as I soaked in His Word. It didn't always feel like it, especially during the low times, but looking back, He was doing so much. And the heart of it all was learning that, more than anything, I need Him to be my everything. As He poured in Himself and His love, I found increasing healing.

No matter how broken you may feel, I believe He can do that for you, too. I know He yearns for you, longing to comfort you in the beautiful way He has for you. Will you surrender to Him and let the God of all comfort minister to your heart?

Prayer

Father,
I invite you into my broken places. I surrender to Your love and Your way of healing. I let go of the things I've been clinging to instead of You. Please forgive me. Help me forgive. Bring Your healing to my wounds. Show me things I need to see and speak Your truth into my heart. I pray for increasing freedom as I learn to receive more of Your incredible love for me.

July 12

Something New
By Janette Brunken
Today's Scripture: Isaiah 43:18-19

Hawaii is the only state completely surrounded by miles of water in the middle of the Pacific Ocean, making it the most isolated landmass in the United States. It's also the state whose landmass expands the most, as volcanic eruptions continually add new ground. New land is formed through this process of high heat and violent forces. So, the Hawaiian island is essentially a body of land in the middle of nowhere, making something new.

On July 12, 2015, I hiked up Koko Head Trail, an arduous 1,048-step stairway hike on the eastern side of the island of Oahu. When I came back down, I was a changed person.

Earlier that year, my family and I moved from the only home we knew to Hawaii for a new start. The years leading up to this day were filled with much stress and heartbreak that came from the consequences of my battle with addiction. Our marriage was at the brink of divorce, and I felt spiritually and morally crushed.

As I reached the top of that trail and looked across the beautiful view of the eastern coast of the island, I cried out to God. The pain of staying the same in my addiction had surpassed the fear of change. God heard my cry for mercy, bent down to listen, and intervened in my life at that moment. It was at that moment that I made a conscious decision to turn my life and will over to the care of God.

When I came back down the mountain, I went home and threw out every bottle of alcohol in the house. I am now standing on new land. You might find yourself in a new place and feel isolated on an island of your own, unable to withstand the violent forces and heat of your personal struggles. But behold, a new land is being formed! God is doing a new thing, and He will make a way.

Prayer

Lord Jesus,
You are the creator of all things old *and* new. Thank You, I am not alone in this uphill battle in life. I pray that You will help me through this and use my struggles to make something new. Help me to have faith that You are already making a way, so I can live my life more fully for You.

July 13

Our Advocate with the Father
By Elizabeth Clark
Today's Scripture: 1 John 2:1

When we sin, we often feel guilt that makes us want to hide from God. Our standing isn't based on our perfect performance but on the continuous work of an Advocate, Jesus Christ. He becomes our Advocate even when we sin. This isn't a license to sin, but an unwavering solution for when we do. A way has already been made for us.

The promise of an advocate is a source of immense hope. "But if anyone does sin, we have an advocate with the Father, Jesus Christ the righteous." (1 John 2:1) This passage is a present-tense reality. At the moment you fall short, Jesus is already at work, speaking on your behalf. His advocacy is based on His perfect life and complete propitiation for our sins. This means our repentance is not the cause of His advocacy, but the result of it. The assurance that Jesus is always advocating for us gives us the confidence to turn back to Him.

I recall a time when I failed, and the guilt was so overwhelming that I couldn't even pray. My first reaction was to try to fix the problem myself. It was only when I read this verse that I realized my thinking was backward. He was already advocating for me, and His advocacy was the very thing that drew me to repentance. Like a parent who sees their child make a mistake, their love is already there to help.

Don't let the shame of sin keep you from your Heavenly Father. When you feel the weight of your mistakes, remember that Jesus Christ is already at work as your Advocate. His perfect righteousness is your standing. You have immediate access to God, not because you earned it, but because your Advocate made it possible. Let this truth lead you to a life free from the burden of unconfessed sin.

How can you practically apply the truth of Christ's advocacy in your daily life when you fail, moving from a place of shame to one of immediate confession and freedom?

Prayer

Lord Jesus,
Thank You for being our advocate with the Father. We praise You that even in our sin, You are speaking on our behalf. Thank You for Your finished work on the cross, which is the basis for our forgiveness. Give us the grace to turn to You and confess our sins, knowing we are already accepted.

July 14

Built to Last
By James Hatcher
Today's Scripture: Ecclesiastes 4:12

A Godly marriage encompasses love, romance, and unity, but it is also about resilience. In a world where love is often treated like a feeling that comes and goes, God calls us to something far more profound—not a contract, but a lifelong covenant.

The foundation of its testimony and resilience comes from its occupancy of two.

"For where two or three are gathered in my name, there am I among them" (Matthew 18:20)

This is the power of prayer in marriage. When we pray together, we are stronger and we are a complete representation of Christ and the church, both of whom still look to the Father.

This is where we submit and allow God to fully be that third strand, and the heavenly bond becomes unbreakable. The world has its opinion about everything, and marriage is not spared its wicked slander. Ignore the world; God's Word says it's a sacred union.

"What therefore God has joined together, let not man separate." (Mark 10:9)

That includes outside pressure, personal pride, or even your own fears. However, we also take this scripture to call attention to our own dialogue within marriage. You'll have disagreements. You'll face stress, frustration, and seasons that feel dry. These challenges allow us to love more like Christ. Every day is a new chance to serve when it's inconvenient, to stay when it would be easier to walk away, to forgive before it's asked for.

God's design for marriage isn't just about surviving together. It is about taking a man and a woman as image bearers separately and joining them through God's covenant, so that together they not only represent the image of Christ and the church, but also bear testimony to the need for unity within the body of Christ.

Prayer

Lord,

Thank You for the gift of marriage. Help me to love with patience, speak with kindness, and forgive with grace. Strengthen the bond between us, help us submit to your kingship. When it's hard, teach us to pray. When it's easy, keep us close to You. Please help us be the image of unity You have called us to.

July 15

Trees of Life
By Shelley Groves
Today's Scripture: Proverbs 13:12

There he was, beaming from the top of his wavy, black hair down to the tips of his polished patent-leather shoes and looking like the charming prince I had always dreamed of. After giving up on the dream of marrying the love of my life, like magic, the day was before me with all the promise of a happy ever after.

I had been a bridesmaid more times than I could count. Maid of honor three times in less than a year. All my friends were married and had their second or third child, and I was still single. The hopes of being a bride had been put aside. People tried to be kind. Say the right words of encouragement. Set me up with their grandsons, nephews, or random strangers, but I knew in my heart that waiting for the right person - the man God had planned for me–was my only choice. So, I waited. I moved on and did my best to be the person God wanted me to be. I was involved in the church and taught a class. I continued my education and developed my skills as a teacher, but my heart was hurting. My heart was sick.

One day, I had no hope. The sadness hung on me like a cloak of darkness and gloom. Then, God brought an old friend back into my life that was like a ray of sunshine. Our friendship deepened and bloomed into a relationship that was more than a friendship. In God's timing, my hope was renewed. When I allowed God to be my priority, he gave me the desires of my heart.

Prayer

Lord,
Help me trust your timing to fulfill my dreams. Help me put you first and allow your desires to become my own, knowing that you want the very best for me. Remind me in days that my heart feels sick, that you can make the best dreams come true when I allow you to direct my steps.

July 16

Faith Re-Aligned
By Veronica Bobo Morris
Today's Scripture: Isaiah 40:31

July is the seventh month. Although the Bible has no reference to the months of the year, it does reference the number seven as a symbol of perfect and divine completion. July is also the midpoint of the year, a time to assess and realign where we are in our faith on the path of spirituality.

On this day in 2017, I would be led to realign my faith. Two weeks prior to July 16th, I was traveling the two hours back to my home. I had visited my hometown that weekend, and the day I would be returning to my home, I drove for two hours with a gripping pain in my side. Trying to focus on the road ahead, I drove with caution and care and prayed the whole time to make it safely to the hospital.

For someone who consistently worked out and ate in a way to maintain a healthy weight and did not present any health issues, I could not understand why I would be experiencing such pain. Not only did I not understand what and why, but neither could anyone else. The hospital was unable to determine a cause.

As I lay in the hospital bed, I would, for some reason, think of the three-day crucifixion of Jesus on the cross. Maybe this was a test of my faith?

I had gone to the emergency room three times in less than two weeks and felt like giving up and dying. By the third trip, I said, "God, I just want to die and be done with this pain."

However, it was the Spirit of God that spoke to me and reminded me to whom I belong and to never give up. At that moment, my faith was renewed, and I believed I would come out of this and recover. And I did!

Prayer

God,
I will always place my trust and look to You for hope in renewing my spiritual and physical strength in all circumstances. You give me the strength to rise above and overcome any obstacles and move forward, no matter how tired or discouraging the situation is. I thank You for the endurance and strength to always persevere with grace.

July 17

The Woman's Testimony
By Cynthia Kay
Today's Scripture: John 4:39-42

The Samaritan woman's testimony shared in John 4:1-42 led many to come and hear Jesus. Then they urged Jesus to stay with them, and Jesus stayed for two more days. This woman's testimony urged many more to come and hear Jesus' words and believe in Him, not just because of her testimony, but also because of His words.

This woman did not tell her whole life story to the Samaritans. She simply told the Samaritans that Jesus had told her everything she had ever done. Remarkably, she shared this truth without a hint of shame as she asked them to come and consider Jesus as the Christ, the Messiah.

The people came because she shared what Jesus revealed to her in this encounter. Not because she recounted to them everything she ever did. I often overshare and sometimes get caught going down rabbit holes while sharing my stories. This passage in John 1:39-42 encourages me to realize I don't have to share everything for my testimony to reach others. Instead, to succinctly focus on what Jesus has revealed to me in my vulnerable moments and lead others to hear or read His word, so they can encounter Christ and believe in Him.

Many Samaritans from that town believed in him because of the woman's testimony. "They said to the woman, it is no longer because of what you said that we believe, for we have heard for ourselves, and we know that this is indeed the Savior of the world." (John 4:42)

Now I focus on sharing what God places on my heart, with vulnerability, while remaining mindful of how He met me in those places and revealed more of Himself—just as He did for the Samaritan woman at the well.

Prayer

Lord Jesus,
Meet us in our vulnerable moments. Reveal to us the truth about who you are and what you've done for us, our dear Savior. Help us face our shortcomings without shame, knowing that with you, there is forgiveness of our sins. May our testimonial stories seek to reveal and encourage others to seek to know You more.

July 18

"God, You're Really Using This?" Redeemed on Purpose
By Melissa Vera
Today's Scripture: Romans 8:28

If you had told me the day I was born that God would one day use my story to speak life and healing to others, I wouldn't have believed you.

I was born on a military base while my dad sat unknowingly at the NCO club. By the time he called, I had already arrived. Fathers weren't allowed in delivery rooms back then, but something deeper began that day—a story of feeling overlooked.

As the youngest of four girls, I was the awkward one with glasses, always trying to earn the approval my sisters seemed to receive so easily. I often wondered if that day was when my mother decided I wasn't enough.

But isn't that how God begins His best stories?

Joseph was betrayed and left in a pit, yet knew that what others mean for evil, God means for good.

Moses stuttered and ran from his past, yet God called him to deliver a nation.

Ruth lost everything but became part of the lineage of Jesus.

Esther, an orphan, saved her people.

David was overlooked by his father, yet anointed king.

Mary Magdalene, once tormented, became the first to proclaim the risen Savior.

I remember being seven, whispering, "I'm pretty," at a church dinner. My mom said to be modest, and my sister replied, "She has to say she's pretty because no one will ever call her that." My mom agreed. Those words shattered me.

But God never wastes a wound. What once defined me has been transformed into purpose. My longing to be seen now fuels my mission, helping others feel known, reminding them that God sees them—and He's not done.

Prayer

God,
Sometimes I wonder how You can ever use my story, but then I remember You used the broken and overlooked—Joseph, Ruth, David—and You can use me too. Thank You for turning pain into purpose and rewriting lies with Your truth. Use every part of my story for Your glory.

July 19

Saved
By Susan Laurie Hutchinson
Today's Scripture: Psalm 69:14

My friend and I headed to the beach, surfboards under our arms, for a few hours of fun. Passing by the lifeguard, he stopped us and said, "It's pretty rough out there. Do you girls know what you're doing?" We gave him a confident "Yes!"

It wasn't long before I found out I was literally in over my head. An intense wave knocked the board out of my grip and out of reach. Another sucked me under, and I was helplessly tumbled and tossed. Many times, I fought my way to the surface to gulp air, only to be sucked back under.

Beneath the water, exhausted and limp, I gave up. I thought I was going to drown. "My poor parents. They will never get over this. I hope Lisa is safe."

The next instant, a firm grip grasped my wrist and pulled me to the surface. I didn't know who, but I was carried, then dumped onto a blanket on the beach. I looked up and there was the lifeguard who warned us, bent over, hands on knees, dripping water, breathing heavy. "Are you ok?" he asked. I nodded.

I looked at the crowd gathered on the beach, watching. Lisa dropped onto the blanket next to me in relief, and I smiled ruefully at her panicked parents.

That was the second time God saved me. The first was earlier that summer when I encountered a college student from Campus Crusade for Christ on the Boardwalk, who led me to Christ. From that moment on, God has saved me countless times throughout the years: from making mistakes, opening my mouth when I shouldn't, holding my temper, stopping me in my tracks, speaking in a still, small voice that only I can hear... and also from stage 4 ovarian cancer. His grace towards me abounds.

What a God!

Prayer

Lord,
You keep running interference for me, and I'm aware I don't deserve any of it. You see me as worthy, I see myself as unworthy. Yet, like the good Father You are, You never stop. Thank You that my life didn't end in the ocean at sixteen. Looking back, I see You had other things in mind for me.

July 20

The Blessing of Staying Faithful
By Tara L. Banks
Today's Scripture: Galatians 6:9

It's the middle of the year. Some of you are on top of the world. Your family is great, your ministry or business is thriving, your friendships are fruitful, and your team is winning. Some of you are in a season of literal waiting—waiting for a phone call, restoration, healing, or the next step. Some of you are sensing the shift in seasons—moving from the bounty of spring and summer into the hard work of fall and winter.

No matter where life finds you, let's pretend we're at a coffee shop and we've just sat down together. Imagine me looking you in the eyes and saying, "Whether you've been in this pursuit of Jesus for three weeks or 103 years, don't grow weary in doing what is good. Whatever God has for you will happen; just know that it will take time to become a reality. Be patient, and don't give up ahead of seeing it come full circle."

We all need that reminder from time to time. We all need to be reminded that if we continue to be faithful to what God has called us to do, we will see the blessing from staying faithful to it. The product of that intentionality will look different in each situation and may even take unexpected forms, but the God who loves us will not leave us in our situation or circumstance. The harvest of the hard work will come.

Patiently waiting on the fruition of God's faithfulness in our lives and allowing Him to complete the good work He has started can be difficult. However, the seeds of faithfulness sown in the soil of time and watered with a deluge of patience will yield the fruit of favor and blessing. You've got this.

Prayer

Lord,
Help me to stay faithful to what You've put in my hands. I want to steward it well and see the fullness of Your faithfulness in my life and situation. May You give me the strength I need to not become tired in doing the good things You have for me that will, in time, be a blessing.

July 21

God is the Greatest
By Dianna Jackson
Today's Scripture: 1 Corinthians 3:7

You may recall the passage of scripture in Luke 22:24, where the disciples began to argue among themselves about who was the greatest. Well, our verse today makes it clear that none of us are, in and of ourselves, great. God is the greatest! Moreover, only God can cause that which has been planted and watered to yield its increase.

In today's world, words like individualism and authenticity can easily evoke schism and strife, as opposed to unity and harmony, especially when promoted without the consideration of biblical principles, godly wisdom, or ample growth and development in God's love.

Whenever faced with the opportunity to engage in such carnal-natured disputes, whether internal or external, may today's verse serve as a gentle and loving reminder that in any given situation, there is neither need nor benefit in ever comparing ourselves to others, and vice versa. We are all planters and waterers. We all serve a critical role as it pertains to the seeding and nourishment process that precedes the giving of God's Increase! So, whether we plant or water, let us do it all for the glory of God. May we be ever so mindful to give him the honor and glory due his name.

Prayer

Heavenly Father,
Teach me to be discerning and understanding when planting and watering. Help me to avoid foolish disputes rooted in strife and confusion. Fill my heart with your love and increase my capacity to give high value and esteem to others. May all that I do bring honor and glory to You.

July 22

An Inheritance of Hope
By Barbara Drewry
Today's Scripture: Philippians 1:3

The most true and beautiful example of hope I have been blessed with in my life is my beloved mother, who died in 2006, but whose kindness, compassion, and selfless love still color and impact every day of my earth journey.

Mama had rheumatoid arthritis from a young age, and it got progressively worse over the next seven decades. Her firstborn was my sister, Kathi, born three months early on July 22, 1952. One year and five days later, on Mama's own birthday, I was born on July 27, 1953.

The three of us adventured through the years, and Kathi and I went on to have our own children, our own grandchildren. Mama was always there, ready to help anybody who needed help in any way. Her sense of humor never wavered, and I never once heard her give in to despair, helplessness, or hopelessness.

When things went wrong, Mama would say, "This, too, shall pass" or, "Offer it up." Mama's countless gifts of love and sacrifice, perseverance, and hope have accompanied me through so many deep valleys and dark nights.

Often hope is a brilliant beacon, like a lighthouse set sturdy among the turbulence of tides and waves. Sometimes hope whispers. When loss or grief threatens to stare it down or break it apart, it stares right back, reverberating through the corridors of my broken, believing, healing heart. And sometimes hope is a tiny flicker of a flame in a night so dark I can scarcely dare to follow on, and yet I do.

Thank you, Mama! Thank you, Kathi! You're still shining! Thank YOU, Jesus! Here's to the adventure and the best journey companions I could have ever had. Save me a spot at the Table of Eternal Love. I love you, forever.

Prayer

Dear Lord,
I come to You today, and every day, with hope in my heart that has ever been Your gift to me. I have known tired hope but never hopelessness. I pray to live each day of my life depending more and more on Your grace and mercy, Your provision and protection. Thank You for loving me!

July 23

The Kingdom Impact of Unseen Obedience
By Yodit Kifle Smith
Today's Scripture: Colossians 3:23-24

I believe we all desire to be used by God. Deep down, our hearts long for our lives to matter in His kingdom. But too often, we attach that longing to the wrong measure. We think God's work is proven in crowds, His presence is louder in applause, His approval greater when the platform is bigger.

I once believed those lies. I thought God's greatest use of me would come when I was seen, heard, and celebrated. But in believing that, I lost sight of the truth: where God has me right now is just as important as where He may one day take me.

When I fell for those lies, I missed the sacredness of my present season. I overlooked the invitation to be faithful, intentional, and missional with the people and work already in front of me.

Because there are always people right in front of us—people longing to be noticed, to be heard, to be loved. And when my eyes began to open, I saw how much kingdom beauty is hidden in the ordinary. Walking alongside a teenager mattered. Obeying the Spirit's nudge to send a text mattered. Meeting my toddler's daily needs mattered.

These may not be moments the world applauds, but our Father treasures the unseen. He gathers every small act of obedience and uses it to touch others and draw us closer to Him. With every quiet yes, He teaches us to trust Him, to hear Him, to walk with Him. Ultimately, it brings Him glory.

So if you're waiting for God to use you in mighty ways, take heart. His measure of significance bears no resemblance to the world's. The mighty work of God is revealed in the daily yes to whatever and whoever He has placed in your life today.

Prayer

Father,
Forgive me for leaning on my own understanding of what it means to be used in Your Kingdom. By Your Spirit, empower me to walk faithfully—seeing, hearing, knowing, loving, and serving the ones You've placed right in front of me. May my life reflect Your heart in both the small and hidden places, for Your glory.

July 24

Named and Called
By Olga V. Seredyuk
Today's Scripture: Isaiah 49:1

For nine months in the womb, I was Julia. In the hospital, as my mother prepared to give birth, that changed. Her own mother, my grandmother Julia, came and gently urged her: "Do not step over the name God will give."

The day after my birthday, July 24th, is a feast day in Ukraine honoring St. Olga of Kyiv, who was the first Christian ruler of Kyivan Rus' and recognized as "Equal to the Apostles." The name Olga also belonged to my father's mother, representing a double legacy I proudly bear.

In my case, at the last minute, Julia gave way to Olga. Olga means holy. Whenever I feel small or unseen, my name becomes a source of strength, reminding me that I am set apart for God's special purpose.

Not everyone feels that way about their name. Maybe yours carries difficult associations, or maybe you've never liked the way it looks or sounds.

Scripture tells us that names matter to God—so much so that He sometimes changes people's names. Abram became Abraham, the father of many nations. Simon became Peter, the rock on which Christ would build His church. Each renaming was never random; it carried a calling.

When I meet someone and hear their name, I enjoy asking who gave it to them and what it means. Your own name has significance, too. Take a moment to learn its meaning and remember how it was chosen for you. Then bring it to prayer, asking God to reveal His purpose in your name and how He may be using it to remind you of your place in His story.

Even if your name doesn't feel like a gift, trust that God calls you beloved. He speaks over you: chosen, redeemed, and mine—the truest names of all.

Prayer

Lord,
Thank You for speaking me into being and for knowing me by name. Teach me to live into the true meaning of mine and to honor who You've called me to be. Glory be to the Father, and to the Son, and to the Holy Spirit, now and forever.

July 25

The Day Anxiety Lost Its Power
By Kay Ashley
Today's Scripture: Revelation 12:11

I could sing before I could talk—and I did, constantly. So much so that my mom would lovingly ask me to take a break. She knew I had a gift. She'd ask me to sing on command, but the moment she did, I froze like water at 32 degrees.

As I got older and tried to use my voice for God, the anxiety only grew worse. The more I leaned into my calling, the louder the fear became. For 17 years, I carried a voice that rarely saw light.

Then in 2016, just shy of 40, I gave birth to my youngest son—and nearly died from sepsis. I landed in the ICU, hovering between life and eternity.

And there, something sacred happened.

The Lord brought back every Scripture I had read about death: saints falling asleep, being absent from the body and present with the Lord. And suddenly—I believed it. I stepped into a realm of peace so pure that there was no panic, no fear, not even a sad thought. Just stillness. Safety. Presence.

And then I heard Him. "If you don't have to fear death... then what is left?"

That question dismantled 17 years of fear.

Friend, if fear is trying to muzzle your gift, hear this; the power of death has been broken. You are safe in Christ. Speak. Sing. Testify. You have nothing left to fear.

Prayer

Jesus,
Thank You for meeting me in the place of fear and replacing it with peace. Thank You for healing what years of effort couldn't fix. Help me remember what You've already defeated so I can walk in boldness and purpose. Use my voice for Your glory. Fear has lost its grip.

July 26

God's Promise in the Aftermath
By Reverend Dr. Juana Jordan
Today's Scripture: Isaiah 66:9

On July 25, 2024, my mother died unexpectedly. On this day, July 26, I woke up an adult orphan: confused, dazed, devastated, and in noticeable silence created by her absence. It felt odd being in the house and not hearing her moving around upstairs or seeing her in the kitchen. It felt equally strange to exist in our home, our hometown, and a reality where my mother is not.

My mom's death left me suspended, untethered, and without an anchor in a world that felt muted and unreal. This is the new, bewildering reality grief creates. It left me with one question. Where is God in this overwhelming confusion?

On the surface, this scripture might seem unrelated to death. It is about birth, new life, and God's work of bringing things to completion. The womb is not a physical one, but here serves as the painful, yet purposeful place of one's grief. It speaks of the nature of God to complete a work, not start it—even a painful one—and then abandon it. God is ever present in the "womb" of our loss, using painful moments to birth something new in us—a new strength, a deeper faith, and a renewed purpose out of the pain. God creates us anew.

So, if you find yourself in the daze of unbearable loss, remember Isaiah 66:9 and that even in your deepest sorrow, God is a God of new life, a God of healing, and a God of hope. Your grief is not a dead end, but a pathway to the new thing God is doing.

Prayer

Lord,
Thank You for being a God who completes what You start. In the quiet of this new reality, I suffer a broken heart and am in a daze. Help me believe Your promise in Isaiah 66:9 that you are at work birthing something new, even when I cannot see it. Comfort me and remind me I am not alone.

July 27

God Who Hears and Answers Prayer
By Brooke B. Stark
Today's Scripture: Isaiah 65:24

Once, on a short-term mission trip to India, our team assessed the needs for water and other essential necessities in the nearby villages. There was a severe drought, and one village reported that they had to walk 3km to obtain water. The team members ventured out in pairs, accompanied by translators, into the village. When we gathered together after our time there, each team member stated that the Lord led them to pray with the people in the name of Jesus for rain.

These Hindus were hospitable, and despite never having heard the name of Jesus before, they gladly accepted the offers of prayer to our God. Do you know what happened that afternoon? Yes, rain! After months of drought, it rained over our hotel, but only in the village where we prayed. No other village received rain.

God revealed Himself to those people. The door for the gospel was opened after that. God used amazing circumstances to cause the villagers to seek more about Jesus Christ and to begin a church-planting work with the long-term missionaries there.

Only through Christ do we have a prayer-hearing and prayer-answering God. This is the difference with Christianity. It isn't a religion. It is a relationship with the Creator-God of all things. Do you know the One True God, the One who controls the rain and bends His ear to His creation? If so, pray for others who need to know Him and watch in expectant faith for God to open their hearts.

Prayer

Heavenly Father,
Thank You that You hear before we call and answer while we are still speaking. Strengthen our faith to pray boldly for others, trusting Your power and timing. Open hearts to know Jesus as Savior and reveal Yourself through mighty works.

July 28

Healing For Heaven's Sake
By Carrie Watts
Today's Scripture: Psalm 147:3

Healing is not a quick fix; it is a journey. The Lord invites us to walk it with Him, step by step. Using the word HEALING, we find a pathway toward wholeness.

H – Holler for Help. Healing begins with honesty. Psalm 34:17 reminds us that when we cry out, the Lord hears us. He welcomes our cries and meets us in our pain.

E – Elevate Your Mind. Colossians 3:2 calls us to set our minds on things above rather than things on earth. Shifting our focus heavenward renews our perspective and lifts us above despair.

A – Align with Jesus's Teachings. In Matthew 5, Jesus shows us the way to live. Aligning with His words not only brings healing but also deepens our faith and purpose.

L – Love Yourself. Jesus calls us to love others as we love ourselves. We cannot pour from an empty cup. As we receive God's love we can love others well.

I – Inspire Others to Heal Early. Your story matters. 2 Corinthians 1:4 tells us that God comforts us so we can comfort others. Sharing your journey may be the spark that leads someone else to freedom.

N – Nurse Your Soul with the Word. Just as a child craves milk, Peter reminds us to crave God's Word (1 Peter 2:2-3). Scripture nourishes, strengthens, and sustains healing.

G – Grow by Doing Hard Things. Healing requires courage. James 1:4 says perseverance makes us mature and complete. Every hard step taken with Jesus leads to deeper growth.

Healing is Heaven's will for you—because your wholeness reveals His glory. For Heaven's sake, let's heal.

Prayer

Dear Jesus,
I pray for every reader of these words. Whatever their pain, may you provide compassion and sympathy for their hurt. Whatever their stage of healing, may You give them strength and stamina to get through the challenges. And for their heart and minds, give them peace. Thank You Jesus, our friend, our father, and our physician.

July 29

Seen, Heard, Celebrated, Promoted
By Gail "Ember G" Sanders
Today's Scripture: Jeremiah 29:11

Today was a sacred turning point where celebration took on new meaning. It became less about an event and more about the belief I'm worthy of being celebrated. Never had I experienced such pure, intentional celebration, and it was just for me. God orchestrated divine encounters that left me breathless with His goodness.

On a call with my friend, she didn't just hear my words; she heard my heart's unspoken cry. I mentioned never walking across the stage for my bachelor's degree or celebrating milestones like earning my real estate license, along with other achievements I never celebrated. She heard what I couldn't give language to. I mattered. You do too!

With the heart of Jesus, my friend planned a surprise private graduation ceremony just for me, along with two others in our friend group. They surrounded me with the love and celebration my soul was craving. God wasn't finished yet! I came home to both my ordination certification and real estate designation in the mailbox.

I experienced how God strategically places people in our lives who see us, celebrate us, and propel us toward our purpose. He's doing the same for *you*. Remember, He knows the plans He has for you. Your breakthrough is coming. Your celebration is coming. Your divine connections are already on their way.

I stepped boldly into my promotion season, and it was just a taste of what God would later reveal about my future. Pursue and possess every promise He's spoken over your life.

Prayer

Father,
Thank You for the divine friendships and strategic connections You've sent my way. Send divinely appointed and spirit-led connections to those reading. Help us all recognize and celebrate the people You've strategically placed in our lives and show us how we can be a blessing to others in the same way.

July 30

Children Are a Blessing and a Gift from the Lord
By Michelle Barringer
Today's Scripture: Psalm 127:3-5

After 36 hours of labor, it felt like the Lord remembered my little boy needed to be born today. On this day, I developed my new threshold of pain forevermore. I didn't know how much I'd need this new measure.

Every year, I tease my firstborn every few hours, beginning the day before his birthday, that I was in labor with him. It's all in fun, but I'm reminded how hard I've worked for the greatest blessings God has given me, my children.

Labor pains were just the beginning of the intense pain that I'd experience as a mother. Raising children is not for the faint of heart. It takes guts, grit, and game. If you have children or have been around children, you know what I'm talking about. Children push boundaries to explore this world in which they were born, and it's our job to hold the line. Whatever their age, children need us to be in the game.

But we need children, too. I believe part of the blessing of children is our own transformation. They help God mold us into better humans. God has molded me into a more patient person because of my children. He's strengthened my resolve and increased my knowledge, understanding, and wisdom.

Yes, children contribute to our pain, but they also enrich our lives. There's more laughter, delight, and curiosity with children.

Did you know that God views children as a blessing and a gift? Have you considered how children contribute to your spiritual growth? How does your faith, values, or experience shape the way you view children?

I have three children. They are a precious inheritance and reward from the Lord. I can't imagine life without them.

Prayer

Father in Heaven,
What joy You bring into our lives with children! Children are the greatest gifts in so many ways. How loving You are to bless us with children in this world. May we see children the way You do, as an inheritance and a reward.

July 31

Mom! Is that a Jet Pack?
By Liz Caffman
Today's Scripture: Galatians 6:2

Four times a week, before school starts, my oldest daughter and I go to our local sports complex to swim laps. Mornings are early, and today seemed to last a lifetime. There are so many things happening in our country, and like others, I feel the weight of the world on my shoulders.

As we were leaving the complex, a group of firefighters were prepping for drills in the courtyard. They were carrying giant bags of gear as well as helmets and items for their drills. As we watched and walked, I noticed that each man was meticulous in ensuring they had not only what they needed but also what their fellow firefighters needed for the day—each one caring for one another. They helped adjust the straps on the bags and suspenders on the trousers. They carried boots and adjusted equipment levels, all while double-checking for one another. Everyone was making sure the other had what they needed.

Half of the group had what seemed like a large tank strapped to their backs, and in a second, my oldest looked at me and said, "MOM! Is that a jet pack?" I giggled (literally) out loud and said, "No, honey. That is an oxygen tank." In which she quickly responded, "A jet pack would have been way cooler."

Bless. I love that kid so much. It was a subtle reminder that sometimes, we mistake what others are carrying. We assume it's something exciting, light, or glamorous, but in reality, it's oxygen—the ultimate survival. Or we think someone else's burden is no big deal when it's actually the very thing keeping them alive in the fire.

Our perception may be skewed, but that doesn't excuse us from loving people well. The firefighters didn't stop to question whether someone's load looked heavy or not—they stepped in to help. They carried for one another, adjusted straps, and made sure no one walked alone.

Isn't that what we're called to do as followers of Christ? Regardless of whether or not they are a believer?

We may not always see clearly what someone else is carrying. We may even laugh or misinterpret it like my daughter did, but love looks past perception. Love says, "I'll help you carry it, whatever it is." And in a world that feels so heavy right now, that's precisely the kind of community God has called us to build.

Prayer

Lord,
Thank You for reminding us that no one is meant to carry their burdens alone. Help us to notice when others need a hand, to love them well, and to walk with them just as You walk with us. Be our strength and our peace today.

August

August 1

The Gift of the Waiting Season
By Rose McCombs Jordan
Today's Scripture: Psalm 27:14

Waiting can feel like standing still, but God is often moving beneath the surface.

For years, I loved serving the city of Mineral Wells through my work. The projects, the creativity, the chance to highlight the beauty of our town—it was deeply rewarding. I loved welcoming visitors, telling the story of our community, and celebrating the people who made it special. Even more, I treasured the friendships that formed with local partners who shared the same heart. Yet even as I served, I sensed God tugging me toward something new.

For nearly four years, that sense of calling lingered without a clear release. I carried the ache of anticipation while still giving my best to the role I held. It was both a gift and a weight. At times, I wondered if I had misunderstood God's direction. At other times, I grew restless, longing for the day when I could finally step into what He was preparing for me.

Then, on August 1, 2025, arrived my last day on the job. Tears came easily: sadness at leaving something meaningful, relief at stepping into what God had long promised. Mixed emotions filled the day, but beneath it all was gratitude. God had been faithful in the waiting and faithful in the release.

When we wait, we often wonder if we've been forgotten. But waiting seasons are not wasted—they grow endurance, deepen faith, and prepare us for the next chapter God has planned.

If you're in a waiting place, take courage. The God who called you is also the God who will carry you into what's next.

Prayer

Lord,
Help me trust You in the waiting. When the road feels long, remind me that Your timing is never late and never wasted. Guard me from discouragement and doubt, and shape me into who You want me to be. When the new beginning comes, let me step into it with courage, gratitude, and faith in Your goodness.

August 2

Our Fruit Nourishes Others
By Heather Cruz, M.Ed.
Today's Scripture: Galatians 5:22-23

Imagine smiles so big they almost hurt. Giggles so loud you could hear them echo across the neighbor's yard. Every fall, my kids would race across the grass with big buckets, eager to pick apples from the neighbor's trees. We made homemade applesauce, apple crisp, and warm apple muffins together—always messy, always sweet.

But then, one year, everything changed. The neighbors cut down their apple trees. They said the fruit was too much. Instead of giving it away, they let it drop, rot, and ferment. The burden of abundance, unshared, became a nuisance.

I often wonder if our walk with Christ can feel the same way. We love Him. We abide in Him. He blesses us with spiritual fruit—love, joy, peace, and patience. But do we share it, or do we let it fall to the ground, rotten and unnoticed by the world around us? God never intended our fruit to rot in silence. He meant it to nourish others.

So, we decided to plant our own apple trees. It took a few years before they bore fruit, but it was worth the wait. Now, we share what we grow—and teach others to grow, too. Fruit multiplies when shared. And when our lives overflow with Christ's goodness, God is glorified.

Let's not waste the fruit we are given. Life is better when we share grace, give freely, and plant seeds in others. That is where hope is found.

Prayer

Lord,
Your goodness amazes us, nourishes us, and strengthens us. You bring hope through Your word, through Your presence, and through the people around us. We confess that, at times, we take it for granted. We ask that You show us where we can share Your goodness with others. Help us to plant seeds of hope each day.

August 3

Blossoms of Hope
By Kelly Hill
Today's Scripture: Today's Scripture: Isaiah 40:8

Life often feels like a harsh season—circumstances shifting like weather, our strength fading like blooms in the heat. There are days when I wonder if anything beautiful can grow from disappointment, uncertainty, or weariness. Yet, even in barren soil, God's Word reminds me that His promises never wither.

When I sit with Him, I picture my heart as a garden. Some places are tangled with weeds of fear, heavy with drought, or trampled by the weight of unmet expectations. Yet He gently works the soil, pruning where needed, loosening the earth, and watering what seems forgotten. His Word is living water, reviving the hidden roots of faith. As I lean into His presence, hope finds a way to push through the cracks—like wildflowers in the most unexpected places.

Each morning, I choose to notice His small blossoms of hope: the laughter of a child, the quiet assurance of Scripture, the beauty of petals turning toward the sun. Even in ordinary moments, His faithfulness is present, growing in ways we cannot always see. I remind myself that the Master Gardener is never finished—that each season, whether one of waiting, struggle, or joy, is a place where He is at work, preparing a harvest of life and beauty.

To behold hope is to trust that God is actively tending our hearts. Even when life feels sparse, we can witness growth, resilience, and joy sprouting in unexpected places. When we pause, we see that His promises bloom quietly yet powerfully, offering a steady reminder that we are never without His care.

Prayer

Lord,
Make my heart a garden of trust, tended by Your faithful hands. May I look for the blossoms of hope in the ordinary and remember that Your Word never fails. May your promises bloom within me, steadying my soul and filling my days with radiant beauty.

August 4

A Godly Life
By Alana Deutschmann
Today's Scripture: 2 Peter 1:3

When I was in the early years of suffering from chronic health issues, I confess, my soul posture was one of apathy and resignation. Sarcasm was a key indicator. "Okay, God, I guess I don't need clear, itch-free skin and a full head of hair to do your will. I don't need a regularly functioning digestive system or copious amounts of energy and happiness to show others your love."

A part of me tried to be earnest and sincere, but it was far more comfortable to wallow in despair and bitterness, pouting in my pity party of one. Envy flared and discontentment reigned. How easily I could read Scripture through the lens of my current circumstances. I hoped and prayed for physical healing to come and so had many others. Instead, I got worse. Salvation can't be earned, but maybe healing can. I don't remember consciously thinking this, but I functioned as if I believed it.

Although I come from a legalistic background, I still took matters into my own hands by researching relentlessly; scheduling appointments with various practitioners; and utilizing different tests, supplements, and protocols.

At some point in the exhausting journey of little help or answers, I continued to pray for healing, and I sensed Him say, "What if I am healing you in ways you couldn't imagine? I am healing you mentally, emotionally, and spiritually. I'm healing your self-image and definition of beauty."

Thus began my inauguration into the wilderness where Jesus brought me back to Himself. I started to see my experience not as punishment but as development and preparation. Faith being refined and purified in the fire of His presence was not pain-free, but it was worth it for producing an enduring hope and a transformation I couldn't have imagined.

Prayer

Merciful Father,
Your grace is sufficient. Keep me tender before You because I am so tempted to harden my heart in my current circumstances. Increase my sensitivity to the Holy Spirit's comfort and guidance and reassure me of Your nearness as I surrender and trust that no amount of time that passes diminishes Your goodness.

August 5

Created for His Glory
By Ada Bontrager
Today's Scripture: Isaiah 43:7

Adam was not a living being until God breathed the breath of life into his nostrils. It was then that he could have dominion over the earth, a relationship with Eve, and with God. Adam taught us the consequences of disobedience. We can also learn the rewards of redemption through repentance and forgiveness.

Abraham and Sarah rushed God's plan and tried to fulfill it in their own flesh and on their own time. We can learn from them the importance of patience. In their old age, God blessed them to produce the promised child of Isaac.

Jacob was a deceitful man. He stole the birthright from his brother, Esau. Jacob stayed up all night wrestling with the angel of God. He didn't give up until he got the blessing from the Lord. He was then given a new name, Israel. Jacob shows us what it means to be persistent.

David was a man after God's own heart. He was righteous (most of the time), wise, and a favored king. David gave in to the lust of his eyes when he saw the beautiful Bathsheba. He then covered up his sin of adultery by killing one of his most trusted army leaders. Despite his sin, David rose to become a man who honored God's appointed leaders.

You too were formed, knit together, and made for the glory of God. You are given a purpose in life greater than you can accomplish on your own. As Esther was created for her time, you are created for this time in this world for His glory!

Prayer

Heavenly Father,
I thank You for creating me wonderfully and fearfully in Your image. I surrender my heart, soul, mind, and spirit to reflect Your glory. Holy Spirit, come and fill this vessel to overflowing.

August 6

When Ordinary Explodes with Extraordinary
By Becky Seamon
Today's Scripture: Genesis 5:21-24, Hebrews 11:5

Hitting the snooze button repeatedly, I simultaneously pulled the covers over my head. The dull list of dirty laundry and unfinished documents made my heart long for a day of adventure. My life felt weary and ordinary, and I could barely muster the energy to face it. Do you ever wish for grand when your day feels bland? Do you dream of more?

My thoughts shift to Enoch, whose most notable achievement is captured in five words. Genesis 5:24 reads, "Enoch walked faithfully with God." At first glance, his story might seem uneventful, with no record of battles won, fame, or riches. But don't be deceived! His walk was a remarkable journey.

It began with knowing the one true God. It was a path of surrender to His way and His will, a life of deliberate communion. It involved pursuing God rather than this world. Enoch's steadfast commitment lasted for 300 years—more than 109,000 days! The story climaxed as God escorted Enoch to heaven before his death. Imagine a long, leisurely walk ending closer to heaven than Enoch's residence. I picture God gently wrapping his arm around Enoch's shoulder as they strolled through the pearly gates together.

Friend, I am learning that fulfillment comes not from what I do, but from who I know. The relationship gives meaning. You will be happy to hear that I eventually got out of bed that morning. My list hadn't changed, but my mindset had. As I worshiped Christ, my tasks became an opportunity for me to walk faithfully, even in my ordinary responsibilities.

Today, I invite you to embrace a relationship with Jesus as Savior, Lord, and friend. Walk faithfully in every stage of life, knowing that ordinary moments can become extraordinary when connected to the Father.

Prayer

Abba Father,
Thank You for the priceless gift of everyday moments, from quality time with family to unhurried conversations with You. Teach me to know You deeply and to walk faithfully in Your ways.

August 7

Trust In the Lord
By Trudy Bosman
Today's Scripture: Proverbs 3:5-6

We were living in Michigan. We had five kids and were members of a great church. However, it seemed like God was nudging us to move to help at a church elsewhere. Steve asked people where they thought a good place might be. Denver, Colorado, was suggested. My husband was self-employed, so we were able to pack up the kids and head for Colorado.

We found the people in the church to be friendly, and the location was beautiful. Yet, it did not seem like the place to be. We had put our house up for sale, but no one came to look at it. We took it off the market and decided God wanted us to stay where we were for the time being.

The following year—and one more baby later—we heard about a pastor who was looking for people to move to Wisconsin and help with churches on and near the Menominee and Stockbridge Reservations. The Pastor came for a visit to tell us more about the work there as well. This was the state we had both come from, and it sounded interesting.

We decided to put a 'For Sale' sign on the lawn, and if the house sold, that would be a sign to us that we should move to Wisconsin.

A few days later, a realtor called and said he had someone interested in our house, and asked if they could come see it. They wanted to visit right away. I told him I had six kids, and it was early in the morning, so they would see it as it was. They came and...they bought it!

We had put it out to God, and he had answered! God will always answer you when you seek his guidance. Sometimes it may take a while, but he who promised is faithful. You can trust Him always.

Prayer

Dear Father,
We are thankful for Your guidance in our lives. Help us to always trust You in all areas of our lives, knowing Your plan is best.

August 8

Running to Win
By Abigail Ruth Miller
Today's Scripture: Hebrews 12:1-3

Do you know where you were on this day in 2008? I do. I had been living in China for over a year and was back home for the summer when the opening ceremony of the Summer Olympic Games began. In Chinese culture, the number eight represents blessings, and thus the Chinese government sought to add as many eights into the day as possible. This is why the games began at 8:08 pm.

Do you want blessings in your life? Do you want to run your race well? The Bible provides us with all the guidance we need. We are all running a race, but sometimes we aren't running to win. We aren't running with our eyes on the prize.

What is that prize that we must keep our eyes on? Our Saviour. Hebrews tells us that we must have our eyes FIXED on Jesus. We must consider, think about, and dwell on what He went through on the cross (in his race) so that we will be able to have perseverance in our own race.

We also must consider Jesus' attitude. He endured much because of joy—the joy of having you. A relationship with you brought Jesus such joy that He endured the cross. Hebrews also encourages us that when we consider Jesus, we will not grow weary or lose heart. Where have you lost heart lately?

Prayer

Jesus,
Thank You for all you did for us in Your race here on earth, keeping Your eyes on the prize of joy. Lord, would You help us keep our eyes fixed on the joy set before us—the glorious moment when we will be fully and completely united with You? We love You and long to be with You.

August 9

Peace in His Presence
By Becca Ramirez
Today's Scripture: Philippians 4:6-7

On August 9, 2016, my family's lives changed in an instant when we were t-boned by someone running a red light. My oldest daughter was injured to the point of needing emergency surgery to stabilize her neck.

After hours of pure adrenaline-induced survival, I felt the weight of what we were facing. My eyes had no more tears to cry, my body was dragging from exhaustion, and my heart felt like it was tearing in two. I didn't know how I was going to make it.

As I lay down, watching my daughter sleep only with the help of pain medication, a presence like a weighted blanket wrapped around me. A hug that permeated through the pain and stress reached into my soul. As the beeping from the machines echoed in the room and the light from the display cast a glow over her tiny face, I felt a sense of peace.

The problems didn't magically disappear. We still awoke the next morning and had to walk our 5-year-old back into surgery, but there was peace in moments that previously held only anxiety.

Sometimes it's not about being taken out of the fire and chaos, but recognizing that you aren't in there alone. God is with us. He has not abandoned us, and He doesn't mind us wrestling within the midst of our trials.

When we continue to seek God, He promises we will find him. Run to Him. Ask Him the big questions. Be intentional about spending time reading His word and praying. When we do this, even if we don't get the answers we want, we find peace and confidence that wasn't there before. Don't be afraid to cry out to God. Tell Him what you want, and know there is no better place than in His presence.

Prayer

Father,
Thank You for always being with us—even in the hardest seasons. Help us to surrender our burdens before You and open our hearts and minds to the peace that comes with Your Spirit. We believe that You work for the good in all things and trust You when we are most vulnerable.

August 10

The Sovereignty of God
By Sharri McGarry, M.A.
Today's Scripture: Psalm 115:3

At sixty-three years of age, I can look back over more than three decades since my kidney/pancreas transplant and only marvel at the sovereignty of God.

Since August 10, 1993, there have been numerous times when death seemed closer than life—hospital stays that left me weak, infections that nearly took me home to heaven, and nights when fear whispered that my story was ending. Yet, every single time, God had the final word. His sovereignty overruled the enemy's lies.

When I prayed for healing, sometimes God gave it. At other times, He gave them the strength to endure. Through it all, He shaped me into someone I could never have become without the struggle. My scars remind me not of what I lost, but of what He preserved.

Today, my heart is full of joy because of His blessings. My parents, husband, family, and friends walked with me through the darkest valleys. God's sovereign hand wove the gifts of two miracle sons and countless encouraging voices into my life, reminding me that He is not only in control but is also deeply loving.

The sovereignty of God does not mean life will always be easy. It means nothing can touch us apart from His wise permission. Even when we do not understand His ways, we can rest in His character. He is faithful, good, and always at work for our eternal security.

If you are facing uncertainty today, trust this: the same God who carried me through decades of fragile health is the God who holds your future. His sovereignty is not something to fear; it is the anchor of our hope.

Prayer

Sovereign Lord,
I praise You for holding every detail of my life in Your hands. Thank You for preserving me through trials and blessing me with joy I never thought was possible. When fear rises or uncertainty looms, remind me of Your faithfulness. Help me trust Your wisdom, rest in Your goodness, and rejoice in Your unfailing love.

August 11

Fresh Starts & Clean Slates
By Shelley Groves
Today's Scripture: Lamentations 3:22-23

According to my husband, autumn must be my favorite season because of all the pumpkins that magically appear in our home each fall. Autumn is wonderful. Crisp mornings. Frosty pumpkins. Cozy sweaters. Warm apple cider. Copper-colored leaves.

School starts in the fall, which is also one of my favorite things. The smell of newly sharpened pencils makes me smile. Lists of books and school supplies appear on refrigerator doors. Backpacks get filled with crayons and glue. School buses rumble down the street. And for me, students move back to campus to begin another semester of their college lives. Some celebrate the start of the new year in January, but for me, it has always been in the fall that the new beginnings take place.

New beginnings. Fresh starts. Clean slates. Each day is a gift, allowing us to begin again. To start something new. To be a better friend. To try again.

I need new beginnings. Sometimes, I need a new start in my attitude. Some days, I am not the person I want to be. I rant at people I care about. I lose my temper. Those days, I'm so much less than I want to be, and feel even worse because the people that I love the most often see me at my worst. I apologize, and they forgive me. However, I keep replaying the ugly things I have said. I need a fresh start.

Fortunately, the Lord gives fresh starts. Lamentations–the book in the Old Testament that is defined by grief and sorrow–provides inexpressible hope. "The steadfast love of the Lord never ceases; his mercies never come to an end; they are new every morning; great is your faithfulness." (Lamentations 3:22-23) God's mercy doesn't give up on us. He has a new batch of mercy every day.

Prayer

Thank you, Lord, for fresh starts and clean slates. In your Word, you promise new mercy every morning. You are faithful to love and forgive us. Today, help me trust the truth of your Word. Please help me to forgive myself and rest in your mercy and grace.

August 12

Waiting During the Storms of Life
By Paige Byers
Today's Scripture: Isaiah 40:31

Last year, three hurricanes hit Florida, and one hit us directly. Flooding, loss of power, running water, and basic necessities overwhelmed us, displacing us along with many others.

I had just been diagnosed with breast cancer. Chemotherapy was ravaging my body. My long, blond hair was falling out in clumps. Fear, my constant companion, sat with me at blood transfusions, MRIs, CTs, and surgeries.

My family was devastated. I was the glue that held us together—now what? We were already dealing with a devastating terminal disease, severe anxiety and depression, and consuming addictions. The future was daunting.

Flood waters receded, yet my immune system remained compromised, and I was forced to isolate and be alone most of the time. The mental toll overwhelmed me. Distraught, a faithful friend reminded me of Isaiah 40. Feeling supernatural peace, I also found solace in photography, capturing God's natural beauty.

Both Isaiah and photography reminded me of God's promises. Many before me felt forsaken and forgotten, and still they endured and rose again. Just like the zoom on my camera, my view slowly changed. Zooming in only provided a close-up of my own tragedies, but by zooming out, I could see a larger perspective.

We are all tossed about in the storms of life, knocked to our knees by gut-wrenching circumstances we cannot control. How do we go another day of fear, hopelessness, or devastation? We remember that our stories are only a part of God's greater plan. Zooming out, we realize trials are just a part of the bigger picture. His promises throughout the Bible demonstrate that He will provide endurance and strength. I can wait patiently for the Lord, soaring as an eagle, and run this race not only with Him, but To Him.

Prayer

Father God,
We know only You can fill us with power and new purpose. Only You can fill us with the breath of new life. Grant us renewed strength of body and soundness of mind. LORD, heal our hearts and comfort our souls. All glory and honor to our God forever and ever!

August 13

Embrace Your Path, Go with the Flow
By Amy Duckworth
Today's Scripture: Isaiah 43:18-19

This passage asks us to let go of our past. While we will not forget the events, they are merely waypoints that leave a mark on our life map.

Instead, we can focus on the endpoints and the goal, that "something new." We are assured that a new plan is being forged for us. God hypes us up for what is to come. We are called to see this new pathway presented in the form of a river. Rivers carve new paths, often finding routes of least resistance but always moving forward. We can grow by jumping into the flow of the river. God has created a new path for us to flow in and gain strength to move forward.

I let go of the belief that my unshared ideas and words would grow stagnant and stuck within my journals. My "something new" came in the surge and flow of words and paint on the paper. I now know that these are my modes of creating, which helped me connect with my creator. I continue to learn and grow on this creative path, following the flow wherever it takes me.

Put this into action by taking out a sheet of paper. At the bottom of the paper, write something you would like to let go of. At the top of the paper, write down something new. Maybe you write about a thing you were.

Fold the sheet in half. Tear the bottom off, crumple it, and let it go by placing it in the trash. Use a marker, pencil, or pen to draw a new path along the edge of the curved or jagged tear. This symbolizes your new path. You had no control over how the tear would move, but your marking tool was able to follow it. May you mark your path and grow with the flow you are destined to follow forward.

Prayer

I pray that I can honestly let go of the past and accept the new path that God has given me. While I may have created my own path, please allow me to see the way forward that is not always designed by me. As these two paths converge, I pray that I can embrace my purpose for doing and stay afloat in the flow of the river path moving forward. Let go and know we can grow and flow with God.

August 14

The Fruit of Righteous Discipline
By Elizabeth Clark
Today's Scripture: Hebrews 12:11

When we face hardships, it's easy to assume God is punishing us. This verse offers a profoundly helpful distinction between divine punishment and divine discipline. Divine discipline is a loving act with a specific purpose—to make us partakers of His holiness. This understanding frees us from the paralyzing fear of being condemned, allowing us to view our struggles through a different lens.

The ultimate goal of God's discipline is beautifully optimistic. Although it is a matter of grief at the moment, the outcome is the fruit of righteousness. The trials we face are not a dead end but a path to a more righteous life and a more profound sense of peace. The very things that cause us sorrow are working for our good.

I went through a season where a series of painful events—a family death, a business failure, health issues, and broken relationships—convinced me God was punishing me. However, as I sought Him in prayer and Scripture, my perspective shifted. I realized that what felt like punishment was actually a loving discipline meant to refine me. These trials were a painful wake-up call, shaking me out of my spiritual complacency. They humbled me and taught me to rely on Him, revealing a newfound peace that I have found in that place of surrender.

Don't be discouraged by the trials that come your way. Your Heavenly Father is not against you; He is for you. The hardships you face are not meant to cause you trouble, but to make you holy. Embrace His discipline as a sign of His deep love and concern for you.

How can you shift your perspective from viewing your current struggles as punishment to seeing them as God's loving discipline? What might this change in perspective allow you to do or feel differently in your situation?

Prayer

Heavenly Father,
We thank You for Your love that disciplines us. Help us to see our present grief not as punishment but as a path to holiness. Give us the grace to be exercised by our trials, trusting that they are yielding the peaceable fruit of righteousness and bringing us closer to You.

August 15

God-Centered
By Erica Lewis
Today's Scripture: Ecclesiastes 12:13-14

King Solomon, the wisest man besides Jesus, tried everything, both good and bad. He wrote a book about all his experiences, and this now cynical old man continually declares everything futile. Yet, near the end of his book, he urges us to take a different path than he did, and instead, to follow God's commands and honor Him with our lives, rather than seeking worldly pleasure.

Solomon sought to demonstrate that life finds meaning only when lived in accordance with God. It's easy to feel like my current season in life has no purpose; after all, I am only in my early twenties, and there is so much more life ahead of me.

However, if I realize that meaning does not come from having large savings or owning my own house, then I can see the real, worthwhile life I'm already living.

Meaning is found when I hear God speak to me, when I make someone else smile, when I honor God while making a hard decision, and so much more. If God's in the center of it, then there is value. After all, our very lives are supposed to display the Great Commission, which is to go and make disciples (Matthew 28:19-20). With such an important task assigned to us, living with God-centered hearts and dreams makes disciple-making a lifestyle rather than another task on the list.

Today, as you begin your day, consider making God the center of your activities. Maybe it's expressing gratitude to God at a meeting or reading your Bible on your lunch break. If God is the center, He doesn't need to be squeezed in. Instead, you're just recognizing His presence was there all along. When the One who brings value is in your life, it's easier to see your value.

Prayer

God,
Thank You that I don't have to add You into my life, but You are already there. Help me to intentionally welcome You into my day. Open my eyes to see Your presence and be grateful for the meaning You bring to my life. Amen.

August 16

Strong at the Broken Places
by Sarah Fry
Today's Scripture: 2 Corinthians 12:9-10

There have been seasons when I've felt so broken that I felt more like a burden than a blessing—too fractured to be useful. But learning about Kintsugi gave me hope. Kintsugi is a Japanese art form that involves repairing pottery with gold lacquer. The cracks are not hidden but filled with something precious, turning the piece into something more beautiful and unique than before. For me, the golden glue has come to represent Jesus Himself. As He holds my broken places together, I don't just survive—I become stronger, because He is the one holding me!

Another image that brings me hope is from Biosphere 2, a 3.14-acre enclosed structure built in the early 1990s to test whether humans could live in a self-sustaining ecosystem. But the trees inside weren't thriving. Scientists discovered the problem: there was no wind. In nature, wind creates stress, forcing trees to grow what's called "stress wood," which makes them stronger and able to withstand storms. Without wind, the trees grew tall but weak.

I think about that when the winds of life feel relentless. Stress and struggle may not be pleasant, but they shape the strength in me that wouldn't exist otherwise. When I feel cracked or weary, I remember that Jesus doesn't discard brokenness. Instead, He binds it with His presence, His strength, His beauty.

So whether it's the cracks filled with gold or the trees strengthened by the wind, I find hope in knowing that weakness is not wasted. My broken places can shine—that's where the light gets in!

Prayer

Lord, I'm weary. I'm embarrassed about my weakness and brokenness. Please hold me together. Please make me strong at the broken places and mend my cracks with Your beautiful self.

August 17

The Faith of A Child
By Dava R. Caballero
Today's Scripture: 1 Samuel 12:24

We had stars in our eyes and the faith of children. In fact, we were barely fledgling adults! Newlyweds at 19, we headed to our sophomore year at a small Christian university in Northeast Texas. We had saved up money over the summer, but our plans for the future still make me cringe. We had no jobs lined up and few prospects, aside from financial aid and low-cost married-student housing. Worst case, we surmised, both of us could work at the nearby McDonald's and make ends meet.

A friend heard from God recently, "What if everything is going to be ok?" Does our faith compel us to truly believe that? Scripture gives us promise after promise of hope and a joyful future. I suppose life has a way of beating us down, and trials bring us to a realization that life can indeed be difficult. But Jesus didn't pull any punches in the area of suffering. He admitted that we would face trouble in this world. However, in the midst of the troubles we are also promised unspeakable joy. That is how we can live out a fruitful, worry-free life.

Thankfully, our childlike faith produced fruit. I landed a blessed position as assistant secretary in Academic Affairs under the mentorship of a beautiful and godly woman. I kept that position for the rest of our college career. My husband secured a Computer-Aided Design job with the university's sister corporation, making significantly more than we had anticipated. God made a way. As life's trials attempt to weigh us down, let us not forget this truth: God is a perfect Provider and a good, good Father to us, his precious children. He is more than enough.

Prayer

Thank You, Holy Father God, that you are more than able to meet every need as we keep our focus on You. LORD, as we mature in You and walk the path You have laid out before us, help us to hold Your gaze and keep the starry-eyed faith of a child.

August 18

The Beauty of Patience
By Breanna Thompson
Today's Scripture: Ecclesiastes 3:11

Patience, one of the fruits of the Spirit, is often a long process, not something that comes easily or quickly. Long seasons of waiting can leave us feeling impatient and hopeless. We ask valid questions of God, but sometimes the answer is not instant. Rather than becoming discouraged, perhaps we can realize that God will use this time to teach us patience. Our tears and sleepless nights do not go unnoticed. He can utilize our pain and brokenness to show us more of who He is.

My own prayers were full of questions. Tears frequently welled up in my eyes as I struggled to come to terms with a diagnosis I was given after years of pain and prayers. My spine is severely compressed due to a genetic condition, and little can be done to alleviate the pain it causes. Despite the uncertainty of what the future may be, God has taught me to see that there is beauty in waiting on Him. My pain has brought me to a low place, but God has reached down to lift my eyes, focusing me only on Him.

The struggle has allowed me to grapple with this question: What if we viewed patience as a means to draw closer to God? He desires a relationship with each one of us. He chooses to reveal Himself to us in different ways as we wait on Him. So many broken things in the world can cause us to drift away from Him. As followers of Jesus, we live knowing that this is not our true home and that one day we will live in eternity. Our broken world will no longer bring us pain. Our unanswered prayers will be brought to light. God will make us whole again. For that, I will wait!

Prayer

Jesus,
Thank You for walking ahead and beside us as we face every moment in this broken world. Please help us to see beauty, even in the midst of trials that shake us to our core. Give us the strength to wait only on You.

August 19

But God
By Tonya Ziese
Today's Scripture: Psalms 116:2

I was 37 years old when "it's cancer" cracked over me like a violent storm. I had been married for 18 years. My babies were six and four. In the quiet, alone moments after the diagnosis, I wasn't feeling strong, brave, or full of faith. I felt scared, uncertain, and overwhelmed by the great unknown. Then I heard a whisper of the One who knows the unknown, and He said, "I've got you."

From the age of five, I knew the bible stories and that Jesus loved me. We had walked together through many seasons—some joyful, some hard and crushing, but this was the fire. Could he really be with me in this deep of a pit, as I stood cloaked in fear? Sitting quietly in these questions, I was drenched in a peace that passed all understanding, and He was there. There was no judgment, no condemnation—just a quiet, enveloping presence.

My cancer journey became my story of how God showed up in the deep valley and taught me to trust him with all of it. He taught me to find joy in the small things and to let go of the illusion of control. I clung to Him and fell into His arms, where he held me, even when I couldn't pull anything together.

If you are walking through a storm right now, I want you to know that God can be trusted to show up. He hasn't abandoned you. He hears the fears you can't give voice to, and he will walk you through them.

There is hope in your valley. God isn't finished with your story and has not abandoned you. Release your fear and doubt and hold on to him for your next steps. He will hold you up and turn that fear and doubt into beauty, and your story will bless others.

Prayer

Heavenly Father,
Thank You for never abandoning us in the seasons of our storms. We are blessed by Your mighty hand and protected by Your loving arms. Use my story to encourage others. Allow them to know that You are with them in doubt and fear, and they can rest in You. Make yourself known in tangible ways as they reach out. Thank You for always loving us.

August 20

The Birthday Habit
By Sandi Banks
Today's Scripture: 1 Thessalonians 5:16-18

It seemed like a great idea. It was August 20th, 1976–the day I turned 30. Being fit, energetic, and committed to a daily running routine, I began what would become my first annual celebratory Birthday Run: Three miles–one-tenth mile for each year.

"That was fun!" I panted as the pedometer reached three miles. "Next year I'll add another tenth mile!" I did, and I loved it.

So, each August 20th thereafter, no matter where I was, I continued the tradition, adding a tenth mile. Many were memorable, but my 49th birthday jog in Vienna, Austria, won the prize.

My friend mapped out a 4.9-mile route the night before to the Little Danube and back. I memorized it. At dawn, I tiptoed out of the hotel room and took off. Two miles later, I saw a sign: Big Danube.

"Ooo, I'll go take a peek!"
Before long, nothing looked familiar. Seems I was a wee bit off-course. Okay, so I was totally, utterly, hopelessly lost.

Foolishly, I'd taken off empty-handed: no map, hotel name, contact information, money, food, or water. And cell phones? A thing of the future. Panic set in.

Hours passed, and I continued to wander and pray. "Lord ... please bring us together."
Eventually, He did. Everyone hugged. By God's grace, I lived to see my 50th. Every August 20th, I rejoice, give thanks, and pray.

Prayer

Lord,
May we who enjoy Your gifts of good health, mobility, and abundant provisions, to any degree, say thank You! We lift those who would love to take a birthday stroll but can't. Give them an extra measure of Your grace today–Your healing, strength, and hope. Let them feel the beauty of Your presence.

August 21

A Tranquil Heart is Life
By Brooke B. Stark
Today's Scripture: Proverbs 14:30, 1 Timothy 6:6

Doctors and researchers tell us that stress, anger, and anxiety take a toll on our bodies. Yet, long before modern science discovered this, God's Word spoke truth—peace in the heart brings life, while envy quietly destroys from within.

Satan loves to plant seeds of discontent. He wants us to believe that what God has given is not enough. So we find ourselves longing for what belongs to someone else—a spouse, children, health, recognition, possessions, or even traits of personality. Maybe we wish we were more outgoing, or more gentle, or less ordinary. Envy can disguise itself in many ways, but the result is the same. It harms our souls, damages relationships, and interrupts our intimacy with the Lord. At its root, envy is sin.

But God does not leave us to battle alone. When jealous thoughts rise, we can immediately turn to Him in prayer. We can hand over our envy and ask Him to cleanse our hearts. The cross reminds us that our value is not found in comparison with anyone else. Because of Jesus' sacrifice, our worth is secure—we are loved, chosen, and redeemed.

You are His masterpiece, designed with care and intention. God delights in His creation of you! That means you can rest, content and at peace, knowing He made no mistake in the details of your life.

We can thank the Lord often for who He made us to be. And when envy comes knocking, we repeat this truth as many times as needed: God is pleased with me, because I belong to Him.

Prayer

Dear Heavenly Father,
Thank You for creating me uniquely and loving me through Christ's sacrifice. Thank You for the gifts You've given me to serve You. Forgive me when I fall short. Be glorified in me as I live fully as Your creation.

August 22

Through
By Maria Burnett-Carroll
Today's Scripture: Psalm 23:4

I had a beautiful, green meadow life, until I had a sudden free fall into death's shadow valley. Overnight, I became a 43-year-old widow with four children to raise. It wasn't the life I planned or prepared for. It wasn't the way my life was supposed to go. I was relocated to the valley, and my only hope was in the One who promised He'd never, ever leave me.

Death's shadow lengthens farther than we can see beyond it, but the Lord knows the way through shadowlands. In fact, He is the perfect One to be with us in this foreign place, bringing comfort, help, and protection that no one else can steadily supply.

People try to help, but only He remains with us through every day and every night. He has been here before and knows how to patiently lead us. He steadily walks, and we follow. His pace is kind. Day by day, we make progress together.

After twelve long years in my death valley life, the word "through" jumped out at me. I realized that, over the years, I had resigned myself to the valley as my permanent home after a tragedy.

However, the Lord spoke to my heart gently and firmly that He never intended for me to spend all of my life in the shadow of death. He was leading me through it to life beyond loss.

Death doesn't get the final word in my story. It doesn't get the final word in yours either. God's goodness always gets the final word in life and into eternity. He is always leading us through every valley, trial, and season of suffering.

Prayer

Lord,
We thank You that you are always bringing life and hope into our stories. You are always lovingly leading us through death's valley to life beyond its dark shadow. Help us trust you as the One who will faithfully lead us through, even when we can't clearly see it happening.

August 23

Strength Beside You
By Laura J. Antos
Today's Scripture: Isaiah 41:10

When seasons of life change and challenges come, true friends reflect God's love by walking beside you. Their steady presence becomes a glimpse of his hand upholding you, shining even brighter when life grows hard. Isaiah 41:10 reminds you that God's love is not temporary; it is steadfast, enduring through both joy and pain.

I've seen this truth in my own life through my sister. She has been by my side in seasons of laughter, like when we sing our favorite Christmas movie songs "Sister" song from the movie White Christmas throughout the years. She has also stood with me in seasons of loss after our parents died. Through it all, her love and strength have been a steady anchor.

Maybe you've had a family member, friend, or coworker who is like that for you. Someone who simply shows up and reminds you that you don't have to walk through life's storms or celebrations alone.

Maybe today you feel the ache of loneliness or the weight of feeling distant from God. If so, remember this: God offers his unfailing friendship and love. His presence is constant when support from family or friends feels absent. And often, he brings new relationships into your life at just the right time, weaving unexpected friends into your journey.

When you remind someone else that God is with them, you also remind yourself. As you share his strength, your own hope grows stronger. Look for someone today who needs that reminder. When you help lift another, you often find that you, too, are lifted.

Prayer

Lord Jesus, Thank You for walking beside me today and blessing me with strength, love, and hope to endure this season of my life. Strengthen not only me, but every person reading these words today. Bring us together in hope, and remind us that we are never truly alone.

August 24

Living Water
By Laurel M. Voss, MSW, MA
Today's Scripture: John 4:14

Many people reach a point in their lives where they ask themselves, Why am I still here? Personally, I've often felt that way. As a hospice social worker, I had many patients ask the same question. Why am I still here?

Some who asked this question were content for their life to end and go to their heavenly home. Others were just tired, in pain, or despairing. There is so much loss in life: the loss of friends, family health, wealth, position, self-image, and even the ability to function on a fundamental level. The struggle can make us weary.

One day, I had a new patient, an elderly lady who lived alone, suffering from end-stage cancer. Her body could no longer take in food or water. My job was to help her adjust emotionally to the fact that her body was shutting down, and the end of her life was very near.

After I introduced myself and discussed her situation, she smiled at me and said, "I don't need drinking water: I have living water."

I had no idea what she meant by that, so I just nodded sympathetically.

Every day for ten days, I visited her. Every day, I found her joyfully singing songs of praise to God. She never once asked me why she was still here, because she *knew* why she was still here. On the tenth day, she was raised to eternal life, and at last, I saw the answer. We are here to praise and worship the Holy God.

In life, we thirst for so many things that deplete us and make us despair, but God refreshes our souls. We are made for worship. Even when we face a fearsome dry land, God is the living water for our weary spirits. Drink and be refreshed!

Prayer

Heavenly Father,
I want to be the kind of person that can continually praise You, even when my body fails, when hope has left the room, when there seems to be no path forward. I will draw upon the living water to refresh myself and praise, until it is time.

August 25

The God of the Impossible
By Kathleen LaFavre
Today's Scripture: Mark 10:27

Several years ago, my husband and I lived on a small piece of country acreage surrounded by farmland and a beautiful private lake. The land had been in the family for generations, and upon the father's passing, the heirs inherited it.

We felt God nudging us to purchase the surrounding property, but when we asked, the answer was firm. "No way. We will not be selling. We know the value." Still, the vision God gave us for that land would not leave our hearts.

So, we prayed. We sought the Lord earnestly and obeyed what we felt Him leading us to do. We took jugs of oil, walked the perimeter of the property, and prayed over it, declaring God's promises.

Months later, we approached the family again. This time, to our amazement, they said yes—at a price far below market value. At closing, one of the heirs said, "I don't know why I'm selling this to you; it makes no sense."

We knew exactly why. What was impossible with man had become possible with God. On that land, we built a sanctuary unto the Lord. Hundreds—if not thousands—came to Christ and were baptized in the waters of that lake. We loved people for Jesus, and God fulfilled the desire He had placed in our hearts.

Never underestimate the power of hearing from God and believing Him, even when it looks impossible. His plans are greater than ours, and His power makes the impossible possible.

Prayer

Lord,
Thank You that nothing is impossible with You. Help me trust Your leadership, even when circumstances seem immovable. Strengthen my faith to believe Your promises and obey Your voice. May my life and all You entrust to me be used as a sanctuary that draws others to You.

August 26

Feeling Invisible?
By Laurie "Sterling" O'Neill
Today's Scripture: Luke 10: 38-42

At a recent workshop, I saw a picture of Martha standing beside Jesus while Mary sat at His feet, surrounded by the twelve apostles. In Scripture, Martha asked Jesus to tell Mary to help her in the kitchen.

Jesus responded, "Martha, Martha, you are anxious and troubled about many things, but one thing is necessary. Mary has chosen the good portion, which will not be taken away from her." (Luke 10:41)

My mind immediately shifted, not to Martha but to Mary. In the picture, Mary was looking up at Jesus, a concerned expression on her face made me pause. How might Martha's words be affecting Mary?

Mary was breaking cultural norms by sitting with the men and learning. Was she feeling shunned after hearing Martha? Again, in the picture, Jesus looked at Mary with compassion in his eyes, his palm facing downward toward Mary, as if saying, "Stay seated!"

Both women were doing what they felt called to do, in the moment. Both needed Jesus.

Martha was in the right place culturally—but distracted. Jesus cared more about her heart than her service.

As I've grown in my leadership journey, I've often felt like I was where God placed me—but not where others always wanted me. I let self-doubt or what they may have thought distract me, leaving me feeling invisible and out of place.

Yet when I looked at Jesus with Mary, I felt Jesus saying to me, "You've always been invited to the table."

If you're feeling unwanted, unseen, or like you don't belong or measure up remember that Jesus is inviting you, sit! Choose the better thing, like Mary because Jesus is more concerned with our souls.

He sees you.
You are not invisible.
You are not alone.
He cares!

Prayer

Jesus,

Thank You for loving me just the way I am. For seeing me! I can come to You anytime. Thank You for inviting me to sit with You. You are gentle and continue to teach me. Lord help me when I get distracted and doubt. Help me remember to turn and see YOU! You do care.

August 27

Leave it to God
By Reverend Dr. Juana Jordan
Today's Scripture: Jeremiah 29:10-11

I had only been at the public relations firm for eight months before its founder asked me to resign. "Juana, you know I love you, but you need to go and do what God is calling you to do," she said. I had never been asked to leave a job before. Months prior, I had been working as a journalist and columnist at the state capital's leading newspaper, a job I held for six years. Being a journalist was my dream job. My vocation for 13 years. When I left, I took pride in the fact that I was still in the communications business.

How quickly things can shift and change, and your faith put to the test. If someone had told me two years later, on this day in 2008, I would be in seminary, starting the first day of my master's program—at 37 years old, no less—I would not have believed it.

When the children of Israel found themselves as exiles in Babylon, far from home and from what was familiar, they did not believe it either. Depressed and in despair, with no vision of a way forward or out, God sends this word through the Prophet Jeremiah.

The passage begins with beautiful words of assurance. We do not have to have it all figured out. We can relax. Even if we feel lost, God remains steady. God is not wringing God's hands, pacing back and forth, saying, "What am I going to do about this?" God responds with certainty—there is a plan. It is to prosper you, give you a future filled with hope.

Words to sleep by. So, leave it to God. Rest.

Prayer

Lord,
Thank You for your assurance that You know the plans You have for us. When our plans change or we feel disoriented, remind us that Your purposes are steadfast. Help us to trust your vision for our lives and embrace the future You have for us, one filled with peace and hope.

August 28

Burning both Ends of the Candle
By Patricia Pate
Matthew 11: 28-30

My dad would often say, "When you were young, while you were struggling with all those painful, frustrating PT sessions, I would become so worried that you would hurt yourself by pushing yourself too much." I would say,

"Come to me, all who labor and are heavy laden, and I will give you rest." (Matthew 11:28

You can relax and let me help you get home.

Mom would repeat the verse to my dad. "That verse applies to you, too. I saw you helping all the displaced people! You've worn yourself to the nubs of your candle. You need rest and prayers."

He would close her laptop and say, "You do all the forms needed. You tackle all the paperwork, all the computer and phone research. You don't stop either. Don't tell me I need prayers and rest.
After all those hours, you need to lean on Jesus as well."

Whether it is physical exhaustion, spiritual weariness, or mental fatigue, Jesus Christ is the hope for everyone who pushes themselves too far beyond their own limits. Jesus heals those whose efforts burn too close to the ends of their candle and gives you complete rest. Jesus comforts all who are exhausted, and He will fill all your caring reserves.

To all caregivers, families, and You who need Jesus's reserves and His caring love, He will restore you and heal you always.

Prayer

May Jesus Christ, our Healer, calm your fears, heal your spirit, and fill your caring reserves. May He comfort and give you rest in order for you to show His love amidst the challenges of these times.

August 29

In All Your Ways
By Abigail Ruth Miller
Today's Scripture: Proverbs 3:5-6

Two of my favorite men both have these verses as their life verses. One is my father, and his birthday is actually today! One reason I love him so much is that he has been an incredible example of trusting in the LORD with all his heart.

My mom was diagnosed with multiple sclerosis when I was two and has also dealt with several other debilitating conditions since then. My parents have had so many decisions to navigate, but they always look to the LORD, and He always makes the path straight.

My husband is starting a YouTube channel called "In all your ways." We often forget that God cares about *every* moment of our days. When we walk to the kitchen, when we walk to the coffee pot, and when we sit down at our computer, we are always to keep Him before us and remember that God is with us.

When I was waiting and praying for my husband for 25 long years, the presence of Jesus was often my only comfort. He led me to serve Him in over 20 different countries while waiting, and He always made the way clear. The day God asked me to give up my fiancé, two years before I met my husband, I saw these verses everywhere. I also meditated on the phrase, "You are for me" again and again. I knew I needed to trust Him, but those moments were the *hardest*. But looking back, I am so glad I trusted the Lord, because He definitely knew best.

Once, I met a famous speaker and told him that I was struggling to obey. His advice was to think about the one you are obeying. Friend, Jesus is kind, gentle, and worthy of your trust.

Prayer

Abba Father,
Would You help us to trust You? Would You help us to remember You in every moment and know that You want to be personally involved in every path we take? Keep us close to *your* heart and help us trust you in the dark. We love you! Help us know how much You love us.

August 30

Grief
By Teresa Montalvo

I did not like death, nor did I understand it. I was introduced to death at a very young age. When I was a little girl, my dog killed my bunny rabbit. Not a pretty picture.

When I was seven, Gina, my six-year-old cousin and friend, died suddenly. She was living in Lubbock, and the mosquitoes were bad that year. Encephalitis was the cause of death. Did I grow up being deathly afraid of mosquitoes?

In 1979, I was one of the lucky ones who was able to dig my way out of the pile of rubble and walk away from a devastating tornado that resulted in the deaths of 42 people. Did I become deathly afraid of clouds that formed in the sky?

In *my opinion*, enough is enough–but God did not put me in charge of the universe and *he did not ask* my opinion!

In the summer of 2020, my life took a sudden turn, and in a span of fifteen months, seven significant players in the game of life walked off the stage. Unwrapping the gifts God gave me in each of these relationships taught me the connection between love and grief.

I had a choice to make, and it would have to be one with no contingencies I could place on God. My greatest challenge was to decide how I would spend the remaining days I have on earth. I could become a bitter old woman, and yes, I have the hair to match, or I could change my retirement plan and let God take the glory. To freely give my life and come alongside others who are stuck in grief is a unique ministry.

Prayer

When grief is thick around us - we can be the ones with an infilling of the Holy Spirit and allow Him to pour it out on others who are hurting. We are all walking each other home. Will that walk be one founded in a greater call? Father God, let me know Your love in my greatest hour of grief!

August 31

Do You Believe It or Not?
Trusting God's Promises When Dreams Feel Out of Reach
By Michelle L. Nelson
Today's Scripture: Hebrews 10:23

"Do you believe it or not? This is a question I have asked myself quite frequently. The "it" I'm referring to is God's promise–His Word.

I have been singing in the church choir for many years. As a result, I have countless songs swirling in my head. Some quote scripture, and others focus on people's experiences and feelings around God. As I sing, I find myself reflecting on my own life and experiences–prayers I've said, disappointments, frustrations, dreams...

Have you ever had a dream that you are afraid to dream? The dream is there, but you're afraid to say it out, share it with a friend, and never mind praying about it.

If I'm being honest, I've had multiple dreams that have fallen into this category. It feels like I literally don't want to be disappointed by God, so I just try to file it in the very back of my mind and distract myself with the next thing. The problem is the dream is still there, even if I can't physically see it. And each time, it leads back to that same question. Do you believe it or not?

It's easy to say that we trust God, but what happens when life doesn't quite line up with our plans–when the dream hasn't become a realization yet? Does our hope go down the drain?

There's an old hymn that talks of our hope's foundation being on Jesus, and that if we put it on anything else, it basically goes out like the ocean's tide.

So, let me ask you one last question. Is your hope placed in something or someone that changes like the stock market, or is it found in Jesus–the One who is the same yesterday, today, and forever?

Prayer

Father God,
Thank You that we can trust Your Word to be true in every season of our lives. We know that every good and perfect gift comes from You, and that includes the gift of hope. When our dreams seem too big and far off, remind us that Your Word never comes back void.

September

September 1

Do Not Grow Weary
By Tyann Beenken
Today's Scripture: Galatians 6:9

My husband farms with his dad and two brothers. When September rolls around, the air buzzes with excitement as what was planted in the spring is now ready for harvest. One day, watching the combines drive into the field around our house, my eyes drifted to our four children who stood watching their dad and grandpa "open up" the field. As I stood looking at them, my thoughts shifted from physical harvest to spiritual harvest.

At times, being a mom is hard. There are days when I feel like I should be wearing a black-and-white striped shirt, blowing a whistle for all the sibling squabbles. On other days, I can hardly keep up with the laundry and toys scattered all over the floor. I begin to wonder if all the time spent trying to teach, instruct, and train our children has made a difference in their hearts and minds. During those times, God, in His kindness, reminds me of His promise in Galatians 6:9–there will be a harvest if I do not give up.

It can be so easy to grow discouraged when we feel like what we are doing is not making a difference, is not noticed, or is even unappreciated. But God sees, and He only asks for faithfulness. Whether you find yourself buried under a mountain of laundry, cleaning floors, scrubbing toilets, or repeating yourself over and over to toddlers and teenagers, continue to plant seeds of kindness, love, and godliness. Do not give in to discouragement, even if you do not see the fruit of your labor now. God has promised a harvest of righteousness if you do not give up, and He is faithful to keep His promises.

Prayer

Abba Father,
If I am honest, I grow weary of doing good when it does not seem to make a difference. In these moments, help me see the bigger picture. Give me the patience and endurance to remain faithful in planting seeds, trusting You for the harvest in due season.

September 2

What if a Hard Start Doesn't Disqualify a Beautiful Life?
By Dr. Shelley Kemp, Ed.D., SHRM-SCP
Today's Scripture: Joel 2:25

Have you ever looked at someone and thought, "How did they turn out so good... after going through so much?"

That's how I feel about my husband.

Today is his birthday—a day I don't take lightly. Because this isn't just the anniversary of his birth. It's the celebration of a life that could've gone so differently, but didn't. He was the oldest of his siblings, raised under a heavy hand. The kind of pressure, fear, and trauma he endured could have left him bitter, broken, or emotionally shut down. And yet... here he is.

Gentle. Strong. Steady.

He loves deeply. He celebrates fully. He leads quietly, but with purpose. And through it all, he's still chasing God's calling on his life. When I look at him, I don't just see the man he is—I see the miracle he's become.

And it reminds me that no beginning, no trauma, no childhood wound can stop the plans of a healing, redeeming God. In fact, sometimes it's the hardest stories that show the most glory.

So let me ask you...

What if your story—or someone else's—isn't defined by how it started, but by how God is writing it now?
What if every scar becomes sacred when surrendered?
What if the greatest evidence of God's goodness isn't found in perfect lives—but in redeemed ones?

Because when God gives the world a man like this, it's worth celebrating—on day one and every day after.

Prayer

Lord,
Thank You for the lives You redeem, restore, and repurpose for Your glory. Thank You for the strength wrapped in gentleness, the calling born through pain, and the beauty that rises from broken beginnings. Help us see others—not by where they started, but by how You are moving through them now. Every life has meaning.

September 3

Perfect Love
By Melissa Lindsey
Today's Scripture: Ephesians 4:32

I breathe in the sweet cinnamon aroma of the warm apple pie as I slide it out of the oven and onto the stovetop. On the counter, there are candles shaped like the numbers three and eight, which will top the celebratory pie later this evening—thirty-eight years of marriage. Apple pie remains his favorite, which is why I've chosen it instead of cake.

After many years of marriage, sometimes we need to put in a little extra effort. We have had bills to pay and children to raise through good times and bad, in richer and poorer, and in sickness and health. I laugh when I read traditional wedding vows because they never mention exhaustion, frustration, emotional meltdowns, or the need for forgiveness.

As humans, over the years of marriage, we will likely let each other down—unmet expectations, crossed boundaries, or forgotten commitments. We will mess up, but with God's grace and our commitment to follow Christ's example of compassion, kindness, and forgiveness, our relationships can withstand the test of time and deepen into an unbreakable bond.

I'm grateful for the years we've shared and the lessons we've learned. The comfort and trust we have in each other bring me joy. Kindness and compassion in my husband's and my hearts don't always come naturally—if you've been married for any length of time, you understand. Life gets messy sometimes, but because our core beliefs are rooted in the idea that we should model the love God showed us, we are guided to show love even when—especially when—we don't feel like it.

God's love is unmatched. It surpasses any love you could ever feel for someone else. He loves us perfectly because Jesus bore our sin debt, making perfect forgiveness possible and, in turn, perfect love.

Prayer

Dear Lord,
Thank You for the gift of love and the power of forgiveness. Help us remember that none of us is without fault, but we are free because of Your unmatched love for us. Shape us into living examples. Let us be kind and compassionate to one another, spreading love wherever we go.

September 4

When Your Prayers Go Unanswered
By Brianna Barrett
Today's Scripture: Psalm 13:1-3

The clock read 4:15 am as I set my coffee down, grabbed my Bible, and my journal with tears streaming down my face and pen at the ready, I scribbled these words in my journal. "Why God? Why haven't you answered me? When God?" I don't know if I had ever been that honest with God about how I felt. I was exhausted, frustrated, and weary, and I couldn't understand why my prayers were unanswered. I had fervently prayed, asked others to pray, and believed that God was going to do what I asked.

The problem wasn't that God wasn't willing, nor that He didn't hear me. The issue was my heart. I was determined that God should listen to my ways.

King David asked these questions in today's verses as he was running for his life from his enemies. But two verses later, his tone changes; he declares he will trust the Lord's unfailing love and rejoice because God rescued him. (verse 5). He ends the psalm declaring that because the Lord is good, he will rejoice.

Jesus asked similar questions as he hung on the cross (Mark 15:34). He questioned God, wanting to know why and if God had abandoned him. Before Jesus' betrayal, He told us how to pray for God's will to be done, not our own (Matthew 26:39b).

When we cease telling God how to answer prayers and begin accepting His will, rather than our own, His unconditional love is revealed. We draw closer to Him as we fully surrender and trust Him wholeheartedly, bringing us peace. It's okay to be honest with God and tell Him how you feel, but you must be willing to submit to His will.

Prayer

Lord,
I don't know how to do this, but I want to submit fully to You. I trust you. I pray that Your will be done in my life, not my own. Thank You for Your unconditional love and peace.

September 5

Becoming Better Humans
By Richard Dubay, Jr.
Today's Scripture: Genesis 2:23-25

The truth is that marriage is fabulously hard.

I don't mean to sound alarming, but it's true.

Think about it: what other institution in our society has decided that it's a good idea to bring together two people from entirely different backgrounds–sometimes with completely separate value and faith systems–into a binding agreement where the goal is for them to stay together, devoted only to each other, for the rest of their lives?

On the surface, doesn't it seem utterly outrageous?

Or... does it? Let's think again.

In what other part of our society do we have the chance, almost daily, to practice forgiveness? To share the deep, intimate parts of life with someone else? Where else can we learn to set aside our own desires and embrace the needs and wants of someone else as our own?

When God created marriage, He didn't mean for us to have an easy life. He didn't intend for it to be all sunshine and roses. He never said, "I will make every day the best day ever."

Instead, when God created marriage, He did it to make us better humans. Sometimes that happens through joy, peace, and love. Other times, it comes through disagreements, trials, and loss. We would never grow if we didn't occasionally learn to share, struggle, and compromise.

When we take marriage at face value, it seems pretty ludicrous. But when we view marriage through God's eyes, we see that we become better people–really, truly better–when we do this life together.

Prayer

God,
Thank You for marriage. Thank You for Your unwavering commitment and desire to help us become better people–people who are more like You.

September 6

When Heaven Meets Earth
By Karen Kay Smith
Today's Scripture: 1 Thessalonians 4:13

Death is something we will all face. A parent, a child, a spouse, a dear friend—sooner or later, we find ourselves standing at the edge of that great divide. For me, September 6 is the day my husband took his last breath. That day broke me, yet it also revealed something sacred.

Scripture doesn't deny our sorrow; it dignifies it. We do "not grieve as others do who have no hope" (1 Thessalonians 4:13). Naming our loss—saying "this hurts"—isn't a lack of faith; it is honest faith. It is how we bring our pain to the One who can hold it. Grief is the price of love, but hope is the promise of Christ.

When my husband's breathing stilled, my heart broke and, somehow, was steadied at the same time. Grief and grace can share the same room. Heaven felt near, as if the veil had lifted for just a moment. Though tears fell, peace lingered too, reminding me that this was not the end of his story. The last breath here becomes the first breath in heaven.

If you are grieving today, know this: your sorrow matters to God. He is not distant from your pain—He meets you in it. Death may feel like a cruel separation, but for those in Christ, it is a doorway to eternal life. One day, every goodbye will turn into a hello that never ends.

Prayer

Father, You see our grief and gather every tear. When loss feels unbearable, draw near. When memories overwhelm, grant rest. When sorrow storms, speak peace. Steady us with Your promises, surround us with Your comfort, and anchor us in hope. Let Your grace carry us forward.

September 7

Turning Darkness into Light through the Years
By Michelle Barringer
Today's Scripture: Isaiah 42:16

The lamp with a glass shade fell. The crash startled us, but we didn't investigate or clean the mess. We agreed we'd deal with it in the morning and continued watching a movie.

After 39 years of marriage, a broken lamp and glass don't rattle us. Besides, it was too dark to see to clean it up. The mess would wait until morning.

When the sun rose, I opened the drapes. The light revealed the mess the broken lamp created. Shattered glass lay everywhere. Glass doesn't land in just one place, so the cleanup included attention to detail and sweat.

Most relationships, especially marriages, go through times of brokenness and shattered emotions. There's going to be darkness, and we can't see where to even begin moving forward, let alone begin cleaning up the relational mess we've created.

We need light to see the path forward. Amazingly, God's word is the lamp that sheds light on our path (Psalm 119:105). It's the Lord who turns our darkness into light (Psalm 18:28). And the Lord smooths the rough places and brings joy in the morning. In fact, He promises He'll do these things.

The reason my husband and I could calmly continue watching a movie with a mess nearby is because God has smoothed unlimited rough places in our relationship. We haven't gone through decades of marriage without experiencing darkness, brokenness, and mess. I'm guessing if you're in a relationship, you have too. Maybe you're in that space now. Believe me when I say, God is faithful, and He keeps His promises. Trust Him.

Today, we begin our 40th year of marriage. We know God will guide us with His light. He will replace any brokenness with something new, just like we will replace our broken lamp with a new one.

Prayer

Heavenly Father, Your light is a lamp to our feet, a guiding beam that leads us through rough and unfamiliar paths. Replace the brokenness and shattered hearts, Lord, with something new. Turn our darkness into light so that joy will come into our lives again.

September 8

Imitate God, Walk in His Ways
By D'Toya Dove
Today's Scripture: Ephesians 5:1

Ephesians 5:1 invites us to become imitators of God to copy Him and follow His example. That's a powerful charge and a daily journey.

As Christ-followers, we are His ambassadors. Whether in our homes, workplaces, classrooms, or even in casual encounters throughout the day, we represent Him. That's why it's so important that we reflect Him well, not just in our words, but in our actions, reactions, and how we carry ourselves.

I encourage you to read all of Ephesians 5. It paints a clear picture of what it means to walk in love, wisdom, and holiness. And the more time we spend in God's presence, in His Word and in worship, the more we are built up from the inside out. When challenges come, we'll respond His way, not out of frustration or fear, but with grace and truth.

Whatever we're full of is what will flow out of us. If we fill ourselves with the world, that's what will show up when we're under pressure. But if we're filled with His Word, His Spirit, and His presence, we'll respond with peace, love, and wisdom because that's what's dwelling in our hearts.

I believe God is going to do amazing things in our lives, classrooms, and beyond. But we must trust Him every step of the way. Eyes have not seen, ears have not heard what He has in store for those who follow Him faithfully. Let's keep walking with Him and reflecting His image to a world that desperately needs hope.

So I'll ask you what I had to ask myself: What are you full of right now? If we want to respond like Jesus, we have to sit with Jesus. Let's be intentional about spending time in His Word, so that we're equipped to respond with His grace when life gets messy.

Prayer

Heavenly Father,
Thank You for Your Word and for showing me how to walk through life, even when things are challenging. I surrender my way of doing and being. I commit to follow Your example and reflect Your character daily, so others may see You through me.

September 9

Embracing New Beginnings
By Jennifer Burchill
Today's Scripture: Isaiah 43:19

September has always signaled a time for new beginnings. The back-to-school rhythms and the arrival of Fall, my favorite season, naturally invite reflection. I find myself looking back at where I have been and wondering what path God is inviting me to follow next.

Sometimes that reflection reveals some of the areas I've let slip. Maybe it's that my health habits aren't what I'd like them to be, my finances need some attention, my faith journey needs direction, or even a relationship that needs tending. I've had seasons when all of those were true. And honestly, the thought of getting back on track can feel overwhelming. Maybe you've felt this too?

When discouragement starts to creep in, it's the perfect time for us to remember that God delights in new beginnings. When we feel lost or stuck in patterns that aren't serving us well, God is already at work preparing fresh possibilities, as He promised, even though we may not yet realize it. He will not just help us dust off old routines, but will bring life to them. Just as He gave hope to the exiled Israelites by promising to do a "new thing," He will clear a path toward a new direction in the areas where we feel lost and provide hope when we grow weary.

God longs to walk alongside us in our new seasons. He invites us to call Him into our fresh starts, to trust Him to restore and renew, not just once, but again and again. As He led His people toward hope and healing, He longs to walk beside us into every new season.

What can you restart or begin anew this season?

How might you invite God to join you in this beautiful new beginning?

Prayer

God,
Thank You for doing new things this season in my life, even when I can't see them yet. Open my eyes to perceive the fresh path that You are creating. Give me the courage to embrace it, the strength to walk forward, and the faith to trust You every step of the way.

September 10

Redeemed: 42 Years Together
By Susan Wheeler Smith
Today's Scripture: Ephesians 4:32

I was 22 when we got married—young, selfish, and stubborn. By our third anniversary, we had separated. We signed divorce papers, but God wasn't finished with us or our marriage.

Shortly after our separation, my husband returned to his family church just as a new pastor, Paul, arrived. Knowing about our situation, Paul was eager to meet me—certain, I thought, to push reconciliation. I resisted at first, but eventually agreed to meet him. He later admitted he feared he wouldn't reach me. Though I was raised in the Episcopal Church, I hadn't attended church in years. Despite my hesitation, Paul encouraged me to join my husband and his family at church. After several counseling sessions, I accepted Jesus as my Lord and Savior in December 1986. As we continued with joint counseling, we gradually began to discuss reconciliation. By kneeling in prayer and asking Jesus to forgive and change me, I found that He wanted "...to do far more abundantly than all that we ask or think..." (Ephesians 3:20).

On September 10, we celebrated 42 years of marriage. Over the years, we raised three children—two of whom are now married—and this year, we welcomed our first grandchild. After retiring, we moved to our dream life on a lake. Throughout, we continued attending church. All our children and their spouses know and love Jesus, and we are embracing the joy of nurturing faith in our grandchildren as well. What I once gave up on became more than I could have imagined.

If you are considering separation, unless there is violence or abuse, seek God's wisdom and surround yourself with godly counsel. Allow Christ to heal your heart. Ask Him for compassion, forgiveness, strength, and discernment. Pray for your spouse regularly, trusting that God can restore even what seems lost.

Prayer

Thank You, Lord, for restoring marriages and love and the reminder that marriage is more than a contract between two people. It is a covenant declared in the presence of a loving God. Remind us to include You in our daily life. Thank You for your intervention and redemption. Thank You for our marriages, our children, and generations to come.

September 11

When the Unthinkable Happens
By Becky Seamon
Today's Scripture: Psalm 46

Twenty-five years ago today, the world watched in horror as tragedy unfolded on screens globally. On September 11, 2001, planes crashed and towers crumbled. Nearly 3,000 souls were lost as the world's foundation became shaky ground from terrorist attacks on the United States.

When tragedy hits, I run to the truth of Psalm 46:1-2.

Perhaps, today, on this September 11, your world is falling apart. Maybe you're facing something unthinkable, such as a medical diagnosis, financial crisis, or the loss of a loved one. Perhaps, you've experienced the sting of rejection—a pain I know well.

However, it was into this brokenness that God responded by sending a Savior. Jesus Christ walked on this earth, was crucified, buried, and resurrected. He is our living hope! He defeated sin, darkness, and the pain of this earthly home. He is the proof that our hurt is not the end of our story, for He has overcome! God promises believers an eternal home free from terror and tragedy. Until then, He is our source of strength. He remains devoted, not distant.

Today, I am more aware of my surroundings due to the events of 9-11. As a Christ-follower, I know that God is actively involved in my life. God brings calm in my chaos. He is present in my pain. He provides truth in my troubles. I can breathe deeply, knowing He holds what I cannot control. No matter what you are facing, I invite you to trust our Abba Father and rest in this living hope.

Prayer

Dear Father,
I praise You, for You are a holy God. I choose to trust You on both the good days and the bad. Thank You for Your protection and deep strength every day. Thank You for carrying me when life is chaotic and complex. Because of You, I will not fear.

September 12

Life Without Anxiety
By Elizabeth Clark
Today's Scripture: Matthew 6:31-33

We live in a world of constant anxiety. It often feels like an unavoidable part of human life. But for those who have a relationship with Jesus, there's good news. He offers us a new, divine life that, by its very nature, is free from worry. We need to shift our focus from ourselves to a different, higher source—the divine life within us.

Jesus teaches that when we make God's kingdom and His ways our first priority, everything else we need will fall into place. This is a breathtakingly generous promise. We aren't trading one worry for another, but a life of constant anxiety for a life of divine provision and perfect rest. This gives us hope of a fulfilled life, free from the crushing weight of worry.

I used to believe my anxiety was a character flaw that I had to fix. This verse made me see that my anxiety was a symptom of living from my own human strength. When I made the conscious decision to turn to the divine life within me, I started to experience a peace that wasn't my own. Now, when a worry comes, I turn to my Heavenly Father. He knows my needs and that my job is to seek Him and His kingdom.

You don't have to fight anxiety alone. You have a divine life that is free from it. Turn to the Lord and seek His kingdom and righteousness. Trust that your Heavenly Father knows all your needs and has already promised to care for you. This is a divine transaction: you give Him your focus and your worship, and He takes care of everything else. Live in the confidence of this divine life, and let Him be your joy and reality.

Prayer

Heavenly Father,
We thank You for the divine life You have given us, a life free from anxiety. We confess our worries and choose to turn to You. We pray that You would help us to seek Your kingdom and Your righteousness first today, trusting that You know all our needs and will faithfully provide.

September 13

Treasured Friendships Out of Obedience
By Joye Waller
Today's Scripture: Hebrews 12:1-2

Moving day. Again. Of all our moves, this one had the appearance of being easy. As we had been staying in a furnished home since our return from living overseas, our physical possessions were limited. Packing was a breeze. A dozen boxes or so, a few suitcases, a mattress, and a washing machine were visible in the small moving truck. What was not so visible were the thoughts and emotions within me.

In the months prior, we had been living in a beautiful city. We had found a church home. I had begun developing relationships and making friends. I had community. And I was comfortable. Pulling up and moving again was not going to be so simple or easy.

I knew that God was clearly directing our steps and leading us to a new place and people. I had moved many times before, guided by God's leading and tender care. And so, I moved again, trusting God to provide the treasured friendships my heart desperately desired.

And He did.

In time, I invited a few ladies into a space with me. We gathered weekly around a kitchen table or patio, opening God's Word, sharing how God was working in our lives. Along with laughter and occasional tears, we spoke of our deep desires and concerns and lifted our prayers to God for what was on our hearts.

Eventually, there was another group of precious ladies. And then another and another. Coffee dates. Gathering for breakfast, lunch, or on the patio while children played. As I opened my life to others, they invited me into theirs. And I got a front row seat to seeing God at work in and through their lives.

In following Jesus, He has blessed me abundantly with friendships throughout my life that I will treasure for all my days.

Prayer

Jesus, Thank You for the gift of treasured friendships. I choose to keep my eyes on you as I follow You in obedience. I desire You to be first in my life. Please help me to hold the things of this world, even relationships, with open hands as You move and work according to your will.

September 14

Forgiveness that Trains Us
By Liz Caffman
Today's Scripture: Titus 2:11–12

Forgiveness is not just something God gives us—it's something He uses to shape us. Paul reminds us in Titus that God's grace has been made public through Jesus Christ. Grace is more than a gift we receive; it's also a teacher. It shows us how to walk away from patterns of sin and selfishness and how to live in ways that reflect God's character.

When we truly experience forgiveness, it changes the way we respond to others. God's readiness to forgive us should overflow into our readiness to forgive those who wrong us. This doesn't mean forgiveness is easy. At times, it feels extremely difficult. To release someone from the debt they owe us can stir up pain and resistance. Yet forgiveness is the very heartbeat of the gospel. Jesus carried the weight of our sin to the cross, declaring once and for all that no failure, no rebellion, no brokenness is beyond the reach of God's mercy.

Forgiveness also frees us. Holding on to bitterness or resentment can consume us. It keeps us tethered to the past and robs us of peace in the present. But when we let God's grace teach us to forgive, we learn what it means to live a God-filled, God-honoring life. This kind of life is not only about what we turn away from but also about what we step into: freedom, joy, and reconciliation.

The message of Titus 2:11-12 reminds us that salvation is not just about eternal life after death; it's about new life starting now. And that new life is marked by grace that receives forgiveness and extends forgiveness.

Who in your life needs to experience God's forgiveness through you today? Remember, we forgive not because the other person always deserves it, but because God first forgave us.

Prayer

Father,
Thank You for making Your forgiveness available to me through Jesus. Help me to receive Your grace deeply so that I may extend it freely to others. When forgiveness feels hard, remind me of the cross and the price You paid for my freedom. Teach me to live a life shaped by grace—turning from bitterness and walking in love, freedom, and peace.

September 15

The Cry of My Heart
By Susan Laurie Hutchinson
Today's Scripture: Proverbs 3: 5-6

There was a time I thought about cancer 1,440 minutes a day. Ok, let's knock off 480 minutes for sleep, but since I didn't sleep much, it's fair to add at least half of that back in. Stage 4 ovarian cancer is enough to keep anyone awake all night.

Lord, I wondered in the wee hours, what do I do? Grief was my overwhelming emotion, throwing up blockades to rational thought or prayer. I knew statistics. I knew my chance of survival, and that fueled my grief. I desired healing. I knew God could heal me, but would he?

Desperate times call for desperate measures. I decided to trust God. Implicitly. No matter what.

Does that sound passive? Believe me, it's not. Implicit trust requires intention, determination, and focus. I ignored all the comments and advice from well-intentioned friends and stayed off the internet. I listened to my doctor, read devotionals, my Bible, and prayed about every decision. An excellent support system of friends and family prayed for me daily.

I enrolled in a clinical trial, kept appointments for blood work, CAT scans, and anxiously waited for the results. Twice, I entered the hospital with infections. It was a grueling time, filled with tears and no promises.

But... the days turned into weeks. The weeks turned into months. The months turned into years. I thought about cancer less, only 900 minutes a day, then 240 minutes a day. Then, one year, September 15th, my anniversary date, passed without a thought of cancer.

Fifteen years later, at my yearly oncology visit, my doctor reviewed with me the national clinical trial data and informed me I was one of two survivors. The wonder never escapes me. God is a God of miracles, even today.

Prayer

Lord,
Your ways are a mystery to me, but my gratitude is overflowing. May I never tire of sharing Your good news with other women going through life's trials, because with You, we walk in hope. You heard the cry of my heart, and I am no one special. You hear everything. I will sing Your praise forever.

September 16

"Even If" Joy
By Jane H. DeLong
Today's Scripture: Psalm 16:11

On this day in 2017, at 11:17 p.m., I had the privilege of witnessing the miracle of birth—the birth of our first grandchild. Such a joyful occasion! I had no idea then the amount of joy this little child would bring into my life! Her name is Charlotte, but I call her my little Lottie-ta-Dottie. She is joy personified.

The world confuses happiness and joy. Happiness is dependent on circumstances. Joy comes from deep within; a settledness in our soul that says, "Even if... I will rejoice." There have been many "even if" moments in my life since little Lottie was born. Since my joy comes from knowing God, trusting His promises, and walking in relationship with Him, I have been able to walk through those trials with rejoicing, not sadness.

True joy is anchored in the unchanging character of God. It's the calm assurance that God is with us in the "even if" moments and He is working all things out for our good. Joy is the quiet confidence that God is near when life feels uncertain. Unlike fleeting happiness, joy is a gift of the Spirit - a fruit cultivated as we learn to abide in Christ.

Today, as you face uncertainties or "even if" trials draw near to God, lean into His promises, let His presence fill your heart, sing praise amidst the trials, and feel His joy welling up inside you.

Prayer

Father God,
Thank You that through Your Holy Spirit, we can cultivate joy in the "even if" moments that come our way. Today, as I face various trials, You empower me to find joy in Your presence and Rejoice because You are with me always, even in the "even if's"!

September 17

We Will See Jimmy Again
By Jim Sierszyn
Today's Scripture: Romans 8:18

Throughout our earthly lives, we hope for many things. We hope for good grades or a good job. We hope for a loving spouse, maybe kids. We hope that we are successful, happy, and safe.

Sometimes our earthly hopes are more specific.

But what does it mean to have hope in the Lord? The bible uses different words for hope. Safety, security, trust. It's something we're waiting for, a refuge or shelter. Our earthly hopes are desires to help us get through today, this week, this year. Right now.

Sometimes it seems God doesn't hear our cries of hope.

But it's not that God doesn't hear our pleas; He does. It's that His plan for us is different. It's eternal.
Our son Jimmy's life was not easy. Born with a severe heart defect, he would endure multiple surgeries and procedures. Countless tests with numerous hospitalizations and years of medication.

Jimmy's life, and ours, was filled with earthly hope. We hoped the surgeries would be successful; we hoped his medication would make him feel better. We hoped he would be pain-free. We wished he could just play with the other kids.

And finally, after 17 years, we hoped his heart transplant would make him all better. But God's plan was different. Things did not go as we had hoped; we did not get the result we wanted. Jimmy was called to his heavenly home shortly after the transplant.

Our earthly hope became eternal hope, to be fulfilled by our faith and trust, our hope in the Lord. Now we wait for our reunion with Jimmy for all eternity. When all earthly hope runs out, we must trust His plan. Have faith, God will deliver us. Remember, our Bible verse tells us, "the sufferings of this present time are not worth comparing with the glory that is to be revealed to us" (Romans 8:18).

Prayer

Dear Heavenly Father,
Hear my plea. Fulfill my hopes according to Your plan. Place on my heart the assurance that my hope in the Lord will lead to eternal life, free from all suffering. I trust in the knowledge that by Your grace all Glory will be revealed in the reunion of all believers.

September 18

Shine in Us Lord
By Heidi Scanlon
Today's Scripture: Exodus 34:34-35

It was a scorching September day. For some reason in the South, high schools feel the need to resume the Fall semester in what feels like the middle of hell. As I sat, trying not to melt, I gazed at the students across the circle from me. "What was up with these people?" I wondered. "Their faces are all so shiny. They all have a look to them."

Not generally caring too much what people in that crowd thought of me, I walked up to one of them, and in a manner that my southern mother did not teach me, I asked, "What is up with you people? You all have this shine to you. It's so weird. All of you on that side of the room."

One of the Connor twins laughed and glanced down at me in a way I would not at the time have recognized as love. He said with a grin, "Oh, it's probably Jesus." I exclaimed, "What?! How can you be so smart and do the Jesus thing?" He looked at me and shot back, "How can you be so smart and not?" What?! Gauntlet thrown.

What followed over the next three weeks was a kind but relentless (so it seemed) pursuit by these students to share the love of Jesus. Either my reticular activating system was on overdrive, or they were everywhere.

I would learn that often when a person encounters God, His face literally shines on them - sometimes making them what I would describe as shiny. Of course, every follower of Jesus has bad days where their face may not reflect the light within them. But I can testify that on September 18, 1982, I gave my life to Jesus because a group of teenagers appeared to have something I did not.

Prayer

Lord,
Let us encounter You deeply through prayer and your Word. Shine Your light through us so others may see Your light on our faces, be drawn to You, and come to know Your love personally.

September 19

In The Waiting
By Tonya Ziese
Today's Scripture: Exodus 14:14

Long years and dark days were the hallmarks of my childless 20s. Those years were filled with questions, disappointments, doctor visits, and medications. Month after month, no baby came. Month after month, I became more withdrawn from family and friends. I questioned God's plan, even His timing and his goodness. I was angry at God. What I didn't know was that in the months and years to come, I would begin to sense a shift, a change in myself. It was a gradual shift, but the very pain that enveloped me became my transformation. To soften the rough edges and cement me in the very real fact that He did love me and He did want to bless me, I just had some lessons to learn first, so I could be ready to receive those blessings.

Those ten years spent in the waiting were preparing me for the exact blessings God would be sending, a girl and a boy. Preparing me to be aware of how precious they were, preparing me to trust so deeply because I knew how much he loved me, preparing me to slow down, let go of the small things and the control I thought I needed and give all to Him, especially the two great blessings He gifted me with and that He loved even more than I did.

I often tell people that if I could go back and change this chapter of my story, I wouldn't. I wouldn't be the woman I am today without that waiting period. It was in the waiting that I became aware that there will always be lessons to learn in the valleys on the way to the mountain tops. The waiting wasn't the breaking of me; it was the building.

If today finds you waiting on unanswered prayers with questions and dark days, know that you are not alone. God will be standing beside you in the fire, in His quiet, patient way, waiting on you and me to give it to Him, as He works things for our good.

Prayer

Heavenly Father,
Thank You for being with us in the waiting, for sustaining and teaching us as we wait on Your time and Your blessings. Help me remember today that You are a faithful promise keeper and only desire good things for me. Use my story to encourage and lift up those who are waiting today, who need to feel Your nearness.

September 20

The Weight in Waiting
By Gail "Ember G" Sanders
Today's Scripture: 1 Samuel 1:19b

For two and a half years, I carried the weight of hope, prayer, and disappointment. I already had one child, so questions plagued me: "What's wrong with me? Why is this so hard now? Am I being punished?"

Familiar with these thoughts and questions? These are lies designed to make you reduce your faith from where your breakthrough is waiting.

I learned that sometimes the stress of what we're carrying blocks the blessing we're believing for. The weight of trying turned intimacy with my husband into a task. The toxic work environment was stealing my peace and affecting my body. When I surrendered control and stopped making our lovemaking about getting pregnant, and I left for a healthier workplace, God began to move. I released control and everything changed. Four months at the new job, I was pregnant.

If stress is stealing your peace, eliminate what you can and find healthy ways to cope. Prayer, Bible study, and seeking God. If control has become your god, practice surrender. Remember that intimacy is about connection.

The truth God revealed became my anchor. His timing is eternal. He sees the beginning and end simultaneously. What feels like a delay is divine orchestration. He is your dependable Heavenly Father who loves you unconditionally.

Isaiah 41:10 reminds us: "I will strengthen you, I will help you, I will uphold you." Whatever you need, ask Him.

The weight of waiting is real, but it doesn't have to arrest your faith. Come to Jesus with your heavy burden. Your breakthrough is on the way.

Whether you're still waiting or have reached exhaustion, God hasn't forgotten you.

Prayer

Father, I come carrying the weight of waiting. Just like You remembered, Hannah, remember me. Help me release the stress and give it to You so I can rest. We surrender and trust Your timing. Thank You for Your promise to strengthen and uphold us. Your promises never fail.

September 21

Just in "God's Time"
By Susan DiParisi
Today's Scripture: Psalm 23

Our California-style rented house just outside the base was rarely quiet. Toys covered the floor, and my three toddlers kept me on the move from dawn until dark. For seven long months, I did it all—meals, tantrums, bedtime prayers and stories—alone while my husband, a Navy officer, was deployed to Afghanistan. Nine months pregnant with twins, it was nearly impossible to take good care of three toddlers. My swollen belly made even small tasks exhausting.

There were days I felt like I was living in the darkest place imaginable, every hour stretching endlessly, every moment a test of endurance.

Just before Ryan's return, my parents drove across the country to be with us. Their helping hands and familiar voices steadied me, and for the first time in months, I felt a glimmer of hope. Still, each night I whispered the same prayer: Please let him come home before the babies do,

Finally, the buses rolled onto Camp Pendleton. Families waved flags and cheered as the service members stepped off. My heart pounded. The toddlers bolted forward, shouting, "Daddy!" He dropped to his knees, pulling them into his arms before wrapping me in a long, tearful embrace.

That night, for the first time in months, Ryan's warmth filled the bed beside me. I fell asleep with his hand resting on my enormous belly, marveling at the timing.

Just before dawn, I stirred. "Ryan," I gasped, clutching his arm. "My water just broke!"

Ryan gathered our overnight bag, and we hurried to the hospital. Hours later, our family grew by two—first a strong baby boy, Nicholas, and forty-one minutes later, a perfect baby girl, Elena.

Ryan kissed my forehead, his voice breaking. "I can't believe I made it." I smiled through happy tears. "God knew you'd be home just in time." And in that moment, our family was whole again.

Prayer

Dear Father, Help me to accept my life as it is. Help me to trust Your divine plan even in times of great suffering. Help me to rest in the knowledge that Jesus is right here with me at all times.

September 22

Freely Give
By Anna Wiles
Today's Scripture: Matthew 5:42

Lord, give me your eyes to see those who are hurting and those who are marginalized. Let me see them as you do, Lord. Break my heart for what breaks Yours.

As I continue to pray this prayer, God continues to answer it. He is transforming my heart and my mind. I read scriptures like this one, and I swallow hard. I read them again and double-check to make sure Jesus was serious.

I read it a third time to see if there is any exception to what he is saying. I don't find any. I hang my head as I think of all of the people whom I have seen on street corners begging for help, whom I have driven right past. I think of those who wanted to borrow something, whom I thought might damage it or maybe not return it at all.

I read the passage a fourth time and repent.

Jesus modeled a kind of radical love that is freely given and freely received. His gift of salvation is for all. No one deserves it.

He has given me every single thing that I have. Who am I to not give freely of the possessions that I have been given for free?

All that I have is yours, Lord.

God is working on my heart daily. He is convicting me and helping me hold out my belongings, my resources, and my strength with open hands. All of this is yours, Lord. It is not mine to judge who is worthy or who has the best intentions because you gave me all of these things even when I was unworthy.

Prayer

Lord, Please open our eyes, so that we may see the world the way You see it. Let us give freely as we have been given. Give us grace for today and hope for tomorrow.

September 23

Strength Through Testing
By Melissa Lindsey
Today's Scripture: James 1 2-4

Heart disease runs in my husband's family. His grandfather died of heart failure at the young age of thirty-seven. His father started experiencing health problems in his early forties and had a quadruple bypass surgery at forty-four. As I write this, my father-in-law is currently hospitalized after receiving his eighteenth stent. My husband hasn't escaped this hereditary trait and has seven stents of his own. It's frightening.

Despite these challenges, I admire both my husband and my father-in-law for their remarkable ability to handle their health issues with grace and compassion. They remain calm and kind to the doctors, nurses, and everyone they encounter, even during their most challenging moments.

Testing is an inevitable part of life that often happens unexpectedly. It can come in the form of a child being off track, a broken relationship, or health challenges like those faced by my father-in-law and husband. When facing these challenges, our human nature tempts us to focus on the pain and sadness they bring. However, James encourages us to see these moments as opportunities for growth rather than just obstacles to overcome.

How can we do this?

When we come out of a trial, we can emerge bitter or better. It all depends on our perspective. And while this is easier said than done, through prayer and petition, laying our trials at the feet of Jesus, God will give us the strength we need.

We must see our trials as divine opportunities—each challenge serving a purpose in God's plan for our lives, shaping us into who He intends us to be. Through testing, our faith is refined, much like gold is purified in fire.

Prayer

Dear Lord,
Please help us understand that life's challenges are for our benefit. Help us look beyond immediate discomfort and our human desires, trusting that You are working in our lives. Please grant us wisdom, endurance, and divine insight into how You use trials to develop us. May our faith grow deeper and stronger, and may our character reflect Christ and shine as a light to the world.

September 24

The Size of Our Prayers and Tries
By Chanda Husser Rigby, Ed.D
Today's Scripture: Luke 1:37

"What if, when we get to heaven, and we see just how big God really is, we are sad because we wasted all of our earthly prayers and tries on small things?" This question tumbled out of my ten-year-old mouth and has since been the impetus that pushes me to strive for big things.

As believers, the size of our prayers and tries should be much bigger than those of an unbeliever. Our heavenly Father is infinitely resourced, and He is faithful to pour out His power and provision to help us accomplish things that we are believing for in His name.

I don't want to waste my life's strivings on small things when I have such a mighty GOD helping me. I want to attempt things that are so big that, if God doesn't come through with His help, I will fall flat on my face. As long as I am operating within His will, He always comes through for me.

As a college women's basketball coach, I am always expecting to win at the highest level... not because of my coaching ability, but because of His infinite capability. We can all benefit from truth gazing at just how big and resourced our loving Father is. This view can grow the size of our prayers and tries, and enable us to accomplish things that others deem impossible.

Prayer

Dear Heavenly Father, help me keep my attention on the truth that You are infinitely powerful, immensely resourced, and always ready to help us. Grow my faith to match Your truth that nothing is impossible for You. Help me attempt big things for You and accomplish big things because of You.

September 25

Just Be Still For Awhile
By Teresa Montalvo
Today's Scripture: Psalms 62:5-6

There goes my mind again, racing ahead of me.

What is a girl to do when there is so much that is demanded from her?

In my earlier years, I was a stay-at-home mom raising two children, and my front door was always revolving. I couldn't hear God. I could not hear myself think. The kids were making messes faster than I could clean up the spilled Cheerios.

The chaos and the noise were real, but I learned the essence of being still before God.

God is creative. When we ask him for ways to meet with him, He will provide an invitation that is uniquely ours. I needed a place of solitude and stillness. I would rummage in the pantry for some stale bread, load my kids up, and go sit by the pond. My kids would feed the ducks. It was a place in the busyness of life where nature was alive. It wasn't far from my house, no one knew to look for me in the cemetery! I was safe! Needless to say, during that season, those ducks were well fed!

The most amazing part was that God would show up and speak to me.

If in the event He was silent, I would walk through the cemetery. I was most attracted to the freshly dug graves, and sometimes I would look at the oldest markers I could find. I would see markers for an entire family. This would quickly sober me up in those early days. I would remember that I was alive! Soon, my life would pass, and what would I do for Christ?

It was a reminder that I was raising the next generation of people who would carry the gospel message to a hurting, dying world.

These invitations were life-giving. They became my safe shelter.

Prayer

Dear Jesus,
I ask this day that You would be with my friend. Meet them right where they are, let them not delay in opening the invitation that You have extended. May their encounter with You settle the chaos that surrounds their life and leaves them incredibly hungry for more.

September 26

God Sustained Me In the Wilderness
By Amber J. Parker, PA-C
Today's Scripture: Isaiah 43:19

I felt overwhelmed and alone as I cared for my husband through a mental crisis. As his primary support person, his caregiver, I was desperate to keep him alive and find the treatment and therapy he needed to get better. It was an intense and exhausting battle for life and one that didn't let up. Caregiving for any life-threatening condition is overwhelming and requires all of one's focus and resources.
It was too much for me alone. But—I wasn't, in fact, alone in my battle.

God was there. He saw me.

Just as he saw and cared for Hagar in the desert, sustained Elijah in the wilderness, and didn't leave Joseph in a pit or prison. It didn't look the way they thought it would—the Lord's provision, protection, and guidance—but God made a way for them and sustained and cared for them.

He did so for me as well. He cared for me and led me through overwhelm, chaos, and uncertainty.

I prayed in faith these words of Isaiah 43:19. I clung to the hope in this verse and asked the Lord to bring forth a new way in this desert and streams in the wasteland.

To bring life again. God heard my cry for help from His holy hill and answered me. He sustained me in the middle of my desert, wilderness season as I cried out to Him to protect, to heal, and to give strength and guidance. Just as he graciously cared for Hagar, Elijah, and Joseph long ago, He saw me and walked through my caregiving journey with me. I am grateful.

Prayer

Lord,
Thank You for being the same God yesterday, today, and forever. I can trust and count on You when the circumstances around me are overwhelming and out of my control. You're Jehovah Rapha—the God who heals, and El Roi—the God who sees. I'm so grateful. Thank You for answering and sustaining us in our wilderness seasons.

September 27

The Giver and Taker
By Hannah Louise Cox
Today's Scripture: Job 1:21

Saying goodbye to someone you love is never easy. Whether the goodbye is the result of a break-up or death, loss is loss, it hurts, and for better or worse, it changes us from the inside out. When I lost my Nana, my life changed; who I was before her death and who I am today are two different women. But God didn't change; instead, He changed me for the better.

Growth comes through pain, and most of the time, that pain comes through loss. Letting go of what we hoped we could hold on to to grab hold of Christ more firmly allows us to continue to grow through the pain. Nothing in our lives is permanent and secure in light of the cross. Only Jesus. The circumstances of our losses don't matter; God is and will always be the consistent, steady presence through the pain. He is the author and giver of life and sovereign over death. You may never know the why of your loss. I don't understand why my Nana had to die when and how she did, but I do know that my faith wouldn't be what it is today if she hadn't died. God used her death and my grief journey to grow me up in my faith.

So, when your world gets rocked and you find yourself on a road of pain you didn't want to be on, remember that God is with you. God gives and He takes away, but He will never leave you alone, whether you have blessings or pain. The Author of your life isn't just present at your beginning and end, but in the dash that takes you from beginning to end. He cares for you.

Prayer

God,
Thank You for caring and carrying me in my pain. Help me to remember that Your ways are not my ways, and there is beauty for me in the journey of grief when I cling to You. You are a present Savior. I love You.

September 28

Finding Joy in Every Day
By Rebecca Thoms
Today's Scripture: Psalm 118:24

We often think that joy is found in life's grand moments, such as vacations, milestones, or special celebrations. Yet the bible reminds us that God is equally present in the quiet, repetitive rhythms of life. Whether it's folding laundry, preparing dinner, or commuting to work, each task can be an act of worship when done with an intentional heart. The mundane becomes meaningful when we remember who we serve. It's not about the task itself but God, who gives it purpose.

Psalm 118:24 is more than a cheerful reminder; it's a call to live with intentional joy. The bible doesn't say we should only rejoice when life is easy or be glad when everything goes our way. Instead, it declares that this day, whatever it holds, was crafted by the Lord Himself.

Every sunrise is an invitation to gratitude. The breath in your lungs, the people in your life, even the responsibilities before you are a part of the day God designed. Some days bring celebration, others bring challenge, but all are woven into His perfect plan.

Rejoicing is not about ignoring hardship, but about anchoring our hearts in the truth that God is good and sovereign, regardless of the circumstances. Choosing gladness is an act of faith: "I trust You, Lord, even here, even now." You don't have to wait for life to be better to rejoice. You can choose joy in a kitchen filled with dirty dishes, in a commute that feels too long, in conversations that stretch your patience, in the heart of the chaos life can bring. Joy is not dependent on excitement but on the unchanging goodness of God. The sacred is not hidden; it's right here, in the ordinary.

Prayer

Lord,
Thank You for this day You have made. Help me to rejoice in every moment, trust Your plan, and see each thing that happens today as a gift from You. Fill my heart with gratitude and joy.

September 29

Love Finds a Way to Stay
By Brianna Johnson
Today's Scripture: Psalm 91:11

Today is my big brother's birthday. I never got to meet him. Kevin passed away just a few hours after he was born. But for as long as I can remember, I've felt his presence in my life. A quiet strength. A comforting nudge. A sense that I've never been alone.

I think of Kevin as my guardian angel. He's never spoken a word, but his presence has been a kind of language I've learned to trust. Psalm 91:11 reminds us that God commands His angels to guard us in all our ways. I believe Kevin is part of that promise—a quiet reminder that we are seen, known, and protected.

My husband and I even went on our first date on this day. It felt special, even then. Like my big brother was making sure I knew he approved of this guy. And now, years later, I often ask Kevin to watch over the three sons we're raising together, especially our oldest, who has a rare genetic diagnosis that presents daily challenges. There have been countless moments when I've whispered, "Kevin, I need your help," or "he needs your help". And somehow, we always find our way through.

I often wonder how deep the ache must have been for my parents to lose him. But I also believe that their love for him didn't just go away. It stayed, and it grew, and it continues to grow every day. I see it in how they raised me, and I hope it shows in how I raise my boys.

If you've ever lost someone far too soon, I hope you know this: their love didn't leave. And neither did God's. The ones we miss are never really gone.

Love always finds a way to stay.

Prayer

God,
Thank You for the unseen ways You protect and guide us. Thank You for the loved ones who remain close, even when we can't see them. Help us trust Your presence in every season and feel Your love through every challenge. Remind us that we're never alone. Not for a moment.

September 30

Death Will Be No More
By Francesca Follone-Montgomery, OFS
Today's Scripture: Revelation 21:3-4

Sadly, pain and grief affect everyone. We often feel lost and alone amid our suffering. However, the message in this quote is quite reassuring. God is with us, we are His people, and He can wipe away every one of our tears.

On this date in 2017, miles away from me, in my hometown in Italy, a fatal heart attack took my father's life. It was devastating for all our family members, near and far. I had never experienced such deep pain in my heart. My husband and my son were also extremely sad, and we decided to go to church to ask God for comfort and guidance.

It was there that the Lord reminded me of His presence in our midst. We bumped into some dear friends who were there to pray for the repose of the soul of their son. We embraced united in tears. The priest, who warmly welcomed us, was from Africa. His beautiful smile brought me such peace and made me feel God's presence as well as my father's love.

Decades earlier, my dad was stationed in Somalia, where he had a spiritually cathartic experience. I had the privilege of being there with him for a whole summer and witnessing God's presence in his life. It was there that I truly connected with my dad and discovered Christ within him, beneath his military uniform.

God let me know then, and reminded me on September 30, 2017, that we are indeed His people. He is in our midst, ready to wipe away our tears, remove our pain, and defeat death. So, take heart and know that things do pass, and that God is with us always. Let Him wipe away your tears, knowing that you are His forever.

Prayer

Lord Our God,
Make Your presence known to us throughout our lives. Let us come to You in moments of joy as well as in moments of sadness. Strengthen our hearts and wipe away our tears. Comfort us and guide us always. Reassure us of Your promise to defeat death as You prepare us for Eternal Life.

October

hope✳books
collections

October 1

Forgive and Forget
By Erica Lewis
Today's Scripture: Psalm 103:12

Maybe you're like me and struggle with perfectionism, causing you to shame yourself for mistakes you made years ago. Sometimes, it seems like the right thing to do. After all, we did disobey God, right? However, endlessly shaming ourselves is not what God wants us to do; there is nowhere in the Bible that teaches us to do that. Psalm 103:12 made it clear that God removes our sins and takes them far from us. Also, Romans 6:6 teaches that our old, sinful nature is dead, meaning it can't possibly be who we are now. How can a dead person be alive? The truth is, when you repent of sinful behavior, which is simply turning back to God, you are no longer living as the person you once were. That's why there is no reason to shame yourself for things that have long been forgiven by God.

The clearest example of this is seen through King David. David was still considered a man after God's own heart, even after committing adultery, because he repented. No longer could he be defined by his adulterous behavior because that sin was declared dead at the moment of repentance. Repentance and walking with God are what define you. Your here and now, not your past, is what God sees and remembers. As you start today, I encourage you to make a reminder for yourself that you are forgiven and a new person. It can be a sticky note, a phone alarm, whatever it takes to make it easy throughout your day to remember that you are different. As you continually practice seeing yourself as a new person walking with God, it will become easier to walk confidently in who you are now, rather than in shame.

Prayer

God,
Thank You that You have made a way for me to die to my sinful self and become a new person. Remind me daily who I am now and help me to let go of my past. Open my eyes to see myself the way that You see me.

October 2

Take No Offense
By Candice Maria Hubbard
Today's Scripture: Proverbs 19:11

The immediate sting of a careless word often triggers a desire to react or retaliate. However, Proverbs offers a wiser path. It teaches that true wisdom is not about seeking revenge, but about knowing when to let an offense go. By choosing patience and forgiveness over anger, we practice a profound form of hope. This is an act of trusting that God is in control and we don't need to take justice into our own hands.

Overlooking an offense shows wisdom, not weakness. It is an act of strength and self-control that frees us from the heavy burden of anger and bitterness. When we choose to let go of a wrong, our hearts become light, and our relationships can heal. This is a hopeful perspective, trusting that peace is possible and that God's plan, not our own efforts, will ultimately make things right.

When we are deeply hurt, it's tempting to hold a grudge. But we can choose a different path, releasing that pain to God. Overlooking an offense is a personal decision to value your peace over winning an argument. It's an act of surrendering pride and trusting God to work for your good.

Let's be encouraged by the wisdom of this verse today. We don't have to carry the weight of every offense. We can practice the quiet strength of patience and the liberating power of forgiveness. God's wisdom equips us to live with grace, knowing that He is our ultimate vindicator. So, the next time you feel offended, take a deep breath and remember that it's to your glory to overlook it. Rest in the hope that God is sovereign and nothing is outside of His control.

Prayer

Heavenly Father,
Thank You for the wisdom to choose Your patience to help us overlook offenses. Help us to surrender our pride and trust that you are in control. Free us from the weight of bitterness and empower us with your grace, so that our lives may reflect your peaceful and forgiving heart.

October 3

The Lord Will Provide
By Shelly Shafer
Today's Scripture: Genesis 22:14

Carrying nothing more than a small handbag and my 4-year-old mother in tow, my Russian grandparents immigrated to the United States, arriving at Ellis Island in 1950. Flashbacks of living under Stalin's reign and surviving a German forced labor camp during WWII made them cling to the truth of the Lord's provision.

They settled in southern Illinois, where we gathered around their small kitchen table late into the night, laughing until we cried or being spellbound by the stories they shared of God's miraculous provisions in the midst of horrific circumstances.

One such account occurred when my grandmother was a young girl in Russia. Once again, three days had passed with no food. As my great-grandmother fell to her knees in prayer, pleading for a miracle to feed her children, a soft knock came at their door. My grandmother opened it, and there stood someone from the underground church holding a basket full of bread and milk. "I was sent by God. May this bless you." The household wept because the Lord provided.

While most of us can't fathom going three days without food, their story is more relevant than we might think, for we have all found ourselves desperately begging God for something: healing, a relationship, financial provision, etc. And yet, the most riveting and life-giving stories are born in hardship and anchored in hope. Oh, the depths of God's goodness! Were we to be the authors of our own stories, how predictable and short-sighted they would be. But when we trust the Author of our lives to provide what we cannot, we collaborate with God Himself, and through His kindness, are drawn closer to His own heart.

Prayer

Lord,
As the Author of my life, may I never underestimate the story You have for me, but may I lean fully into Your heart. I trust You in whatever circumstances I may face. Thank you for always being the Lord who provides, for it is You and You alone who sustains me.

October 4

Peace be with you!
By Francesca Follone-Montgomery, OFS
Today's Scripture: John 14:18, 26-27

In the Catholic tradition, today has always been a celebration of Saint Francis of Assisi. He left his family of origin to follow Christ's example, letting the Holy Spirit lead him in peace and love for all, which is why he is associated with peace and love for all creation.

I have always felt a special connection to him. Not only am I named after him, but he is traditionally considered the patron Saint of my native country, Italy. Also, in most Catholic families, we celebrate family members named after the saints.

I recall that my baptism godfather, Zio Franco, and I would have a friendly competition to see who would call the other first to exchange our feast day wishes. He and my dad reminded me of Saint Francis in that they also communicated peace when greeting people.

After losing both, I developed a strong desire to follow their example and strive to bring peace to others in a Franciscan way. Strangely, I felt that peace on October 4, 2017, when we buried my father in a beautiful cemetery in Italy. I am confident that the Holy Spirit allowed me to feel that Franciscan inner peace to enable me to smile and comfort the people around me.

Looking at some roses over my father's casket, I imagined that Saint Francis was welcoming my dad in Heaven. That's when I heard in my heart my father saying, "A rose for my little girl on her feast day!" I took a rose, and to this day, I keep it framed with a photo of my dad. It is a reminder of that strengthening calmness the holy Spirit gave me, and of my father's loving Franciscan way to bring Christ's peace to others.

Prayer

Heavenly Father,
As by the example of your servant, Francis of Assisi, we ask you not to let us dwell in the darkness. Rather, send us your Holy Spirit to bring light into our hearts. Let Him guide us to be one with your will for us, and show us ways to bring Christ's peace to all we encounter.

October 5

When...Grateful!
By Dawn Reselle Fowler
Today's Scripture: Phillipians 4:11-13

I was wondering and thinking about the right time to say it and believe it. I was trying to think about the best time to express my gratitude:

Maybe...after the disappointment leaves, after the day calms down and becomes more peaceful, after everything gets better in my professional life, after the tears are gone and the struggle is over, or after I feel better and everything comes together, I will express gratitude. I decided the perfect time to be grateful is now.

I think sometimes we wait too long to say thank you. We are looking for convenience and a better time to do it. Actually, I think showing gratitude in the middle of doubts, pain, uncertainty, anger, and confusion is the ideal time. It helps us to understand the process of learning gratitude and how God molds us into His image.

During my college years, I faced some difficult times, and many times I questioned God. I wondered if He would answer my prayers while facing so many challenges like health issues, lost loved ones, limited money, peer pressure, and the list goes on.

Then, one day, I started thinking about being more grateful. I was going to church with my mother, and the pastor was talking about the importance of gratefulness. The preacher said, "Gratefulness helps you to focus on what you have and not what you do not have." I was thinking to myself, "That is not enough, and God needs to show me something else."

Learning to be grateful has helped me in so many ways that I now make a daily mental list of things to be grateful for. This is where I will encourage you to do the same thing. Let gratefulness lead you in expressing all the ways that God blesses your life. Our world can get so busy that we forget about the things that are most important. Remember, be grateful in everything!

Prayer

I pray that God will reveal His beauty, hope, and faithfulness to you, inspiring gratitude. May His unconditional love create an overflow of gratefulness in your life. May being grateful allow you to see things that you did not see before and bless you in ways like never before. May God bless you and keep you in everything!

October 6

From Awkward to Eternal
By Karlie Fiore
Today's Scripture: John 10:27

Has the Holy Spirit ever asked you to do something that you really didn't want to do? These little nudges from the Lord usually come at the most inconvenient times and places, like a hospital bed, far from home in Nepal.

As I lay hooked to my IV, I wished more than anything that I was in a single room instead of sharing with a complete stranger from Germany. We learned a lot about each other very quickly. I learned about Chiira's broken upbringing and how she stopped believing in the Lord because He had allowed terrible things to happen in her life.

Between coughs, I felt the Holy Spirit prompting me to color a picture from my devotional coloring book for her. I thought to myself, "Absolutely not, that is so embarrassing!" After fighting it out with the Lord, I finally listened and allowed him to speak through me as I wrote a personalized note on the back of the coloring. I don't recall what I wrote because at the time, I didn't think it would matter.

The next morning, I woke up next to an empty bed. I learned that Chiira had requested a new room. Was it my picture? Did I color too much outside the lines? Did I insult her? I had gotten my wish of being in a room by myself, but now I was missing her company. I never saw Chiiara again.

Months later, to my surprise, I opened up my Facebook to a message from Chiiara. She wanted to let me know that she had started praying again, and she was seeing the Lord begin to move in her life! May this be an encouragement to you that no matter how inconvenient or uncomfortable it may be, it will change your life (and perhaps someone else's) when you learn to recognize and obey the voice of your heavenly Father.

Prayer

Lord,
Your Word says that Your sheep hear Your voice and that they know You. I pray that I may recognize when You are speaking to me. Help me to slow down enough to notice your gentle nudges that will lead me in the way I should go. Lord, I pray for the strength and the courage to act when You speak.

October 7

Fear Less, Trust More: God is with You
By Amber Bishop Mornes
Today's Scripture: Deuteronomy 31:6

Fear has a way of gripping our hearts. Maybe it's a diagnosis, financial uncertainty, a broken relationship, or a situation completely out of your control. I know that fear—I felt it after a hit-and-run left me struggling with brain issues. The fear was so heavy, I was even afraid to admit how scared I felt.

In those moments, we long for reassurance. We want to know that God truly sees us, protects us, and won't abandon us. And His Word reminds us again and again that He does. In fact, the command "Do not fear" shows up in the Bible 365 times—one for every day of the year.

The enemy would love to keep us tangled in fear, whispering lies. You're not good enough. God doesn't really love you. Why would you deserve His help? Fear often disguises itself as unworthiness, leaving us doubting God's grace, protection, and unconditional love.

But God says otherwise. He calls us His own. He promises His presence, and He reminds us that we don't have to carry life's burdens alone.

When fear creeps in, tell God exactly what's on your mind. Be honest about your frustrations, your anxieties, and your desire to control the situation. As you release those fears, God gives you His perspective and His peace. He doesn't always remove the challenge immediately, but He always promises to walk with you through it.

Today, think of the situation that weighs heaviest on your heart. Write it down in your journal. Then make a choice. Will you spend your energy worrying, or will you spend it remembering that the Lord is your helper? One path feeds fear. The other grows faith.

Prayer

Dear Lord,
Thank You for being my strength. You know my doubts, my fears, and the weight of the unknown. I surrender my desire for control and trust Your higher ways. Help me to accept your unfailing love and take each step with courage, knowing You are with me always. Build my faith where fear wants to take hold.

October 8

Promise and Provision
By Dava R. Caballero
Today's Scripture: Isaiah 43:19

The first women's event I helped host was fraught with drama, and I was shaking in my shoes. The three-day retreat encountered issues with sleeping arrangements, personality conflicts, and general grumbling and complaining. For years, I had dreamt of a place where women could gather for healing of mind, body, and spirit. I discovered that healing is sometimes a messy business.

Prayerfully, we carried on, beginning each session with praise. Each day concluded with the hymn "Oh Gracious Light." Indeed, faithful Jesus showed up with great grace and broke through the shifting shadows. Despite difficulties and my inexperience, God met us there. He created order out of the chaos.

One woman observed that our dates coincided with the Feast of Tabernacles, a Jewish tradition that commemorates their deliverance from slavery and their time in the wilderness. It is preceded by the high holy day of Yom Kippur, which calls for repentance and forgiveness. How very appropriate. Our journey with Jesus may seem chaotic at times, but He is always leading and guiding, righting our wrongs, and redirecting our steps.

The Israelites coming out of Egypt were often caught grumbling and complaining, even after God miraculously provided light in the darkness and water from a rock. Nevertheless, He continued to show Himself faithful and able to meet all their needs. Those with faith were eventually ushered into the Promised Land.

God always makes a way; we must only open our eyes to see it. God always provides; we must only trust in His love for us. God always multiplies our obedience and moves miraculously as we surrender whatever we have in our hands to give.

Prayer

Jesus, Light of the world,
Shine upon us. Teach us to rest in the womb of our anointing, where each part of our journey is knit together according to your perfect plan. Thank you for the promise of your presence and the promise to fulfill your call on our lives.

October 9

I Found Jesus in the Psych Ward
By Josh Parker
Today's Scripture: Judges 7:2

I've always been fiercely independent. "I can do this myself" was my default position. As someone who naturally relies on competence and self-sufficiency, the concept of surrender felt foreign—even threatening.
Then God began reducing my army.

After years of battling combat-related PTSD, addiction, and suicidal ideation, I found myself trapped in a chaotic psychiatric facility. Every human solution I came up with had failed. Therapy alone wasn't enough. Medication, alcohol, and autonomy weren't enough. I was stuck in a place with no real treatment, threatened with months of involuntary retention in a facility that preyed upon those in mental health crisis, milking their insurance for all it was worth. I felt trapped.

Just like Gideon, whose army God reduced from 32,000 to 300 men, God had stripped away everything I relied on—every "soldier" in my arsenal of self-reliance. But that's exactly where He wanted me.
In that unlikely place, through a Christian roommate, my faithful wife, and a dusty Bible, God met me with a peace I'd never before experienced. For the first time, I saw the power in surrender. I had an encounter with the Living God and laid down my will, accepting Jesus as my personal Savior. There was unexpected comfort in giving up the control I so desperately tried—and failed—to hold onto.

God reduced my army so I couldn't boast that my own strength had saved me. In complete helplessness, His power became undeniably clear.

Sometimes God allows us to reach the end of our rope not to abandon us, but to show that His strength is made perfect in our weakness. When we finally stop trying to orchestrate our own rescue, we discover the peace that can be found in true surrender—and the hope that comes from trusting His infinitely better plan.

Prayer

Father,
Help us release our desperate grip on control and find peace in surrender to Your perfect will. When we reach the end of our strength, remind us that Your power is made perfect in our weakness. Give us the courage to trust Your plan, even when we can't see the way forward.

October 10

The Abundant Life
By Lori Parkerson
Today's Scripture: John 10:10

In the midst of a hurried task, consumed by my own created urgency in the moment, I glance at the clock to gauge how much time has ticked by and am immediately beckoned back to centeredness by the numbers glowing up to me—sharp and symmetrical from the digital screen, the tiny center dots pulsing each second for steady emphasis, "10:10."

Have you recognized in your own faith journey that the Holy Spirit speaks in so many ways? Gently, and often surprisingly, He speaks to me through the numbers on a clock, or a passing sign on the road. Through a bird alighting in my view to lock eyes with me just as I peer out the window. Through an unexpected text from someone I was just thinking about praying for. He speaks in these subtle, quiet, and unassuming ways, always to say, "I am here." And in them, I draw my breath, and recenter on the only true reality. He is with me. He is here.

In my mind, I've called these moments "noticing synchronicities" and the pursuit of continually being aware of God's presence, the "10:10 Life." What did Jesus mean in John 10:10 that he came so we may have life more abundantly? And, how do we grab on to that essential promise and truth? Isn't it always more of Him? Not holding on to the parts of life that steal, that kill, and that ultimately destroy our vision for a life poured out to Him, for Him to pour into us—until our joy overflows?

As the clock ticks away my time, the more I relish the simple, the pared back. In all life's joy and grieving, the to-do lists, callings, and all the many versions of myself over the years, He is *here*. Beckoning us to draw on His peace and provision. This is abundance.

Prayer

Father,
Today we pray that you would remind us of your presence in each moment. That we would grasp what it means to live a profuse and copious life. That we would be bold enough to grasp onto the promise of an abundant life in You. Thank You for giving us this life. We give our lives back to You for Your Glory forever.

October 11

The Unseen Hand of God
By Ada Bontrager
Today's Scripture: 2 Corinthians 4:16-18

As we sat in the doctor's office making plans for an anniversary trip, life quickly came to an abrupt stop.

"Dan, the cancer came back. You need to have surgery, and if this surgery doesn't get rid of all of the cancer cells, you'll need to have chemo and radiation."

I can replay this conversation as if it happened today. Becoming paralyzed by fear, I started planning a life without my husband and started asking the question that everyone asks when faced with a difficult situation. God, why would You do this? How could You allow this? The thoughts quickly consumed me as if I wasn't in control of them anymore.

The Lord reminded me of 2 Corinthians 4:18.

The reality, what we were seeing, was that cancer could take my husband's life. What we weren't seeing was that God was working things out in the spiritual realm, setting us up for the next assignment He had for us.

What I didn't see was that a close friendship would hinder us from accepting the call of God in our lives. I realized that that friendship led me to a fear of man that controlled every thought, word, and action that came out of me. It paralyzed me.

But God....He redeemed me! He showed me who I am in Him. If my husband's health hadn't been compromised, I may not have found the freedom that came from wholly relying on the Lord for my future. Our prosperity comes from his plans and purposes.

Prayer

Heavenly Father,
I will find joy in the trials You allow in my life. Even when I can't see what You are doing and when I don't know Your plans, I will trust that You are working it out for my good and Your glory.

October 12

Finding Rest for the Weary Soul
By Elizabeth Clark
Today's Scripture: Matthew 11:28-29

Life is full of toils and burdens. Our first instinct is usually to fight against them, trying to fix things in our own strength. We also seek rest by trying to escape our circumstances, but this only leaves us perpetually restless and exhausted.

Jesus offers a different kind of rest, one not based on the absence of our struggles but on a change in how we carry them. The secret to this inward rest is to take His yoke and learn from Him. A yoke connects two things, and by taking on His, we are yoked to Christ, who is perfectly in sync with the Father's will. He doesn't promise to remove our burdens, but to connect us to His life of rest.

For much of my life, I tried to fight against frustrating situations, which left me perpetually restless. But as I began to practice submitting to God's will, I discovered that yielding to Him brought a quiet, inward rest that was independent of my circumstances.

When we embrace His meekness and lowliness, we find that true peace is an inward condition, independent of our external circumstances. This rest is a guaranteed outcome of learning from Christ and submitting to God's purpose. It's a profound peace that no amount of fighting or complaining could ever provide.

What are the situations in your life that cause you to resist or feel anxious? How can you practice submitting to God's will in those moments to find His promised rest?

Prayer

Lord Jesus,
Thank You for the promise of rest for our souls. We confess our tendency to toil and resist. Help us to learn from You and to take Your yoke upon us. Give us a meek and lowly heart so that we may submit to the Father's will and find Your peace in every circumstance.

October 13

Faith, Grit, and Grace: A Grandmother's Enduring Legacy
By Colleen Ann Ruggieri
Today's Scripture: 2 Timothy 4:7

Today, on my great-grandmother's birthday, I honor her as the woman who inspired my faith, as the one who wove a legacy that death cannot erase. My father, a pioneer house flipper in the 1960s, moved my family eight times before my 18th birthday. I learned not to grow too comfortable in any house, but Grandma's place became my haven, offering a sense of home where my spirit could rest in the arms of Jesus.

I was born when she was in her sixties and grew up captivated by her stories of resilience. A young widow in the 1920s, she raised two children, endured Great Depression bread lines, and worked at Isaly's, a store famed for chipped chop ham and Klondike bars. Through hard work and determination, she eventually owned her own store, bought a house, and opened it to boarders; her home became a sanctuary. Grandma's life taught me the true meaning of turning trials into triumphs.

In her golden years, she guided me to live in the Word, as we prayed together and read Psalms from her KJV bible. Her backyard, alive with peonies, roses, lily of the valley, and lilacs, whispered God's presence to me. Freshly washed sheets fluttered on her clothesline, revealing the sacred in ordinary tasks. We gathered grapes from her arbor, making jam in her kitchen for shut-ins—yet another example of her gentle ministry of love. During her 80th summer, our church chuckled when a police officer spared her a speeding ticket because she was headed to babysit for bible study.

My great-grandmother's life was grit wrapped in grace. Her example was an invitation to live with heaven in mind. As autumn leaves fall, I'm comforted knowing that she's sitting next to our Savior, still calling me to sing the songs of Jesus.

Prayer

Heavenly Father,
Thank You for the faithful mentors who have led me to Your radiant truth. As I cherish their memory and timeless guidance, please grant me the strength, courage, and wisdom to fight the good fight in my trials. Lord, though I miss my loved ones, help me to trust that we'll one day reunite in your eternal glory.

October 14

Seal Upon My Heart
By Kristy Mabe
Today's Scripture: Song of Solomon 8:6-7

Crossing the wooden drawbridge into the stone castle, I paused to help lift the DJ's cart of electronic equipment. Surprised, he offered his thanks and then kept rolling. Following behind the bridesmaids, I trudged up the stairs to dress and primp for photos. Ready and waiting, I eased out onto the upper balcony to peek down below as the florist hung flowers along the great hall's entrance.

Every minute was merry until the music started and nerves cramped my stomach. My legs felt like jelly, all I imagined was falling down the huge staircase during my entrance. At the bottom, I'd never been so happy to hold my brother's hand.

As I walked up the aisle, clutching my bouquet with a red rose heart for loved ones lost, my gaze landed on my almost husband. Then and there, time froze. Everything was right in my world.

A distinguished friend presided, another read selected scriptures, then we spoke our sentiments. In front of the gathering, I confessed to rescuing my fiancé from a dragon, not to mention meddling to get engaged. Tired, I'd given up and let God take control. That night, my boyfriend proposed. Now, ten years from the day of our first date, we vowed to love each other until death.

Sitting at the sweetheart's table, I read my place card. Everyone had one I'd specially crafted based on the two movies that inspired our theme. Mine said I'm merely a servant in a fine dress.

Truer words couldn't have been spoken. God created me to help others. As I fought the urge to straighten our leaning wedding cake, I knew I'd delight in wearing the seal of both men I loved. One would be a cross, and the other my new monogram, thanks to the silver band around my ring finger.

Prayer

Dear Lord,
Embolden us to show our love and praise for you outwardly for all to see. No matter how dire our circumstances, help us pledge to walk in Your way. Strengthen our faith as we embrace the love You have for us, which allows us to wholeheartedly trust in You.

October 15

What if God Sees More in You than You See in Yourself?
By Dr. Shelley Kemp, Ed.D., SHRM-SCP
Today's Scripture: Psalm 127:3

Have you ever wondered if you're really cut out to be a parent? Or questioned if your life—your mistakes, your mindset, your past—disqualifies you from being someone's mother?

I know that feeling. I lived it.

I never thought I'd become a mom. And to be honest, I didn't think I wanted to. I was driven, focused, and—at the time—very self-centered. I had built a life that revolved around my goals and my pace. Motherhood didn't seem to fit into that picture.

But then, God gave me a son, and everything changed.

He became the best thing that's ever happened to me. Not because I suddenly became perfect, but because I finally saw what love beyond myself looked like. He gave me a reason to wake up and pour into someone else. He softened me. He grew me. He made me better.

Through him, I learned that God doesn't call us based on how ready we feel—He calls us based on what He knows we're capable of. He knew that this little boy would not only bring light to my life, but also become a light in the lives of everyone around him.

Let me ask you again, what if God sees more in you than you see in yourself?

What if the very thing you're afraid of—becoming a parent, starting a business, going on a mission, ending a relationship—is the thing that will help you grow into the best version of yourself?

What if, instead of disqualifying you, your past is the very reason God is calling you to nurture new life?

He believes in you. He has a plan for you. And in time, you will too.

Prayer

Lord,
Thank You for trusting us with the gift of life. Remind us that even when we feel unworthy or unsure, You see our potential. Help us embrace the calling of motherhood—or any assignment You give—with courage, humility, and love. Shine through us, Lord.

October 16

Learning It For Ourselves
By Tara L. Banks
Today's Scripture: Matthew 16:15

I enjoy learning new things, but I know it's one thing to watch someone drive a car, parent a child, or write a book. It's entirely different to do those things on your own.

This is also true with our faith. What we know personally about Jesus and how we live out our faith in Him, matters. Most importantly, our faith must be grounded in what we know and believe as individuals, not in what we observe in others or what we hear from the latest podcast, a sermon series, or from Instagram.

In three of the gospels, Jesus challenges the disciples in their personal knowledge of who He is. The disciples begin to rattle off all that they have heard about Jesus and what others have said. In my imagination, I see Him stop and turn, looking directly at each of them and then serving up the punchline, purposefully emphasizing the word "you."

Jesus loved the masses, but in that moment, all He wanted to know was based on the individual. Did the disciples know the Truth for themselves? They had been around it, eaten miracle lunches because of it, and done wonders on behalf of it, but did they know it for themselves? Did they truly know Him?

Peter responds with the personal revelation that Jesus was the Son of the Living God (Matthew 16:16-17). When he does, I imagine Jesus smiling a broad smile and giving Peter a gentle slap on the back, pleased that he knew the Truth for himself.

Prayer

Lord,
May we learn the truth of who Jesus is and the life He has for us through reading and studying Your Word for ourselves. Help us to understand, memorize, and consume the daily bread it offers us. May we be like Peter and have a fresh and clear revelation of you today.

October 17

Can I Ask?
By Kathy Gustafsson
Today's Scripture: Jeremiah 33:3

I was recently on a flight with a momma and her two littles. The questions started flying from the kids before we left the ground. "Will Dad be there to pick us up? Did you remember the snacks? Where are my earphones? How high will the plane go?" Their mom was patient to listen and answer, even as the questions echoed down the hallway towards baggage claim.

I'm discipling a young lady who has many questions about God and faith. How do you know God has a sense of humor? What does it mean to bless God? What if my struggle is exactly what He wants to use to reach others? Her questions certainly keep me on my toes! What a joy to be able to share the deep truths I have learned with a sister who is growing in her faith.

Thankfully, we have a God of endless patience who welcomes our questions. Moses asked God's name. Hannah asked for a son. David asked for victory, for forgiveness, for guidance, and to build a temple. Martha asked Jesus if he would make Mary help with dinner. James and John asked Jesus if they should destroy an unwelcoming village.

Whatever the question you have for God today–big or small, silly or serious–*ask*. He will hear you. He will answer you. He will use your questions to teach you more of His character. He will answer to draw you into a deeper relationship with Him. He will tell you great and incomprehensible things you do not know.

Prayer

Heavenly Father,
Hear my voice as I call to You. Answer my plea and guide me into Your truth, Your wisdom, Your grace. Thank You for listening to my questions and grant me patience to wait on Your answers. I know the author of the universe will author the perfect answer to my question.

October 18

Cherish the Sweetness
By Shelley Groves
Today's Scripture: Psalm 34:8

Believe it or not, today is National Chocolate Cupcake Day. No, I'm serious. I'm not sure who makes this stuff up, but it's true. I can get fully on board with a day that celebrates eating chocolate cupcakes. I mean, really, an official day on the calendar that not only makes it a day about chocolate but encourages me to partake! It's an excuse to find your favorite bakery or pull out that mixer and get to work on some yummy chocolate deliciousness.

I believe there needs to be more moments that we set aside time to celebrate. If you are anything like me, it is easy to get overwhelmed and sucked into the negative messages we take in all around us. Watching the evening news is not for the faint of heart. Scrolling your feed can easily become a downer. Just showing up and doing your part at work can be too much. Life is hard.

But King David knew that. He knew that amid life's discouragements, we must stop and remember that our God is good. In Psalm 34, he celebrates the goodness of God. Scholars believe this psalm was written after David escaped King Achish by pretending to be insane.

David knew hard days. He knew days that could mean the end of his life, but he also knew how to praise God. He knew how to celebrate God's goodness. He looked for reasons to have Chocolate Cupcake days. He looked for the sweetness of God in everyday life. David knew that God was his refuge. He had tasted the goodness of the Lord.

Prayer

Thank you, Lord, for Chocolate Cupcake days. Days we stop and celebrate your goodness. Help us remember to celebrate your goodness and faithfulness, even on the days that seem too overwhelming for us. For when we focus on your goodness, we realize that the world around us isn't too big for you.

October 19

First Sighting
By Susan Laurie Hutchinson
Today's Scripture: Jeremiah 29:11

At seventeen, I was eating at a pancake house with a friend when I spotted him at the counter. His good looks caught my attention, so I playfully put my glasses on and stared. He became uncomfortable and left with his friend. I went into the mall, pretending to make a phone call, while watching him window-shop. When he left the mall, I rejoined my friend.

"No go," I told her. I shrugged, laughed, and went back to eating, not giving it another thought. I waitressed there, so when I came into work the next day, the hostess said, "A guy came in last night looking for you. I know him; we went to high school together. He's coming back." Oh no, I thought with embarrassment.

It took more than a handsome face to hold my attention. Mike was funny, hard-working, open, honest, and without guile. He was country, I was city. He was Irish Catholic, I was German Protestant, he was leather jackets and motorcycles, I was theatres and museums. He was a hunter, I was horrified. So opposite, but oh, did we fall in love. I gave up college to marry, and never looked back. My plans changed, but I'm sure it was God's plan all along. He took my teenage silliness and grew it into something solid and priceless.

Three kids, eleven grandkids, many gains and losses in life later, Mike commemorates every October 19th with a "Happy Anniversary." If we're apart, he will call or text. He calls it *first sighting*. And, it still makes us smile.

How often in life do we make plans that never happen? Too many to count. There are my plans, and then there are God's plans for me.

I've discovered I do much better when I follow God's plan.

Prayer

Lord,
It's good I don't know the future, because I would have no reason to trust You. My best plans often go awry, Yours never do. I'm so thankful to be walking through life with the perfect partner for me. His handsome face is a bonus.

October 20

It's Just a Storm
By Gloria Delaney
Today's Scripture: 1 John 5:14

Life can feel calm one day and turn to turmoil the next. The storms of life often catch us off guard. Recently, I faced a heart blockage that required open-heart surgery. Though my family was fearful, I chose to trust God—and He gave me peace and a quick recovery.

God knows every detail of our storms—their beginning, their end, and their purpose. Your storm may look different—perhaps a child caught in addiction or another unexpected hardship. God knew it was coming, and He charged you to pray. The storm reveals your faith level and proves God's trustworthiness.

1 John 5:14 reminds us that the Lord listens to what we ask. Do you believe His Word? Do you know He hears you? If yes, then you can rest assured—what you ask in His will is already being worked out.

Sometimes we repeat the same prayer, but God may be testing our faith. When we choose to believe that He hears us and is faithful to His Word, we can shift from pleading to praising. Even when we cannot see it, God is moving in the background.

God responds to faith. When He sees your trust, He acts on it. Whatever storm you face today, hold on to this truth: He hears you, He is faithful, and He will fulfill His Word.

Prayer

Lord,
Thank You for being faithful in every storm. Strengthen my faith to trust that You hear me and are working on my behalf. Teach me to move from fear to confidence, from asking to praising, knowing Your Word is true. I place my storms in Your hands today.

October 21

Stillness in the Fall
By Joy Caswell
Today's Scripture: Lamentations 3:22-23

Autumn is a time of the year that naturally calls us to slow down and reflect. In today's world, we are so distracted. We lack direction, which is affecting everything around us, our emotions, jobs, and our families. When we slow things down to regain our perspective, we can see and feel God most clearly.

We find hope everywhere, a sunrise or sunset, in nature as the animals are preparing for winter, leaves falling from the trees, and in the little moments that pass by so quickly. When life feels overwhelming, when everything seems hopeless, remember that God's mercy is always there.

Every morning, like a song in our heart, all we need to do is receive it. His goodness is not seasonal; it is eternal. Remember that change will always come our way. How we respond to it depends on the strength of our faith, which fills our foundation. Strong foundations can weather any storm. God's grace and mercy are new every morning.

As a society, we must learn to repent and follow God. We need to reconnect with God and shut out all the harsh, bitter, and angry world. Do not let a bitter world disconnect you from everything that matters. Reset and stand firm on the promises of God. You will find more peace, hope, and love than you have ever known.

In the book of Lamentations, we find a series of poems that describe the consequences of sin and God's judgment for those sins. These lessons show us his everlasting mercy and faithfulness. It is a small part of the Bible, but it offers us many valuable lessons. It is never too late to start prioritizing your faith foundation. If you need to follow someone, follow Jesus. He will always walk beside you, guiding you with grace and mercy.

Prayer

Gracious Heavenly Father,
Help me to embrace this season of change. Help me to trust in You and not in my own understanding. Father, help me to see You in everything around me. Please help me to let go of yesterday's struggles and to receive the gift of today with joy and a grateful heart. Show me how to build a solid foundation in faith.

October 22

A New Generation
By Mary Thissen
Today's Scripture: Psalm 105:8

For years, I had attempted to have children with my husband. But with three miscarriages and an ectopic pregnancy, it had seemed that I was not meant to hold a child in my arms on this Earth. I knew the promises of God, and I believed I would meet my children in the afterlife of Heaven, but my arms and my heart still felt empty.

However, in the fall of 2019, I felt the Lord calling me to open my heart just one more time to the possibility of pregnancy. In my heart, I heard the Lord say, "Will you trust me just one more time?" As I pondered the Lord's request, I came to the conclusion that I would forever regret not trusting him with the one thing I wanted more than my life itself.

"Yes, Lord, I will trust."

Medical appointments were made, and a treatment plan was put into place. By the grace of God, I became pregnant on the very first attempt! But fear and a constant sense of foreboding came from my mind and the world as I grappled with the possibility of losing another pregnancy. In addition, the COVID-19 pandemic had swept the world, bringing quarantines and unprecedented circumstances. It seemed as though God had stripped away anything else to trust in so that I would learn to place my trust only in him.

But, as the verse says, God's promises are for a thousand generations, and he heard my cry. On this day in 2020, I delivered twin boys. God had taken my other children to him and doubly blessed me in one pregnancy. Sorrow lasts but a little while, and joy follows.

Prayer

Lord,
Help me to believe that Your promises are indeed for a thousand generations. Let us remember the marvelous deeds You have committed in our lives. Let us always proclaim Your greatness to the world in the way in which we live and love.

October 23

Finding Courage When Your Heart Would Rather Fear
by Laurie "Sterling" O'Neill
Today's Scripture: Psalm 27:1-3

I've never faced the adversaries David did, but mine do feel encompassing, often leaving me without confidence. I've faced a prodigal child, cancer, aging parents, losses of loved ones, betrayals, etc. All of these stirred fear in my heart.

Walking through cancer, fear became my constant companion. Yet, each morning I woke up determined to fight. I journaled my fears, wanting, like David, to place my hope in God.

I remembered and praised who God is, my Light and my Salvation. I named my fears and thanked God for what He would do. Like David, I trusted that my enemies, my fears, would fall away. I spoke truth to my heart, clinging to confidence.

I wanted God to answer me in my time of trouble, and He did. Each day, I sought Him, and He revealed Himself in small yet faithful ways to strengthen me—through my doctor, a kind word, helpful information, or Scripture, among other things.

Did I know whether He would heal me? No. Even Jesus prayed in the garden to be spared from the cross, yet surrendered to the Father's will. God sent an angel to comfort Him, just as Jesus sent me comfort.

Now, to find courage when my heart wants to fear, I endeavor to seek my Heavenly Father. I journal, praise, name my fears, give thanks, and speak truth into my heart.
Where can you start today?

Prayer

Jesus,
Today I face _____. You are my God of light, my salvation, and my _____. Whom shall I fear? Thanks for being my Lord. I pray You will answer _____. Thanks for giving me exactly what I need. Please forgive me when I forget You. I bring all my thoughts before You, knowing You love and know me best.

October 24

Rest in the Dwelling
By Sheila Krygsheld
Today's Scripture: Psalm 91:1

Life is in perpetual motion regardless of the stage we are in. As women, we have varied responsibilities of holding jobs, balancing finances, prioritizing health, possibly raising children, and/or helping a spouse, and much more. Many of these things are absolutes; they must happen. And yet the mental gymnastics of anxiety, worry, and fear of the future cloud our thinking and leave us exhausted. Thus, our minds and hearts suffer. We have the tendency to become a skeptic about God and his promises.

The shelter of the Most High is not a place we visit. Visiting is stopping in, but dwelling is staying or living as a permanent resident. Dwelling in the shelter of the Most High is to live in his refuge and safety, to permanently reside there, and it gives the feeling of being home. There is fellowship in the dwelling. What happens when we reside in his shelter of being home? We rest. In the dwelling, everything is known, and it is going to be just fine.

Shadows can be scary. When a storm approaches and the sky is bright in one part of the sky and dark in another, we go to safety and take cover. When we are in the shadow of the Almighty, dwelling in his shelter, storms do not shake us. Why? Because there is rest in God's shadow. He is there, right with us, holding us, offering rest that can be ours for the taking.

When we visit God in his shelter, we intend to leave. When we dwell in his shelter, we stay and are given rest in his covering. He longs to meet us in the dwelling.

Prayer

Lord,
Help me to create a space in my busy life to dwell...to live in Your shelter. I want to relax and let You wash over my soul so I can be the woman You have planned for me to be. Help me to consciously dwell in Your shelter, so I can rest in your shadow.

October 25

Perfect Otherworldly Peace
By Sheila Krygsheld
Today's Scripture: Isaiah 26:3

In this verse, the Israelite nation's southern kingdom, Judah, was facing a takeover by the Assyrian empire, a brutal people with the reputation of being inhumane to those they conquered. Isaiah was calling on Israel to return to their covenant with God and to trust him.

The Hebrew translation of "perfect peace" is literally "shalom shalom." This kind of peace is supernatural, extraordinary—absolutely perfect in all that perfect can be. It is completely indescribable because God is the giver of such peace, and humans can do nothing to obtain it...except trust. That kind of peace is only attainable when the level of trust is so great that the receiver has nowhere else to go except God, and their trust is complete in him.

Sixteen years ago today, my daughter was in a dreadful car accident. I will never forget the feelings I had of constant fear of the unknown. I had nowhere to turn for peace about the situation except to God, whom I trusted to handle the situation to its end. I had to give up control of worry, anxiety, and uncertainty, and trust God that he had my daughter through the accident, recovery, and beyond. Peace ensued. An otherworldly perfect peace that passed any kind of understanding. (Philippians 4:7)

As permanent as the accident has been burned into my memory, the perfect peace God gave is far more indelible.

Prayer

Lord,
Perfect peace seems unattainable in my life right now. I give You control over the things in my life that are burdening me, and I trust You to bring incomprehensible peace into places that seem to be void of hope.

October 26

Confession Frees You to Be Known
By Lesley Swanson
Today's Scripture: James 5:16a

I didn't plan on confessing anything that weekend. It was just an ordinary fall women's retreat, and as a mom of young kids, a weekend with women learning about the Word felt like a dream. I don't even remember what the topic was. But one of the nights, I felt compelled to share the secret I had been hiding for years—my abortion.

I decided to tell my friend and our pastor's wife, Jenny, and her response stunned me. She simply asked, "So you don't think God wants to use you?" Her words felt like a holy smack, shaking me awake to a truth I had resisted for too long: God could still use me. That night became a turning point. What I thought disqualified me, God would redeem for His glory.

Confession has a way of loosening shame's grip. We fear rejection, so we stay silent. But James 5:16 tells us that confession brings healing. It opens the door for God's grace to flow in new ways. That night, what I had kept secret finally came into the light. And instead of rejection, I found compassion, friendship, hope, and prayer.

Friend, maybe you've been holding onto something you believe disqualifies you from serving God. Confession feels risky, but hiding is heavier. When we take the risk of being known, we discover the freedom of being forgiven—and the joy of being useful again.

God isn't finished with you. In fact, He delights in using those who know His grace firsthand. Don't be afraid to walk in the light. Healing and hope are waiting on the other side of confession.

Prayer

Lord,
Thank You for the hope that comes through confession. Forgive me for the times I've let shame keep me silent and afraid. Give me courage to bring hidden things into the light, trusting that Your grace is greater than my sin. Use my story—even the broken parts—for Your glory and the good of others.

October 27

Guiding the Next Generation
By Linda Lowe Erley
Today's Scripture: Deuteronomy 6:6-7

I am the grandmother of eight–the absolute joys of my life. I can rest more easily in this role than I did as a young mom stepping into unknown terrain, praying each morning over my husband, myself, and our three sons' impressionable hearts–that God's truth would take root.

When they were toddlers, I began praying for the friends they would choose, the decisions and choices they would face, and the women they would marry.

Now, as I watch the men our sons have become, I am grateful to God for the legacy woven through our trials, challenges, and mistakes. We didn't always get it right, yet God was faithful. Today, I see our sons and their beautiful wives raising their own children, and the fruit of years of intentional prayer and time invested. This legacy–planting seeds of God's truth in the hearts of our children–can continue from generation to generation.

Are you a mom, dad, grandmother, grandfather, aunt, uncle, teacher, or neighbor? Each of us carries a responsibility. What life-giving seeds are you planting in the children God has placed in your life? They grow up quickly. Seeds can be planted anywhere–while making mud pies, during car rides, baking cookies, through bedtime prayers, and in a church community. The opportunities are endless. Now, as grandparents, my husband and I continue this same calling.

In what ways are you being intentional with your words, actions, and prayers? What we pour into their hearts will overflow into their own words, choices, and priorities.

We have a choice. Will you allow the world to shape the next generation's values, hopes, and identity? Or will you intentionally guide them to live differently–to live "upside down" from the ways of this world, firmly grounded in God's Word and truth?

Nurture the next generation!

Prayer

Dear God,
You have entrusted these lambs to our care. Show us how to plant seeds of Your love in their hearts. Help us be intentional in our words and actions. We thank You that You are our Great Shepherd who counsels and guides us. Teach us to do the same with the children You've placed in our lives.

October 28

Know Who I Am Remember Who You Are
By Carol Sammarco
Today's Scripture: Psalm 46:10

Know Who I am Remember Who You Are

Remember before you were born of flesh I breathed my breath
Creating you my child
Remember before you were a daughter or a sister a son or a brother
You were my child
Remember before you were a wife or a mother a husband or a father
You were my child
Remember before you were a friend or a disciple
You were my child

Know I have held you so close in the dark times
And rejoiced in the light even though you were unaware of My presence
Know I wanted so badly for you to feel the capacity of my love
Even when you were numb
Know when you make mistakes and fall
I pick you up forgiving you completely so you can forgive yourself
Know when you attempt mercy for others and tire of the struggle
You can give it to Me and I will give you rest
Know when you are too weak from the battle
I have already won it for you
Know when you are wounded and broken
I can put all the pieces back together perfectly
Know you couldn't save yourself born of sin
So I sent you a savior
Know when you opened your heart in answer to My Son
I rejoiced with all of heaven

Remember these things always
Knowing that nothing will ever separate you
From the vastness of my love

I created this world
Parted the Red Sea
Resurrected my Son all just for you

Remember who you are
My precious child

Know who I AM
Your Father in Heaven

Prayer

Precious Lord,
Help us to remember our identity through Christ as Your beloved children, chosen and created with a purpose, redeemed through grace. Teach us also to know your voice, trusting your heart as our unchanging and merciful Heavenly Father, anchoring our hearts in your truth, shaping our words, our choices, and our worship. And wrap us in the comfort and peace of your everlasting love.

October 29

Practicing Silence
By Alana Deutschmann
Today's Scripture: Habbakuk 2:20

Does silence intrigue or terrify you? Do you love it or loathe it?
In my experience, silence is less about the absence of noise and more about the quality of presence.

My pursuit of silence came during a wilderness season of suffering. I was questioning everything I thought I knew and believed about my faith. Silence was part of my healing, but it was also a revealing process. I couldn't escape my sin or my truest thoughts and feelings about what I was enduring. Of course, distracting myself into oblivion could help temporarily, but once external stimuli decreased, I was left with the internal noise.

What I didn't know was that my raw honesty and accusatory questions were actually paving the way to greater intimacy with Jesus. Because He sent us the promised Holy Spirit, we have the gift of communing with him all of the time; indeed, our very bodies become the host of the Holy One if we entrust our lives to Him.

Over time and with practice, awareness of my thoughts, feelings, and bodily state, along with nature and my surroundings, increased my capacity to be present right where I was. This brought clarity, wisdom, discernment, and humility because I was able to attune to the presence of God and truly listen. As a side effect, I noticed that I was better able to be present with others. We all know or have been one of those people who are physically present but a world away. So, friends, can I urge you to try it? Begin slowly. Start with one minute or five. If it's too much, you may need to practice this with a safe person. Let silence beckon you to explore the mystery, beauty, and richness of fellowship with our Triune God.

Prayer

Father, Son, and Holy Spirit,
Help me hone my awareness away from distraction and chaos to honor your presence within and all around me. I want to clearly see and hear you so that I can know myself as your beloved creation and, in turn, offer a ministering presence to the people I encounter today.

October 30

Messy Middle
By Rachel Anne Maverick
Today's Scripture: Philippians 4:6-7

How do you live right where you are when anxiety weds you to an uncertain future?

Perhaps you're waiting on oncology results. Maybe your company is facing layoffs, or your tender marriage has grown tenuous. While regret taunts us with the intricacies of our every mistake, anxiety propels us into futures that are frightening because they're unknown.

Nothing is scarier than uncertainty.

When we're not berating our past selves for our mishaps, we're too often promising peace to our future ones: after the negative test results come back, we vow to embrace peace. If we keep our jobs, our lives will flourish with peace and abundance. Or only when we avoid a disastrous divorce will peace sprout wings in our lives.

The problem is that we skip the messy middle altogether. We avoid rooting ourselves where we stand because that ground is too uncomfortable or worrisome to hold with trembling hands. We exist in a world that abhors discomfort.

But what if by missing the messy middle, we also forgo the beauty God has to offer in the present moment?

He doesn't want us to lament the past or to be anxious about the future. Rather, we're to cast our lots onto God, our peace in uncertainty. Because He promises to guard us, we cannot only withstand the messy middle; we can flourish right in its midst.

Prayer

Father,
Please cradle my messy middle. Fix me precisely where I'm planted—my anxious heart and mind rooted in your capable, steadfast love forever.

October 31

Bless Me in the Silence
By Robin Keahn Heim
Today's Scripture: Romans 8:26-27

I love a good cemetery.

My grandmother's backyard on Dewey Street in Royal Oak, Michigan, shared a chain-link fence with the Oakview Cemetery. Summer through late autumn, five-year-old me would lean against the tree by the fence, sitting for hours absorbing the calm. Sometimes quiet, sometimes chatty. Innocence isn't always a given in the first years of a child's life. My mother divorced twice; I missed my father, was confused about my stepfather's inappropriate behavior with me, and did not totally understand that my mother had abandoned me for a chance at a dancing career. God met me in the solitude at the edge of the graveyard. He listened to my tiny voice regarding big issues. He read my heart when I didn't know how to verbalize the feelings that clouded my childhood. I was too young to know the immensity of what I had experienced. God comforted. The I AM simply *was*—in the hushed shade between both worlds, living and dead.

He will meet you when and where you need Him, even if it is behind the steering wheel of your car, as you catch your breath between tears, mourning over the death of a marriage, a career, a loved one. When others are being congratulated on the birth of a child, a milestone birthday, or receiving an award, your happiness is tempered by the sadness that comes from having no one to celebrate you. When you are unable to speak out loud. When you have no bandwidth left to think. When you have no strength to move. He will hear you in your silence. He will gather your thoughts. He will lift you up. The Great I AM *is* and will always *be* with you.

And I will always love good cemeteries.

Prayer

Lord,
Life in this world is challenging. Humans are complicated and complex. Circumstances and situations can interfere with the happiness You so wonderfully and fearlessly created me for. Do not leave me alone with a full heart and no voice. Keep company with me. Help me work through my pain and embrace my joy.

November

hope*books
collections

November 1

For He is Good
By Amy Leigh Hughes
Today's Scripture: Psalm 107:1

I have to be honest, "gratitude" makes me a bit squirmy. It feels simplistic and naive, and maybe even a bit cliché. I can't help but see the gaps, the lack, everything that's missing. I am constantly aware of the broken state of the world, and it can be difficult for me to appreciate goodness when it's so imperfect and fleeting.

Instead of just rattling off the same generic, yearly list of things I am supposed to be thankful for, I want to name why I should even be thankful in the first place.

Psalm 107:1 tells us why we give thanks. The good things we have are not by chance; they are given to us because God is a good God and he loves to give us good things.

This gives a deep purpose to my gratitude. I can be thankful for each day because it was hand-crafted by a merciful God. Every breath is a gift. The world is still going to be broken, but the hopeful truth is that God provides goodness even in the midst of brokenness. In fact, there cannot be any good thing apart from God.

For me, the key is to be as specific as possible. I can be generally thankful for my son, but when I hold him and hear his little heartbeat, I am filled with awe and thankfulness that there is a God who set that muscle in motion and keeps it beating every second.

I wonder how many things I take for granted every day that I've never even thought to thank God for.

Prayer

God,
Open my eyes to Your abundant blessings all around me. Remind me daily that You are the source of all goodness. Thank You for Your unending mercies, and help me to recognize the beauty that You've hidden in each moment.

November 2

Eternal Life
By Francesca Follone-Montgomery, OFS
Today's Scripture: John 3:16

Growing up in a Catholic family in Italy, today has always been a day for us to honor our loved ones who have passed away. There is an Italian tradition of visiting their sites in the cemetery and praying for them in a special way. Our public schools would even have days off to allow families to be together on this date.

One year, my father brought me to Sicily with him, so we could honor his parents' place of repose there. Our family had a designated place in the cemetery that was almost like a chapel with tombstones on the walls. As we approached it, the wind was blowing, and I felt the presence of the Holy Spirit around us. I could almost hear my grandparents' voices thanking me for being there. My dad was sad, yet serene.

During our stay in Sicily, his sister and brother-in-law hosted us in their home, and the family gatherings were so spiritually enriching. I could almost feel the love in my dad's heart as it radiated through his smile. The food was amazingly delicious and all homemade. The table conversations were filled with respect and an awareness of the sacrifices that our loved ones had made to provide for their families. One of them was a priest, and everyone remembered with joy his faith-filled, generous heart.

Those memories showed their love and their faith in the promise of Eternal life. I treasure those moments in my mind as a lesson learned about people whose lives were spent in acts of care for others and in preparation for the life to come after death. I encourage you to take the time to appreciate your loved ones and to spend some time honoring those who have had a special place in your life.

Prayer

Heavenly Father,
Thank You for all our family members and close friends.
Thank You for those whose memories we hold dear in our hearts.
Please keep in Your presence those whom You have called home to You.
May they rest in peace and may they experience Eternal Life.

November 3

Firsts
By Susan Laurie Hutchinson
Today's Scripture: Romans 8:39

"There's a first time for everything." My dad's voice runs through my head as I study the face of my firstborn after he is placed in my arms. I was 20 years old with no clue how to be a mother. This is on-the-job training.

Many aspects of life are essentially on-the-job training. The first time you take a step, ride a bike, get behind the wheel, fall in love, have your heart broken, or get your feelings hurt, the list goes on.

Experiences, the good, the bad, the ones we look forward to, and the ones we dread, mold and train us. As I studied my child's beautiful face, anxious thoughts filled my head about my responsibility for his well-being.

Here I am, now at the other end of the spectrum—looking back through life at a multitude of firsts. The first time I stepped on a platform to speak. The first time I saw my words in print. The first time one of my kids totaled a car. The first time I had chemo. The first time we dropped one off at college. The first time I drove a boat, held a grandchild, and lost a parent. The first time a friend let me down. The first time a friend passed away. The first time I cried with grief, and the first time I leaped with joy.

I think about the most important first. I love Jesus because He first loved me. He is the reason I never face these firsts alone. My hand is always held. My heart is always protected. My spirit is always calmed. Jesus loved me first so that everything else would fall into place.

What a difference that makes in every circumstance of life, whether it's a first or a repeat.

Prayer

Thank You, Lord, for loving me first. Thank You for awakening my awareness of You in the everyday and for always being there for the joys and sorrows of life. Your presence makes all the difference.

November 4

Generational Storytellers
By Jane H. DeLong
Today's Scripture: Psalm 145:4

As I write this, our fifth grandchild is due on November 4th. She already has a name. Her parents have chosen to name her after her paternal great-grandmothers. They named her big sister after her maternal great-grandmothers.

I love that they have chosen to keep the memory of their grandmas alive through the generations. As they raise these girls, my prayer is that they will tell them stories of their great-grandmas that inspire them to emulate some of the best qualities of these women who raised their grandparents.

Generations are important in the Bible. There are whole chapters dedicated to the naming of past generations. God values individuals and the contributions they make to those who come after them. He commands us to tell the next generation about His works in our lives.

Psalm 145:4 paints a picture of a faith that moves forward–flowing from one generation to the next. It's a reminder that what we've seen God do in our lives is not only for our encouragement but also for the building up of those who come after us.

When we speak of God's goodness to the next generation, whether that's our children, grandchildren, or spiritual sons and daughters, we are adding another link in the chain of His story. The lessons we've learned through trials, the moments of answered prayer, and the times when His presence sustained us; these are seeds that can grow into faith in someone else's heart.

The world wants to forget past generations, but God calls us to be storytellers of His faithfulness. Intentionally sharing what He has done isn't just recounting history; it's building hope for the future.

Today, become a generational storyteller and share what God has done in your life with someone in the next generation.

Prayer

Heavenly Father,

Thank You for the people who came before me, those who poured into my life by sharing what You had done for them. Help me to be faithful in sharing my story with those coming behind me. May I be a generational story teller, proclaiming Your mighty works to the next generation.

November 5

Beauty from Ashes
By Angie Hanson
Today's Scripture: Isaiah 61:3

New beginnings often arrive when we least expect them. After seasons of loss, the thought of hope or love returning can feel far away–even impossible. Yet God delights in redeeming broken places, surprising us with joy that grows from the very soil of our sorrow.

Today is a date I once couldn't have imagined celebrating. After the losses I'd endured, the thought of opening my heart again felt both impossible and disloyal. But God has a way of writing stories we never saw coming–and on this day, I married my husband, Chantz, stepping into a new chapter filled with hope, love, and laughter.

Isaiah 61:3 reminds me that God doesn't simply help us get through sorrow; He transforms it. Beauty from ashes doesn't mean the past is erased–the losses are still part of my story. But in His mercy, God weaves new joy into the fabric of our lives.

Loving again didn't diminish the love I still hold for those I've lost; it expanded my capacity to love. It showed me that resilience doesn't mean forgetting–it means trusting God to keep building, even when some foundations have cracked.

If you're in a season where new beginnings feel far away, hold on to the truth that God is still at work. He can take the pieces of a life that feels broken beyond repair and create something you never thought possible. Joy may not look the same as it once did, but it can still be full and good.

Prayer

Father,
Thank You for redeeming the broken places in my life. Help me trust You with my story, even the chapters I don't understand. Fill me with courage to embrace new beginnings and gratitude for the joy You bring. May my life always reflect Your restoring love.

November 6

Losing My Mind in the Waiting
By Brooke B. Stark
Today's Scripture: Isaiah 26:3

We were blessed with a beautiful, healthy daughter. Yet alongside that joy came deep loss—a stillborn child, a miscarriage, and the ache of unanswered prayers. Our hearts longed for more children, and we prayed for years. Surrendering to God's plan wasn't easy, but He gently gave us contentment as we watched others welcome child after child.

The truth is, God alone satisfies the deepest longings of the heart. He may fulfill our desires, or He may lovingly reshape them to match His own. That reshaping is not rejection—it is redirection into His perfect will.

In His time, He opened a new door—foster care. Our first placements, a tender two-year-old girl and a lively three-year-old boy, became a part of our lives forever. The beauty of adoption wove them into our family with a kind of peace only God could orchestrate. Even the timing of our daughter's age made sense—she was old enough to help care for her younger siblings. What once felt like waiting without end suddenly revealed itself as purposeful preparation.

Looking back, I see that God wasn't just working in my circumstances—He was working in me. He taught me to rest in His wisdom, to trust His timing, and to allow Him to write a better story than I ever could have imagined.

Peace is found when I stop grasping for control and instead fix my mind on Him.

Prayer

Father,
Thank You for keeping me in perfect peace when I fix my mind on You. Teach me to trust Your timing and rest in Your will. While I wait, shape my desires to reflect Yours. Fill me with patience and joy.

November 7

God-Led Decisions
By Charmaine Perkins
Today's Scripture: Mark 14:36

Decision-making can be hard. I've often had struggles with indecision. There were times when making the right choice felt just as scary and immobilizing as making the wrong one, especially when the right choice meant I would have to make a sacrifice on my part as well.

I recall feeling the weight of a difficult decision in college, as I tried to choose my major. Another time when I was deciding on the right job, and more hard decisions came when navigating difficult relationships. At each of these times, I was terrified to move forward, initially thinking I would make the wrong choice. Then, I prayed, asked God about what to do, and then asked for the strength to do whatever He was telling me.

As God continued to give me wisdom in my choices, I pushed myself each time to remain confident, knowing He would lead me. The right decision would always be right for me if it were God-led.

When God gives us wisdom regarding our decisions, if life's obstacles, the opinions of others, or our own fears arise, we can stand firm knowing Who is leading us.

Though fearful and overwhelmed with anguish in the garden of Gethsemane, Jesus grounded himself in prayer and submitted to the Father's will. His decision to die for our sins meant great pain was in store for him, but He knew it was the right choice. He pushed himself to make a hard decision that led to glorious victory!

Perhaps you need to make an important decision regarding your family, such as a financial move, a career pivot, or another significant life change. Pray and ask God to lead you in the direction that's right for you. Then, when He does, stand firm on it.

If it's a God-led decision, it's the right decision.

Prayer

Abba Father,
I want to make God-led decisions. I ask for wisdom when making my decisions and submit to Your perfect will, knowing that Your plans for my life are the right plans. Lead me, oh Lord.

November 8

The Strength of Long-suffering
By Matasha Montgomery
Today's Scripture: Job 1:21

Life can be hard, nothing is predictable, and nothing is straightforward, especially when we choose God. An active enemy is waiting to devour, if possible. Trials can boil us in the fire and stretch our faith, and at times push us over the limits. Hardship can be overcome by long-suffering with virtue and steadfastness. Job has set an unparalleled example; As we read his story, it exemplifies long-suffering and faith. The suffering he felt was unimaginable. He was stripped of everything he held dear, yet he was unmovable in his faith.

True wealth lies in our relationship with God. Job's declaration is not one of defeat but of unshakable faith. When we persevere in pain, it can deepen our faith and strengthen our character. These trials can cultivate us like pure gold, purifying our hearts and preparing us for greater blessings.

Let's reflect on when you had to withstand long-suffering. How did you handle that ordeal? Did your faith help you to persevere? Contemplate how these episodes shaped you and strengthened your trust in God. Are you currently facing a difficult situation that requires patience and perseverance? God will hear your prayers. Bring your burdens to him and ask for fortitude, patience, and the grace to keep moving on.

Job's story is a strong testament to faith's power in the face of adversity. It continues to nudge us and let us know we will not understand everything or why we suffer. We must trust in God's sovereign plan. Long-suffering is not an indication of weakness, but of might and vigor. God is with us. Keep that hope, even in the darkest of valleys. Take heart and be still, dear one, you are never alone.

Prayer

Lord,
Help me to know you are near. All I see is chaos, and I only feel my pain and don't feel you around me. It feels like this fallen world is caving in all around me. All I know is loss and suffering. Please, Holy Spirit, give me the strength to stay strong and continue in my faith. With your embrace, I can only hold myself steadfast in your arms.

November 9

Distracted by the Details
By Becca Ramirez
Today's Scripture: Luke 10:38-42

I swear I wasn't a bridezilla, or at least I tried not to be. I just wanted everything to be perfect. The florist kept inserting her own opinions. The church refused to move the drum kit from the stage. I had a vision to execute, so two days before I would marry the love of my life, I was tying ribbons onto wedding favors alone. I was so caught in the details that I isolated myself rather than celebrating with friends and family.

The story of Mary and Martha often portrays Martha in a negative light, as if she were doing something wrong. She wasn't wrong; she was distracted. Scripture tells us that Martha was the one to invite Jesus into her home. She wanted to honor Jesus, and as such, she wanted everything to be perfect. She was caught up in the details but missed the main point. Jesus' comparison to Mary was not meant to shame her, but to redirect her. Mary was sitting at His feet as a disciple, and Jesus welcomed her there. She was open to receiving what He had for her, and He wanted to share it with Martha as well.

How often do we get distracted by the details that we miss the point? We're doing good things, but are we focused on God things? Are we so caught up that we're missing the opportunities to interact more with Jesus?

When I walked down the aisle at my wedding, I wasn't worried about drums on the stage or even the flowers. I was focused on the man who was waiting for me, and that was all that mattered. Consider whether the details are adding value or distracting us from the main thing God has for us today.

Prayer

Jesus,
Please forgive me for the times I've been distracted. Help me focus on You and have an open heart to receive all You have for me. I pray for discernment in separating the God things from the good things and ask that You help me prioritize You today. Thank You for always being there.

November 10

Who Is Watering Your Soil?
By Sara Copley
Today's Scripture: Hebrews 10:24

Recently, my daughter and I attended a mother-daughter retreat, where we planted tiny succulent plants. Succulents are finicky, and I fully expected them to last only a couple of months. To my surprise, nearly four months later, they're still alive!

One morning, I came downstairs to find my husband watering the plants on the windowsill. I couldn't help but smile. In that simple, everyday moment, God spoke to me in a profound way. I realized I had assumed I was doing all the work—yet, just like the succulents, my growth hasn't happened in isolation.

It was a humbling reminder: we rarely flourish on our own.

So I ask you—who is watering your soil?

Life can make us feel like we must achieve everything alone, that growth and success are solely the results of our own effort. But God often places people around us to nurture, encourage, and support us. Every cheer, prayer, text message, act of kindness—these are the waters that nourish our roots, foster growth, and sustain us through the seasons of life.

As we ebb and flow through life, we are reminded that it truly takes a village in all stages of life.

Who are the gardeners in your life? And who might God be calling you to water in return?

Prayer

Father,
Thank You for the hands & hearts You've placed in my life to help me grow. Help me never take for granted those who are watering my soil. Give me gratitude for their love and support. For those who lack encouragement or feel unseen, fill their lives with Your love, guidance, and peace. Help us all to flourish, rooted in You, nurtured by Your grace, and strengthened by Your Spirit.

November 11

Still Waters at Dawn
By Pauline Pyne Arthur
Today's Scripture: Psalm 46:10

Listen! Can you hear it? The birds sing in the early morning, their voices rising with the dawn's first light through the rustling leaves. The lake rests quietly beneath the trees, and a new day unfolds. In these still moments, when you slow down and simply behold, you catch glimpses of His creation: the birds among the branches, the flowers in bloom, the colors of the season. Each detail whispers of His love. He awakens you to cherish the beauty He has given.

Yet even as the morning dawns, the weight of the day presses in. Obligations pile up and seep into your thoughts. Time feels fleeting, and as the holidays draw near, anxiety rises with the urgency to get it all done. But when the world pulls you into a hurry, God calls you back to stillness.

When you step into that sacred place, each pause becomes a declaration of trust that He orders your steps. His Word draws you deeper, and worship rises naturally through prayer, through song, through thanksgiving for all He has done and all He will yet do. When you align your pace with His rhythm, the day unfolds in strength and purpose.

God loves you! He cares for every circumstance and calls you to spend time in His presence. There, in the quiet moments with Him, your soul is refreshed as you cast all your care on Him. Through the Holy Spirit, His grace and peace abound! As you leave that quiet space, your heart feels light, your spirit renewed. You have stood at the throne of grace, embraced by the love of Jesus.

Where in your day can you create a sacred pause to rest in His presence?

Prayer

God,
Thank You for Your gentle presence that greets us with each new dawn. As we begin this day, open our eyes to what You want us to see, our ears to what You want us to hear, and our lips to what You want us to say. Truly, Your mercies are new every morning, and Your grace is our refuge and strength.

November 12

Take a Nap & Eat a Cookie
By Shelley Groves
Today's Scripture: 1 Kings 19:4-8

I've been a teacher for a long time. I've been a student for even longer. I've been a wife, a mom, a minister, a caregiver, and a friend to the grieving. All that to say, I know what it's like to be tired. So tired that it doesn't matter if there are dirty dishes in the sink or my teeth aren't brushed before I crash on the nearest horizontal surface. The kind of tiredness that surpasses exhaustion. The weariness that comes when you can't take another step.

As a college professor, I often see this kind of tiredness hit students around this time of year. The adrenaline that kicks in right before finals isn't quite here yet. Thanksgiving feels miles away, and fall break is a distant memory. It's hard to push through when you've got a bad case of the "don't want to's".

Poor Elijah knew this feeling. He'd been doing what God had called him to do. He had been bold to stand against the prophets of Baal and saw God bring down fire from Heaven to burn up his offering. He had defied Ahab and Jezebel. He was obedient. But he was tired. In his weariness, he ran away and prayed that God would let him die. Not long after this, he hears from God in a still, small voice after amazing manifestations of God's power.

However, before that happens, scripture says that he lay down and went to sleep. An angel woke him and told him to eat. Then, he went to sleep again. God knows we need rest. He even included honoring the Sabbath in the 10 Commandments. Sometimes the most effective spiritual warfare is to take a nap and eat a cookie.

Prayer

Lord,
Please give me wisdom to rest. In a world where I feel the need to give of myself and help others, help me remember to take care of myself so that I am able to minister from a healthy place. Guard my heart from guilt that would condemn me and let me hear Your voice instead.

November 13

An Accomplished Fact
By Elizabeth Clark
Today's Scripture: John 20:22

Understanding the Holy Spirit can feel complex, but this verse simplifies it. The Lord's breathing of the Spirit in John 20 is for life and inner strength, and the blowing of the Spirit in Acts 2 is for authority. These are accomplished facts for every believer. Just as we don't need to feel His crucifixion to believe it, we don't need a specific feeling to believe we have received the Spirit.

The Holy Spirit is an accomplished fact in your life, not a feeling you have to chase. This truth gives us great optimism. We are fully equipped for both our inner life and outward service. The breath of the Spirit gives us the very life of Christ, and the blowing of the Spirit gives us the power to move in His will. We can face any challenge with the confidence that we have everything we need.

I have often wrestled with this, waiting for some grand feeling to confirm the Spirit was truly within me. I'd read about the disciples and wonder why my experience wasn't so dramatic. But the Lord gently reminded me, "Do you believe I died for you, even when you don't feel it? It's an accomplished fact." This same principle applies to the Spirit. I no longer have to feel a rush of wind or an intense emotion to know.

Don't be discouraged if you don't feel a dramatic spiritual experience. You are equipped with both the life of Christ and the authority to move for Him. The Bible is the report; your faith is the key. Stand firm on the fact that the Spirit is an accomplished reality.

How does the understanding that the Holy Spirit is an "accomplished fact" change your perspective on spiritual dryness or a lack of feeling in your walk with God?

Prayer

Lord,
Thank You for the accomplished facts of the Spirit's breathing and blowing. We choose to believe Your report and not rely on our feelings. Strengthen us by the Spirit of life within us and empower us with the Spirit of power upon us.

November 14

The Heart of His Timing
By Irina Brcic
Today's Scripture: Ecclesiastes 3:11

I walked into a coffee shop and was greeted by a smiling friend, ready to congratulate me on our second baby. I was thankful, but I dreaded the question: "So, what are you having?" When I said I didn't know yet but was hoping for a girl, he replied, "It's going to be another boy. I just don't see you having a girl."

His words stung. Inside, I thought, "Who do you think you are?" I prayed that God would prove him wrong and give me the daughter I longed for. For months, it consumed my thoughts. When the ultrasound confirmed that it was another boy, I was crushed. Guilt and shame weighed heavily—I didn't know how to reconcile my disappointment with the gift of a child I knew I should treasure.

Yet slowly, God worked on my heart. He reminded me that every child is fearfully and wonderfully made (Psalm 139:14) and that His gifts are always good (James 1:17). My son was not "instead of" a daughter; he was exactly who God intended him to be, a perfect reflection of His plan for our family.

Then, five years later—on November 14—the Lord surprised us with the sweetest gift: a baby girl. At that moment, I saw God's timing in a new light. His "wait" had never been a "no." It was an invitation to trust Him more deeply.

If you find yourself in a waiting season, take heart—you are not alone. From Abraham to Hannah, Scripture reminds us that God always delivers in His perfect time. Hold on, friend. Your longings, tears, and whispered prayers are seen. The One who writes your story is faithful, and His timing—though often mysterious—always proves good.

Prayer

Lord,
Thank You that You see the desires of our hearts even when others don't understand. Teach us to trust Your timing and to receive every gift with gratitude.

November 15

Just When You Think It's Over
By Elise Daly Parker
Today's Scripture: Isaiah 43:19

I stood in my dining room. Outdated cabbage-rose wallpaper had been stripped from the walls. Spaces where the antique dining table and chestnut buffet stood were empty. Sheer curtains replaced the damask drapes.

I lamented the quiet. Once full of four lively daughters—singing, laughing, arguing—the house felt hollow. So did my heart. Kids grown, my husband and I were leaving our home of 24 years. How could this chapter be over? What's next? How can anything ahead be as wonderful as what's behind?

Milestone celebrations once filled the rooms—holidays, birthdays, graduations—along with the everyday activities that infuse a family home. A strong breeze fluttered the curtains, shaking me from my memory trance. I sensed a still small voice, "You're closing this door; I'm opening new windows." I remained quiet, reflecting. Blessed assurance settled my mind, body, and spirit.

My husband and I had been cranky and impatient with each other recently. I felt sad, sifting through boxes, books, trinkets, deciding alone what would stay or go. Junk to others was treasure to me. How could I part with them?

I felt a shift, and the promise of a new day dawning. There was so much ahead—time to embrace the future.

I shared my God encounter with my husband. We had a long talk, laced with laughter and tears. We could move ahead, together. Our focus pivoted to our next chapter. With a renewed sense of teamwork, side by side, we sorted through our children's old books, papers, and artwork.

Dread about downsizing turned to anticipation. We would find our next home—ideal for us, with space for kid and grandkid visits. We found the perfect place! That first weekend, our kids and extended family came to celebrate among unpacked boxes. We were already making new memories.

Prayer

Dear Lord,

Sometimes we reach a crossroad. We're confused about how to navigate what's next. We feel fearful and anxious about the unknown. But you are always doing something new and have good plans for us. Help us remember this and trust you to lead the way.

November 16

He Heals the Brokenhearted
By Brooke B. Stark
Today's Scripture: Psalm 34:18

The healing of the Lord is unlike anything else—it is deep, complete, and reaches into every hidden place of our lives. His restoration doesn't just touch the surface; it seeps into the wounds we carry, the griefs we cannot put into words, and the burdens that feel too heavy to bear. While ultimate wholeness will be fulfilled in eternity with Him, His Spirit is already at work today, bringing healing to our hearts and minds.

As we walk closely with Jesus, we discover that He is always working for our good and His glory. He invites us to abide in Him—resting at His feet, soaking in His Word, and allowing His presence to soothe the raw places within us. This abiding is not striving; it is simply letting Him work inside us.

When facing grief, trauma, or wounds that feel overwhelming, it is wise to seek counsel and take steps toward healing. Yet, true restoration always begins with the Lord. He knows us more intimately than we know ourselves, and He is faithful to mend what feels beyond repair.

Christ's power not only forgives sin but also heals the scars it leaves behind. Though life in a fallen world still holds hardship, He gives daily strength and victory, one step at a time, until the day we see Him face to face.

May His nearness comfort you today, and may His healing presence bring restoration to every hidden pocket of pain in your heart.

Prayer

Dear Lord,
Thank You for seeing every tear and knowing every hurt. Please bring healing to the broken places in my heart. Restore me with Your peace and help me forgive as I have been forgiven. Let Your love shine through me.

November 17

It's the Most Wonderful Time to Praise
By Angie Leigh Edelen
Today's Scripture: Philippians 4:6-7

I love November because collectively, as a society, we are reminded to be thankful. This gives us a reset and time of unity that is not always so obvious.

Biblically, God tells us to praise Him in all things! When we walk through the valley, it can be easy to struggle with knowing what to say when we start to pray.

As a fellow valley traveler, I can assure you, He will grab your hand and walk you up that hill to the other side. Praise will flow out of your mouth like water trickling in a stream! He is faithful, and His promises are ones that you can take to the bank. For every valley I have found myself in, He has been there and true to who the Bible says He is.

We have praise, no matter what our physical eyes may see, in Jesus. He died and was resurrected for the good days and bad! Even if this season is hard I feel you. I have been there too. You can always have hope in the one who is our hope, Jesus.

Prayer

Jesus, I thank You for Your friend who reads this today. I ask, Lord, that You show us Your love and hope in the midst of our day. Father, show us Your hand in all that we see as we navigate through our path.

November 18

Hidden But Seen
By Sarah Odom
Today's Scripture: Romans 8:28

Have you ever found yourself in an unforeseen situation and unsure what to do next? Sometimes our hearts take us to places we never thought we would go. When that happens, do you ever want to hide from God and hope that He will not find you?

I found myself in an unplanned pregnancy at the age of 17 and wanted to run and hide from everyone and God. As a young high school girl who had her whole life ahead of her, what were my options if I wasn't ready to be a mother?

After reading Romans 8:28, God instilled a courageous heart within me to walk into New Life Pregnancy Center and learn more about adoption. This was not going to be easy. The thought of placing my baby with another family and the unknown of what happens after, would be terrifying. But I couldn't let fear overtake me. I needed to be fearless and trust that God would work out the details for not only me, but also for my baby. Fast forward 20 years, and my son and I have a beautiful relationship! God found me in my hiding place and created beauty out of the brokenness.

As much as we may want to run away from God and the situation we are in, we must have faith, hope, and trust that He is working out the details for our good.

So today, no matter what is happening, know that God loves you deeply and is working out the details. Over time, you will see something even more beautiful if you keep your eyes on him. He is our hope, and He is our peace.

Prayer

Lord Jesus,
Thank You for Your grace, mercy, and unconditional love through a time of crisis in my life. I pray for those reading this today–that Your Spirit fills them with courage, faith, and hope. Guard our hearts and minds as we journey through the day. May we focus our eyes on you.

November 19

Here Comes the Bride
By Trudy Bosman
Today's Scripture: Revelation 19:6-8

I was attending a Bible college in Michigan. It was my birthday, and my boyfriend took me out to the airport restaurant to eat. When the meal was over, he said to me, "I talked to your dad, and he said it was ok." Then he pulled out a small box and asked, "Will you marry me?" My heart was pounding and swelled with joy as I said, "Yes!"

Later, as we drove back to the dorm, I thought about the joy and anticipation I felt for the wedding and the life that was to come with Steve. Wow! This was like the joy and anticipation we should have for the wedding supper that is being prepared for Christ and His bride, the church, for me.

Just as Steve chose me to be his bride and share his life, Christ has chosen me, as part of the church, to be His bride and be with Him forever. Steve had talked to my father, but Jesus willingly gave his life so that I could be his bride. I would wear a special wedding dress on our wedding day. Christ made sure I would be clothed in fine linen, bright and pure as His bride.

I hope I remember this every time I attend a wedding. As I see the bride smiling and eagerly joining the one she loves, may I be reminded of the heavenly bridegroom who waits for me.

Prayer

Jesus,
Thank You that You loved me enough to pay for my sins. Thank You for choosing me to be Your bride. I look forward to that wedding feast You are preparing and to being with you forever.

November 20

When God Restores What Is Broken
By Julie D Davis
Today's Scripture: Psalm 143:8-10

There are moments in life when everything changes in a heartbeat. I remember sitting in the middle of a storm I never thought I would face. The dreams I once held seemed shattered, and I couldn't understand why God had allowed me to follow this path. Questions filled my mind—Did He see me? Did He care? Had He forgotten His promises?

Yet in those quiet, painful mornings, I began to notice something. God was near. Through His Word, I found comfort. Verses I had read before came alive with new meaning, reminding me that He had not turned away. Slowly, the heavy fog of disappointment and sorrow began to lift, and in its place, God planted hope.

It wasn't instant, and it wasn't easy. But little by little, He restored my soul. He gave me the strength to face each day and reminded me that His plans are always good, even when I don't understand them. My days were filled with a joy for life I hadn't had for quite some time. Then, on this date, in His time, He surprised me with blessings beyond anything I could have imagined—including the gift of a loving, godly husband to walk beside me in this new season of life. Together we serve Him with grateful hearts, attempting to live each day to the fullest, knowing that His ways are higher than ours. Although we don't always understand God's ways, we can trust He loves us and wants the very best for our lives.

When life feels overwhelming, remember this: God sees your pain, hears your cries, and longs to walk with you and restore your soul. He truly does provide us with abundance (Ephesians 3:20). Trust Him—He is faithful and working for your good, even now.

Prayer

Father,
Thank You for never leaving me, even in the hardest seasons. Help me to trust You when life feels uncertain and to rest in Your arms of love that never fails. Restore my joy, renew my hope, and keep me close to You each day.

November 21

The Reciprocal Law of Refreshment
By Michelle Barringer
Today's Scripture: Philemon 7

On this day, I became a grandma. I remember the anticipation. My heart burst when I held my first grandchild, a little boy who changed our world and filled it with joy. So much so that I referred to him as my "Joy Bomb."

I remember calling his parents several times that first year, asking if he could play. My heart instantly refreshed spending time with him. Now, nine years later, I have half a dozen grandchildren, and each one refreshes my heart.

Recently, I read Philemon, a one-chapter book in the Bible. Verse seven prodded my heart. Paul was writing to his friend Philemon, Apphia, and Archippus, a fellow brother in Christ. Paul commended them for refreshing fellow believers.

Can you imagine how they must have felt reading that their love gave Paul great joy and encouragement? After all, it was Paul who was known to be the refresher. That must have refreshed them, too. Did you know the Bible says that whoever refreshes others will themselves be refreshed (Proverbs 11:25)? This is the reciprocal law of refreshment.

Have you considered that when your heart needs refreshing, there's a cure for it? Refresh someone else's heart, and yours will be refreshed, too.

Recently, I was challenged to ask some people in my life if I was refreshing to them. I want to be a heart refresher, a joy bomb, just like my grandchildren are to me. But am I?

Are you a heart refresher? Can you name three people who would say you refresh their hearts?

And who refreshes your heart? Name those people. Then do what Paul did, let them know.

Let's become heart refreshers, joy bombs to others. In return, I'm confident our hearts will be refreshed and filled with joy, too.

Prayer

Father God,
Refresh my heart and help me to refresh others, too. May joy and encouragement flow through me so that others may experience refreshment. May I reciprocate joy and encouragement just like You designed.

November 22

Is Life a Dash or an Ellipsis?
By U. R. Heard
Today's Scripture: Genesis 1:27-28, 2:15-17, 3:6, 3:17-19

I numbly stared at the two dates, a dash between them.

I wanted to hold on to the belief that God sovereignly holds the times of our lives in His hands. But the dash with the second date under our son's name pulled mercilessly against that truth.

It had been years since the car accident, yet I was still struggling with the brevity of our son's life. It felt cut short. Premature.

Over the years, I had taken many broken pieces to my heavenly Father in prayer. But this question persisted in my heart, unasked.

With tears streaming down my face, I finally poured out what had been plaguing me. "He was finally serving You. Why did You cut short his ability to serve You?"

He is still serving Me.

The prompting to my heart surprised me. Could that be true? Did that line up with Scripture? I was reminded that God gave Adam & Eve work to do in Genesis 1-2 before the curse came in Genesis 3, so work itself is not part of the curse. Sweat and difficulty in our work are part of the curse, but not work itself. Because work was enjoyed before the curse, it is likely that we will have opportunities to enjoy productivity in heaven and eternity.

It was time to apply an eternal perspective to our son's life. My heart felt lighter as I pondered the encouragement in this new perspective. He didn't experience a job ending. He had a job transfer! He is still serving the Lord! Present tense.

The dash between the two dates was not his reality. Jesus's salvation had added an eternal ellipsis to his life. His life and work are ongoing and will always be throughout eternity. I wonder what he is doing today!

Prayer

Father, You know all things. You see all things, even in our hearts. Prompt us with any question or hurt that is buried in our hearts, keeping us from Your hope. You are the God of all hope. Speak to our hearts from Your eternal perspective as we face loss. Especially the heartbreaking loss of a child.

November 23

Who Goes There?
By Kati von Schmitten
Today's Scripture: John 14:26-28

My aunt tapped away, photo after photo. I didn't recognize a single person. It was a Thanksgiving tradition to whip out the photo albums and pore over the memories. One small problem: I struggle to recognize faces. I was in my twenties before I learned the name: prosopagnosia. Show me a photo of my friends or family, out of context, and I won't know who's who. As I grew, I learned to recognize people by their body language, hairstyles, accessories, and even clothing.

Recognizing the Holy Spirit works similarly. We can't see this presence with our eyes, and guidance doesn't always come in bold, obvious ways. Instead, we learn to notice subtle cues: the peace that settles our hearts, gentle nudges in our decisions, the conviction in our conscience, and the fruit that grows in our lives. Even when circumstances around us change, this presence remains recognizable if we pay attention.

But what does that actually mean? It's that "gut" feeling. Intuition, gentle warning, an inner pull, these are all ways the Holy Spirit moves. It's not the ego urging you to speak harshly; it's the sense of peace saying to act in grace. It's not the desire to gossip; it's the prompting to quietly bless someone who needs it. The Holy Spirit aligns us with God's presence and guidance if we just choose to listen.

Just as I had to learn to recognize a friend, recognizing the Spirit requires practice, patience, and attentiveness. Over time, those subtle nudges become familiar. It gets easier. When we learn to notice them, we begin to walk in a deeper rhythm with God, responding with wisdom, love, and grace.

Prayer

Heavenly Father,
Thank You for sending Your Spirit to guide me, even when I cannot see or hear in the ways my eyes and ears expect. Open my heart to recognize Your gentle nudges, the quiet whispers of peace, and the subtle ways You lead me toward Your will.

November 24

Blessings Every Day
By Laurie Ostby Kehler
Today's Scripture: Psalm 103:2

Today is the night before my birthday. And if you're like me, sometimes we want our loved ones to make a big deal out of us.

Secretly, we all want to be noticed. We all want to matter. And all too frequently, we are let down in our expectations.

A few years ago, I decided that that year's birthday would be different. I wasn't going to subtly hint at certain gifts or events to happen. I wasn't going to hand over the keys to my happiness on whether or not I was celebrated enough. I would be proactive.

I wrote down a list of all the things I was grateful for. And the number had to add up to my age. So at 45, there were 45 reasons. At 100, (God willing) there will be 100 reasons to have a "happy" birthday.

Since this date is close to Thanksgiving, it's the perfect time to recount your blessings—whether it's your birthday or not. Choosing your age helps you move beyond "family and friends" as we so often repeat around the table.

The Bible encourages us to note these things in Psalm 103:2.

You can start with all the things you take for granted: a roof over your head, something to eat, the ability to see beauty, the ability to hear the birds, not living in a war zone, the list is endless. Then you can move on to all the promises of God in Scripture, such as never leaving or forsaking you (Hebrews 13:5).

The Psalms are full of instances of gratitude. Dig through them for inspiration. As your list grows, your happiness and hope grow, because you'll see how great His faithfulness is.

Prayer

Thank You, Heavenly Father, for Your kindness and faithfulness all the days of my life. Help me to see all the blessings that surround me each day. Teach me to notice all the little things that You put in place to delight us—birdsong, fragrance, and laughter. And thank You for your Word, filled with promises of steadfast love.

November 25

A Noble Wife
By Melissa Lindsey
Today's Scripture: Proverbs 31:10

Our son and daughter-in-law's wedding was scheduled for June 2020. Plans were made, a venue was booked, and friends and family were coming from out of town. Everything was ready to go. Then the COVID pandemic decided otherwise.

The wedding day - possibly the biggest and most important day of a woman's entire life.

When the shutdown occurred and the venue was no longer an option, our son called three weeks before the wedding to ask if they could move the service and the reception to our backyard. My first thought was, "We have only three weeks to get ready for a wedding?" followed immediately by, "Oh my goodness, how is Sydney going to take this?"

As it turns out, Sydney was okay. Disappointed, yes – but Bridezilla she was not. She expressed that being married in the company of close friends and family was what mattered most, and she let go of everything else. This was the first of many times I've been more than proud of her for how she has handled an unexpected and less-than-desirable situation.

Proverbs 31:10 tells us that a noble wife is worth far more than rubies. She is diligent, wise, and compassionate with a spirit of service and love. She creates a home filled with peace and happiness.

Our culture sometimes measures worth by worldly standards, but the Bible reminds us that actual value lies in our character and our faithfulness. Earthly treasures will be left behind, but our character and faithfulness endure forever.

Prayer

Dear Lord,
Thank You for the Bible, Your holy word, and for showing what it means to be a noble wife. Please give us the strength to encourage those around us. Let us build others up with our words and let our actions reflect Your love and grace.

November 26

Hope in God, Alone
By Janet Rico-Everett
Today's Scripture: Psalm 46:11

I ticked off everything I was doing right:
- Spending daily personal time with God.
- Eating right, walking five miles a day, and losing weight.
- Consistently attending the fertility doctor appointments.
- Enlisting everyone to bathe our request in prayer.

Nothing was working, and with every monthly reminder, I grew increasingly bitter. Why would God deny me a baby?

One evening at my home Bible study, I listened to the lesson I didn't do. Lay down all my hopes? That sounded faithless and defeatist. When an elderly saint revealed that she had miscarried and knew how I felt, I said acidly, "Yes, but you will get to see your baby in Heaven one day." The next day, one of the guests gave me a tongue-lashing for the way I responded, ending with, "You need a come-to-Jesus with the Savior, Himself!" That evening, I cried on my dining room floor for eight hours, wrestling with the Lord. And all that time, the Holy Spirit brought to my mind, "Put your hope in God."

My hope was misplaced. God is not our Spiritual Santa, there to fulfill our desires, even when they are good ones, but only those that fall within the boundaries of His will. Focusing our hope on what we want binds our faith to the event, object, or circumstance instead of God Himself. Only He knows the life events that will benefit us and build His kingdom. In the meantime, He can fill every hole and satisfy every longing with Himself, but only if we let Him.

That night, I laid down my hopes to become a mother and allowed God alone to be my hope. Two years later, after thirteen years of marriage, without planning or preparation, God gave us a son on November 26, 2003, Ian Keith Everett.

Prayer

Father God,
I confess that my hope turned into an obsession, and my fellowship with you became a means to an end instead of my greatest joy. Forgive me for not trusting you to satisfy my emptiness. Fill me with Yourself until no holes exist. For my good and Your Glory, I surrender my desires to Your will.

November 27

Choosing Joy
By James Hatcher
Today's Scripture: James 1:2

On the surface, this scripture may not seem to provide much solace during our painful times. However, we cannot miss God's sufficiency in this scripture in our time of trial.

It's so easy to miss what God is saying to us. God does not just command us to do something; he also says, "I see what you're going through." God acknowledges us when He says 'count it' because He knows what we are going through isn't joyful. He knows it is messy and hurtful.

Jesus is looking at the same thing as you and acknowledging that it's a mess and there is pain. This is amazing! Jesus isn't asking us to pretend it didn't happen or justify it. And hear this: he isn't saying it didn't happen! He is saying, yes, that's terrible, but it's mine. He is telling you, 'I want that.' He is whispering, 'I can do something with that.' Be encouraged; your Jesus came to this earth to pay the penalty he paid, so he could say, "All your pain is mine!"

It's easy to disregard verses like James 1:2 as cliché in our darkest hours. We may even want to use them as an excuse to distance ourselves from the gentle presence of the Holy Spirit. In these moments, we need to remember that Jesus wants us to turn to Him and choose joy–not joy because the situation is joyful, but because He is joyful. He wants us to be like David: turn to him, surrender our response, and choose His joy.

Prayer

Prayer.
Lord, thank You for acknowledging my hurt. Thank You for meeting me in my darkest time. Jesus, I surrender all the pain, hardship, and brokenness to you. Please help me find Your joy and Your peace in all my hurt.

November 28

Living in the Fullness of Eternity
By Shawn-Dennise Parisi
Today's Scripture: John 5:24

The news came in the early morning hours; Connor had taken his life. So many times, we prayed God would save him from himself, but this never crossed our minds. As I entered a home filled with insurmountable grief, I heard a father calmly sharing the news no parent would ever want to speak and the sobs of a mother's shattered heart. My thoughts turned towards the future. Every photo taken would have a person missing. Every celebration a void. The hopes and dreams these parents had for Connor had become a never-ending chasm of grief.

Eternity is not something to hope for; it is something to have hope in. Jesus says, in John 5:24, "Truly, truly, I say to you, whoever hears my word and believes him who sent me has eternal life. He does not come into judgment, but has passed from death to life." Connor, together with Jesus, lived in the fullness of eternity.

The impact of losing Connor is felt every day. His legacy serves as an enduring example of eternal life. Connor's desire to aid others with mental health and addiction issues continues through his family's work to remove the stigma and support those in need. These words from Connor's heart, "You are loved, you are never alone, I believe we all have an impact," speak the truth of what eternity is.

Eternity thinking is not a concept. It's our Kingdom Calling, the impact our lives have on individuals and the world. Connor understood his kingdom calling. The inception of Honor Connor has allowed his family to embrace an eternal perspective, help others, and fulfill Connor's kingdom calling and eternal purpose.

As we hold onto the hope of God's eternal perspective, who has set eternity in the human heart, we are offered assurance amid uncertainty.

Prayer

Father God, We praise You for Your glorious grace and unfailing love. As we walk into this day, may the joy of the Lord be our strength, knowing the confusion of this world does not reflect Your glorious kingdom and our eternal home. May we reflect Your light and be an expression of Your love for all to see.

November 29

Deeply Rooted
By Brenda Kaker
Today's Scripture: Lamentations 3:22-23

Years ago, I had the privilege of traveling to Israel. One afternoon, standing on the mountaintop of Masada, I looked out across the vast wilderness that surrounds the Dead Sea. It appeared so silent, desolate, and lifeless. Yet even in its barrenness, it possessed a strange beauty. I remembered the date tree farms we had passed on our way—a reminder that life was near—but from where I stood, I could see only wilderness.

As we descended from the mountain and traveled along the edge of the sea, the Lord opened my eyes to something I hadn't noticed before: scattered across the dry land were several trees living in the midst of the desert. I wondered how they could survive in such a harsh place. With no river nearby and no irrigation system to sustain them, they must have roots reaching deep—drawing from hidden springs below the surface. And in that quiet moment, the Lord whispered to my heart: "That is how deeply you must be rooted in Me. Even in the wilderness, if your roots go deep, you will live and thrive."

I recalled Colossians 2:6-7: "...as you received Christ Jesus the Lord, so walk in him, 7 rooted and built up in him and established in the faith...."

Friend, the wilderness is not always what it seems. From afar, it may look empty and overwhelming, but if we look closer, we see signs of God's presence—His quiet leading, His steadfast love, His hidden springs of life. Perhaps the wilderness is not a place of abandonment but an invitation to sink our roots deeper into His unfailing love. His mercies are new every morning. His faithfulness never wavers, and we can discover the sweetness of His lovingkindness even in the desert places.

Prayer

Heavenly Father, I praise You for the gift of a new day and for Your goodness and mercy. Remind me of Your faithfulness, and nourish my soul with the sweetness of Your lovingkindness, even when the wilderness feels overwhelming. May my heart rest in You, and may my steps today reflect Your beauty, grace, and truth.

November 30

A Mother's Legacy Continues
By Leslie Bake
Today's Scripture: 2 Timothy 1:5

She wasn't training for a marathon, but just before mom went for a run, I remember watching her spend a few minutes sifting index cards, and when I asked what they were, she told me they were her Bible verses. She would select one card, pocket it, and leave. I didn't realize it as a self-absorbed teenager, but jogging with scripture in hand was her time with the Lord.

Throughout my high school and college years, she wrote letters to me every week, which included scripture, encouragement, and her prayers for me.

Four years ago this month, she passed away from ovarian cancer, and I discovered three rubber-band-bound packs of those scripture-filled index cards tucked behind some books earmarked for Goodwill on her bookshelf. I had no idea she had that many and kept them for more than 30 years!

Now that I have two children of my own, I am deeply grateful for my mom's legacy of faith. Today, I do my best to challenge my young ones to learn scripture. A whiteboard is mounted in our kitchen on which I write a short "verse of the week." At dinner time, my second-grader and sixth-grader see the verse, and I point it out, asking one of them to read it out loud. On the headboard of each child's bed, I scotch-taped index cards with the same verse on the kitchen whiteboard. Part of our bedtime routine involves reinforcing the verse and praying it. They may not yet understand the meaning or purpose of this, but we are starting spiritual conversations in this way, and I pray that they are internalizing God's word at a younger age than I did.

Prayer

Dear Heavenly Father, Thank You for providing me with a Godly mother who modeled for me the discipline of memorizing scripture. I pray for the wisdom and creativity to do the same for my children, and I pray that they understand and appreciate these conversations and experience Your presence in their lives as they grow.

December

December 1

Living Proof of Grace
By D'Toya Dove
Today's Scripture: Isaiah 43:2

Sometimes the greatest evidence of God's grace is this: you're still standing. You've walked through fire, pressed through pain, and survived seasons that felt like they would break you. But they didn't. Why? Because grace carried you.

Isaiah 43:2 doesn't say we'll avoid deep waters or fiery trials; it promises we won't be consumed by them. And if you're reading this, that means you've lived through things that tried to take you out... but didn't. You're not just surviving, you're becoming.

Maybe you're still in the middle of your storm. Maybe you're walking into your breakthrough. Either way, you are living proof of God's sustaining power. Your story, the one with the broken pieces, the hidden tears, and the quiet victories, is evidence of His faithfulness.

So when fear tries to creep back in, when old voices whisper doubt or defeat, remember this: you're not who you used to be. And you're not walking alone. The same God who brought you through before is the same God who is carrying you now.

You are living proof of grace.

Prayer

Heavenly Father, Thank You for carrying me through seasons I thought I wouldn't survive. Thank You that I am living proof of Your grace and unfailing love. When anything contrary to Your Word tries to rise, help me remember all You've brought me through and to combat every lie with Your truth.

December 2

The Beauty of Yes
By Ada Bontrager
Today's Scripture: Matthew 7:13-14

You get to decide which path in this life you want to venture down.

One path has few people traveling its narrow trail. It's quiet, serene, and peaceful like walking in the morning mist with only the sound of your footsteps.

The other path looks fun and so enticing, with loud crowds of people drawing you in and encouraging you to join them. It can be intriguing and it can be tempting...

What is the difference between these two paths?

One path will lead you to life everlasting, and the other to destruction and death.

On the crowded path, you can do everything you want and live your life as you wish. You can follow your dreams, go after all the riches of the world, chase fame, luxuries, companionship, and what seems like freedom. There is no one to hold you back. This life seems easy and exciting. The gate at the end of this path is wide, and many have chosen this path.

The other path is peaceful with gentle guidance, structure, and a sense of order. And there He is..your gentle Savior, Jesus, softly inviting you to come and follow Him. He doesn't say it will be easy, but He promises to walk with you every step of the way. On the beautiful, narrow way, you get to experience so many wonders – miracles, healing, signs, and moments that reveal God's power, all flowing from your faith. All because you said YES to following Jesus and to enjoying a wonderful life everlasting.

Prayer

Heavenly Father, I say Yes to You and to Your ways! Please give me the courage to stay on this narrow path that leads to life. And please give me the boldness to invite others to come with me.

December 3

Unexpected Redemption
By Jane H. DeLong
Today's Scripture: Isaiah 9:6

Watching my children become parents has been a great joy, but none so much as our middle child. He is affectionately known as our double-stuffed Oreo since he's the middle of five children. He is the child who outwardly pushed the limits and sent us to our knees more than any other! But through it all, God promised we would see His redemption in Andrew's life.

Andrew introduced us to his new girlfriend in 2021, and when she left, he told me, "I think I could marry her." The change in his lifestyle became evident the more time he spent with Maddison, and in October 2023, they were married. On December 3, 2024, their first child was born. Watching Andrew with Lenorah Nell has been so beautiful. God's gift of redemption seldom comes the way we expect.

When God set in motion His plan to redeem humanity, He didn't send a king. He sent a baby. A small, fragile child, dependent on another human, would be the One to bring redemption.

From the moment of the first promise in Genesis 3:15, all of history waited for Him. Generations passed, kings rose and fell, prophets spoke and were silenced. And then, in the stillness of a Bethlehem night, redemption cried His first cry.

God's rescue plan came swaddled in human skin, showing us that His ways are not our ways. Through the weakness of a child came the strength to save the world. God entrusted the power to defeat sin and death to a Child born in a stable. His unexpected redemption.

Today, look for God's unexpected ways as you go about your normal routine.

Prayer

Father God,
Thank You for sending Your Son to redeem me. Help me embrace Your ways, even when they come in unexpected packages. Keep my heart tender, my faith strong, and my eyes fixed on Jesus - the Child who grew up to become my Redeemer.

December 4

Knowing God
By Dava R. Caballero
Today's Scripture: 1 John 3:1a

I love babies. Something happens to me when I set eyes on them. Emotions overwhelm me, and I tear up with a mix of joy, awe, and gratitude for the gift of new life. Before I had my own grandchildren, I was curious how different the emotions might be. I'd long heard others proclaim the overwhelming joy a grandchild had brought them. Experiencing greater emotions than I already held for newborns seemed outlandish.

When the time came, it was indeed a joyous occasion. Watching my daughter give birth affected my very soul. Yes, I cherished my beautiful grandson, but it didn't feel much different than the love I felt for all babies. I kept it all in my heart and took note. Fortunately, I was able to help care for him when my daughter reluctantly returned to work after maternity leave. That is when the miracle happened.

This child wrapped his tiny little hands around my heart in a way no other child had – even my own. I wondered what the actual difference was and how my perspective had changed. While journaling with Jesus one morning, it dawned on me. It was our relationship. That's what changed. That's what was different. I began to know him, and he began to know me.

It also became apparent that this relationship differed in that it was free of the trappings and insecurities of raising my own progeny. I could joyfully give of myself and then leave him in the care of his parents.

This attitude of joy and surrender models our relationship with our heavenly Father. We can have a sweet experience with Him and know Him on a certain level. But as we spend intimate moments with Jesus, we encounter Him more fully. Then we experience that precious holy communion.

Prayer

Heavenly Father, Thank You for Your great love. Thank You for pursuing a relationship with us. Help us to grow in grace and knowledge of who You are and to rest in surrendering our lives to You as Your beloved children.

December 5

Unified
By Erica Lewis
Today's Scripture: Galatians 3:28

Being a pastor's kid my whole life, I've seen a lot of division within churches. Instead of joining together for the sole purpose of worshipping God, people come to see their cliques and snub those not in their group.

Yet, Jesus doesn't support cliques, and Paul made that point when he declared we could no longer separate ourselves based on things like status or gender.

The reason we can't support cliques is that division is against the very nature of God. How can we worship God if we're going against His nature? Jesus avoids division by looking past how we define ourselves. He looks at me and He says I'm His beloved, much like the two lovers declare about each other throughout the Song of Solomon. He doesn't turn to me and declare, "My beloved female, theatre buff, writer, pastor, blogger, teacher!" and then turn to you and spew a string of facts about you, clarifying which group of people you should be consorting with.

Rather, He sees you and loves you just the same as me, no divides needed. To be unified in worship for God, we need to let go of the labels of our careers, hobbies, and likes and dislikes. Instead, we should love God so much, following His word and His truth, that all that matters is that we're all God's beloved and striving to live with Him.

After all, Scripture calls us to be unified and glorify God through our unity (Romans 15:5-6). Today, rather than striving to separate yourself by what you do, remember that you're God's beloved. Your purpose in life is to honor Him with your life. When our priority is living for Him, it becomes much easier to live in unity as people of God.

Prayer

God, Thank You that I'm not a sum of what I do. Please help me to see myself and others the way that You do. Remind me daily that we are all Your beloved. Alert me to the divisions I make and help me to be a person of unity who strives to honor You. Amen.

December 6

Legacy of Love
By Susan Laurie Hutchinson
Today's Scripture: Joel 1:3

My mom was 94 when she passed. With only six days' notice, it was a surprise. Living alone in a six-bedroom home, she drove, shopped, cooked, gardened, and FaceTimed family. Five months prior, she kayaked with my sister!

Multiple myeloma wasn't on our radar. Mom never complained about pain, until one day I saw her struggle putting on socks. Alarmed, I drove her to the hospital.

After three days, she came home. In early 2021, immediately after the peak of COVID, Hospice nurses were scarce. The family lined up to greet the ambulance with smiles and applause, and we faced her bed to the garden, a big picture of my dad within sight. Everyone kicked into gear, singing hymns, praying, sharing funny memories, and expressing love and gratitude. I held her hand and stroked her face as she did for me when I had cancer. She rallied out of her morphine fog, acknowledging everyone individually with a smile.

For three days, I watched my mom's legacy in action. With loving, attentive gentleness, eight of her grandchildren put busy professional lives on hold to care for her around the clock. Without nursing experience, they administered morphine, moistened her mouth, repositioned her, held her hand, emptied her bag, read, and sang to her. At night, they slept around her bed on recliners and blow-up mattresses. There was good-natured teasing about who was her favorite.

The truth was, they all were.

As I left to go home at night, I'd pause to watch them settle. I was witnessing the fruit of a life well lived—the life of a woman who loved well and honored God with her unconditional love and forgiveness.

And I wondered... Lord, will that be me someday? Those are big shoes to fill.

Prayer

Father, You have given me the best example of serving others. As I long for the sound of her voice, may I long even more for grace to extend to others. May my legacy be a reflection of my mother and of You.

December 7

Welcome Home, Children
By Trudy Bosman
Today's Scripture: John 14:1-3

I enjoy being invited to special celebrations, but have usually been a person who sits on the outside of the crowd - watching, observing, sometimes participating. I am glad to be invited, but most times feel more like an observer than a "special, so happy to have you here, wonderful" type of guest.

In the past, when I thought about heaven, I knew God would let me in. Jesus said he was preparing a place for us and would be with Him forever. I just kind of figured He would say to me, "It is nice to have you here, and I have a little place over there for you." I felt that would be fine for me.

Then one day, I heard a song on the radio by the Gaithers called "Welcome Home Children".

It suddenly came to me that God was not going to just let me in. He would be happy to see me! He would welcome me with open arms and a big smile. It made me realize that I am special to God. I was loved and important to Him. Joy just filled my heart.

Even if I am a sideline person here, I know I have a loving heavenly Father who is eagerly waiting for all of his children to come home. He has prepared a wonderful place for each one.

Prayer

Dear Father, I look forward to Your welcoming open arms. How great it is to know that I am a "special, glad you are here, wonderful" child of Yours. I love You. I can't wait to see You.

December 8

A Caterpillar Soars
By Sandi Banks
Today's Scripture: 2 Corinthians 5:17

Every December 8th, I celebrate the day I awoke as a "new creation." I had found Jesus. I was no longer a caterpillar. Now in Christ, I was a soaring butterfly.

How different my life became!

Growing up in Denver, I had three things:

1. I had Religion. Our single-mom family was church-centered but not Christ-centered.
2. I had a Bible. I read it twice, but out of duty, not devotion.
3. I had a fear of death. Every Easter, I focused on Jesus' crucifixion, rather than His Resurrection.

Years later, I visited my old friend Charlie. "You're different, Charlie. What happened?"
He smiled. "Once I had religion; now I have a relationship with Jesus."

I wanted what Charlie had and surrendered my life to Christ. That dry, dusty Bible became my lifeline. Decades of my personal journals told of God's amazing grace in my life—through losses of my daddy, my baby, and my husband. He brought people to me who needed to hear.

People like Joe, the inmate in a Kansas prison, who thanked me for telling him about my Heavenly Daddy. "He'll never leave me, always love me!" Yes, Joe!

Norma, the nurse whose story of heartache was my story.
"God carried me through, Norma; He'll carry you too . . .." She went home a new creation.

Miriam, the young girl beside me on the plane. She was scared to fly. "Oh, Miriam, I had an awful fear of death. Then I met Jesus..." God moved in her heart. Miriam walked off the plane, free!

Prayer

Thank You, Lord, for entrusting heartaches and losses to us so we can use them to point others to You. Please put people in our path who need to know that nothing we experience could cause a wound too deep for our Abba Father to heal. Praise!

December 9

A Hopeful Response
By Sabrina French
Today's Scripture: Luke 1:1-80; 1 Peter 1:3-9

When my husband and I found out we were pregnant with our daughter, I found myself being wary of hope. After years of struggling with infertility, managing my hope while in fear of the pain of disappointment had become second nature. Having lost our first child in a miscarriage a mere three months prior, the news of this pregnancy had my mind working overtime to manage the hope in my heart to make sure it didn't get too high.

I imagine Zechariah was also in the hope-managing business when Gabriel told him Elizabeth would have a son. During this divine encounter, Zechariah responded with unbelief and doubt, explaining that he and his wife were too old. Zechariah's disbelief and lack of hope made him unable to speak.

Mary received similar miraculous news from Gabriel about conceiving the long-awaited Messiah, yet her response differed from Zechariah's. While both Mary and Zechariah asked Gabriel, "How?", the posture of Mary's heart sought understanding due to being a virgin, rather than being rooted in doubt. Gabriel explained the "how" to her, and Mary trusted the word of the Lord from Gabriel and believed in it. Mary's faith in God and hope in the coming Savior resulted in an open mouth full of praise.

Our resistance to hope, which paves the way for doubt, will close our mouths like it did Zechariah. But when we, like Mary, trust in God's Word and place our hope in Jesus, our living hope as Peter describes, we cannot be disappointed. Even amid trials, our hope in Jesus prepares the way for praise to overflow from our lips.

Prayer

Father, I thank You that I have been born again to a living hope through the resurrection of Your Son, Jesus Christ. I lay all my disappointment, fear, and pain at your feet. Restore my hope, and let my mouth overflow with praise like Mary's.

December 10

When You Can't Go Home for Christmas
By Mary Ann Esque
Today's Scripture: John 14:2-3

I have often contemplated the centuries of Israel's longing and hope for the Messiah. They were not quiet about their requests for deliverance and a place to call home. No, they cried out to God and sought His comfort, and sometimes they tried to create their "home" in all the wrong places.

I also wrestle with my own deep desire to find a place that I can call home. This is most challenging around my December birthday and the Christmas season, which resurrects my difficult memories of deaths, illnesses, and relational dysfunction. So what do you do when you can't go home again?

I love the way that Jesus responds to this question in John 14, where he says that he goes to prepare a place for us, and there's more than enough space for everyone. Our home with him is secure and can never go through foreclosure. Jesus says our home is not just here on earth. It's an eternity where we know love and belonging.

While that is not my earthly reality, I have to trust what I know to be true. God is good. God keeps his promises. God is in control. I need to stand firm in these foundational truths and cry out to God when I am overwhelmed by whatever I'm facing. If that's where you are today, then know that God sees you. He genuinely cares about your situation and the challenges you face. He is already working on your behalf, even if you don't see it yet. That's a promise you can take to the bank.

Prayer

Jesus, for all who struggle to find a home, you are Emmanuel—God with us. You, who are enthroned in cosmic glory, delight to wrap Your arms around us when we feel lost and broken. Be with us. Remind us that we are home with You and in You.

December 11

Your Invitation to Flourish in God's Presence
By Josie Muterspaw
Today's Scripture: Isaiah 55:1-3

God is a relentlessly inviting God, and Isaiah 55 carries one of the most beautiful invitations in all of Scripture: to come closer and flourish in His presence. Deep in our souls, we crave connection and long to feel welcomed, wanted, and fully known. God is masterful at creating such a space—where our hearts feel invited in.

In the whirling busyness of the world around us, God is always speaking—inviting us to draw near, to listen closely, and to receive the restoration, nourishment, and joy only He can provide. But in today's fast-paced world, we are growing increasingly disconnected from our hearts, where He longs to meet us. With dwindling attention spans and constant distractions, encounters with God in the deep places of our souls are becoming rare. And yet, it is there we learn to flourish.

Safe in God's presence, we learn to embrace how He sees us and give Him space to gently uproot anything that clouds our view. Just as a seed needs good soil to grow, our hearts need to be tended and cultivated so we can be receptive to the love God desires to give us. When we step away from the noise and draw near, God meets us there—renewing what has been depleted and nurturing us from the inside out.

Verse 3 of Isaiah 55 ends with a beautiful promise—a promise of His faithful, steadfast, and unfailing love. What, then, is God asking of us? Simply this: pause, turn your heart toward Him, and come closer. He will do the rest. For the one who flourishes is the one who has learned to incline their ear to His voice and entwine their heart with His. And when we do, His steadfast, transforming love awaits us.

Prayer

Lord, I come with a thirsty heart, longing for more of Your presence. Awaken me to the depth of Your enduring love and the nearness of Your nourishing presence—always available, always faithful. You created me to flourish in communion with You, and all You ask is that I come. So here I am, drawn by Your grace and love.

December 12

Ask and Open Your Heart
By Laura J. Antos
Today's Scripture: Matthew 7:7

There are times in your life when you ask God for something with all your heart. You may plead for healing for a loved one, a new job, relief from stress, or restoration of a broken relationship. You knock again and again, yet sometimes it feels like silence is the only answer.

My grandma was a caring, loving, and faith-filled woman who taught me the importance of faith, as well as the value of inviting God into one's life. For one of my birthdays, she sent me a card in a bright pink envelope with a "LOVE" stamp on it, which I still have. Inside was a letter reminding me of Matthew 7:7. She shared with me that no matter if I was having a happy day or in a moment of despair, to always "ask" God to guide my steps, my thoughts, and my actions.

The challenge isn't just to ask, but also to be open to the blessings God has in store for you. Oftentimes, you pray for something specific: a healed relationship, relief from stress, or the recovery of someone you love. Sometimes the answer doesn't come in the way you expect. I prayed persistently for healing for my mom's dementia, yet her illness worsened. Over time, I began to see that God was giving me something else—strength to endure, grace to keep showing up, and glimpses of peace, even in the midst of heartbreak.

When you ask, you place your heart in God's hands. In some ways, he is your own personal love letter. When you open yourself to his answer, you find he provides more than you imagined. His love will hold you while you wait, and his wisdom will give you what you truly need.

Prayer

Lord Jesus, Thank You for always hearing me when I pray. Teach me to ask boldly and to trust fully. Provide me hope in the moments when my prayers feel unanswered or when I struggle to understand Your ways. Open my heart to receive your answers and blessings, even when they look different from what I expect.

December 13

The Blessed Hope
By Elizabeth Clark
Today's Scripture: Titus 2:13

The blessed hope of the Christian is not a wish for a better future, but a living reality. It's the very power that sustains and motivates us daily. When we're united with Christ, our hope isn't a distant idea; it's a present reality that changes our perspective and gives us strength for today.

Our hope is for an active life, not a life of passive waiting. We don't just wait for the day our hope is realized; we live that hope every day. This changes how we see our challenges. Instead of seeing struggles as obstacles, we see them as opportunities to live out this new life, intertwined with Christ's divine strength. Our hope enables us to be patient, loving, and faithful, knowing our ultimate joy is secure.

My life as an innkeeper, wife, and mother sometimes felt like an endless list of tasks. The pressure to do everything perfectly left me feeling overwhelmed and empty. My hope was tied to just getting through the day. But one morning, as I rushed to start the laundry, this thought based on Colossians 1:27 came to mind: *Christ in you is the hope of glory*. It was a powerful reminder that I wasn't doing things alone. I began to intentionally pause and pray, *Lord Jesus, live in me today*. My perspective shifted. The endless tasks didn't disappear, but I started to experience divine patience and peace.

You can live this life of present hope, too. The anticipation of Christ's return is the life-force that enables you to be patient, kind, and loving today. Your hope isn't in your own striving, but in the indwelling Christ. This blessed hope brings joy and peace. The future promise of glory is your present reality, making every day a testament to the hope living within you.

How might embracing the present reality of Christ's hope change the way you approach your daily challenges this week?

Prayer

Lord Jesus, Thank You for being our blessed hope. Help us to live in this present reality, letting go of our striving and embracing Your divine life. May the anticipation of Your return be the source of our strength, patience, and love today.

December 14

Start Right Where You Are
By Maria Burnett-Carroll
Today's Scripture: Judges 6:14

There are times when I feel unqualified for my life. I am simply not enough. I just don't have what it takes to handle everything that is coming my way. I need more strength, more faith, more preparation, more optimism, more wisdom, more endurance...and the list continues to grow. My discouragement and overwhelm weigh heavily.

Several years ago, during a hard season as a single mom, a friend encouraged me with God's message to Gideon in Judges 6. Repeatedly, Israel is being attacked, and Gideon is feeling hopeless. God sends an angel to tell him to go forward in the strength he has. To Gideon, his own strength is laughable. He protests that he is weak. But God reassures him, telling him He will be with him.

Their interaction brings the hope we all need to hear. God isn't asking us to be more than we are today. He doesn't expect us to have everything figured out or even have the strength for what we are facing. Like Gideon, God knows we often feel defeated before we even try.

Instead, He gently invites us to go forward with whatever little bit of strength we can muster, trusting that He is with us. He will add His strength to what we lack. It isn't complicated. Even if it is one small, faltering step at a time, grace says to simply start where you are. Whatever strength you have, right here and right now is where you honestly begin with Him.

Prayer

Lord, I don't think I have enough strength for today, but I am going to move into the day with what I have. Thank You for being with me in all the ways I am going to need You. Help me live today knowing that my weakness doesn't define me. You love me, so you will strengthen me.

December 15

A Christmas Prayer
By Teresa Montalvo
Today's Scripture: 2 Corinthians 12:9

As I sit here savoring a few moments of silence, I am reminded that there was much activity swirling around Your birth. Troubles were all around, loved ones had passed, leaving an empty chair at the dinner table.

Financial difficulties meant people did without. Political uprising on every side filled the atmosphere. Taxes were due. Sickness and disease were among the people. Relationships were difficult due to surmounting differences of belief.

I am reminded, again, that there's nothing new under the sun. Help us to not be ashamed of our weakness, but to boast in it. I ask that You remind us that in our weakness, You are strong.

Would You please touch my friends and family right where they are? Heal them, heal their broken hearts, shattered dreams, give them fresh hope, a light that is dawning brightly with joy unceasing.

I pray this Christmas season would be filled with tiny sparkles of miracles that turn into glimmers of hope and faith increased. I ask You, Father God, that they remember the promises You have spoken over them. Your promises are yes and amen! We are Yours forever & always!

Thank You for our place in history, but most of all, we thank You for your son, Jesus, who was born in that lowly manger!

Humility was cloaked and delivered in an unexpected package! A gift that would never cease to give us an abundance of returns! The greater story was about to be revealed...death and resurrection mean we have eternal life!

Help us to remember the bigger picture. You're a Holy God, the God worthy of all of our worship, praise, and adoration.

Prayer

When we are weary and overwhelmed, may we remember that we can come and cast everything at Your feet because You care for us. When it seems the darkest, may we remember that the light shines brighter! I also ask that, like Mary, we ponder these things in our hearts.

December 16

When Winter Fell
By Irina Brcic
Today's Scripture: Revelation 21:4

It was a cold December evening, the kind of night when families should be gathered close in love and warmth. Instead, the phone rang with news that shattered our world. Our oldest brother—still so young—was gone. We knew he was ill, but nothing prepared us for that call. Shock numbed us first, then grief poured in, wave after wave.

Illness had been clouding his mind for years, day by day stealing pieces of his laughter, his dreams, his joy. We all longed for a different future—a life free from suffering, a chance to grow strong beyond the toxic environment we lived in. Instead, we were struck with grief, robbed of the tomorrow we prayed for. How can this grief possibly reconcile with

God's promise of hope and love?

Mary and Martha knew that grief. Their brother Lazarus grew sick, and when he died, the sisters cried out: "Lord, if you had been here, my brother would not have died" (John 11:21). Their words echo the ache of our own hearts.

Yet even in that moment of heartbreak, Jesus did not stand far off. John 11:35 tells us that He wept. The Son of God entered their sorrow, tears on His own face. Then He whispered hope into their pain: "I am the resurrection and the life. Whoever believes in me, though he die, yet shall he live," (John 11:25).

Prayer

Heavenly Father,
Your promise carries me still. Grief may mark our days, but faith marks our eternity. Loss reminds us of what was taken, but Christ reminds us of what will be restored. Until then, help us walk with our eyes fixed on heaven, where healing is complete.

December 17

Love That Conquers, Strength That Holds
By Julie D. Davis
Today's Scripture: Romans 8:37–39

Subtle changes in a loved one can be easy to dismiss, but sometimes those changes lead us down an unexpected path.

This was the day my mom was diagnosed with Alzheimer's disease. The weight of that reality settled heavily on our family. Her memory—once sharp with birthdays, milestones, adventures with grandchildren and stories of God's provision—has slowly faded. She had been a registered nurse and when not caring for her patients was intensely involved with her church. As her daughter, it has been so hard to see her change. I miss my mom.

Yet, what remains shines even brighter: her unshakable connection to the Lord. Scriptures and hymns still flow when she hears them, a reminder that God's Word is eternal and cannot be stolen.

Though the disease takes pieces of her earthly memory, it cannot touch the eternal truth that she is loved, chosen, and held by God. Romans 8 assures us that nothing—not illness, time, or even fading memory—can separate us from the love of Christ. That truth equips us to walk through uncertain seasons with confidence.

We may face circumstances that feel overwhelming, but in Christ, we are more than conquerors. His faithfulness will carry us, and His love will sustain us until He calls us home.

Prayer

Father, Thank You that nothing can separate us from Your love in Christ. When life feels uncertain or painful, remind us of Your steadfast faithfulness. Help us walk with hope, anchored in Your promises, and strengthened to love and serve others even in difficult seasons.

December 18

Where Will You Run?
By Linda Lowe Erley
Today's Scripture: Proverbs 18:10

In ancient times, fortified towers stood as strongholds of defense and safety. Some rose 30 to 150 feet, built from the strongest materials to endure for centuries—remnants still stand today, like the expansive Tower of David in Jerusalem. Perhaps this is why God used such an image in His Word as a reminder for every generation: "The name of the Lord is a strong tower; the righteous man runs into it and is safe" (Proverbs 18:10). But how can a name be a strong tower?

In biblical times, a name represented one's character. God's names reveal His attributes—who He is to us. And oh, how many names He has! So, when life presses in—when attacks come from every direction—look up. His tower is waiting. Run toward it. He calls you to take refuge in Him.

Every year this month, my husband and I celebrate our wedding anniversary. This year marks 43 years together, and we give thanks. Marriage is not always easy—it takes "three," with God at the center.

Many times, we've run to that tower. There, high above the worries of the world, we found His comfort, shared our burdens, sought His presence, and listened for His words of life. From that high place, God gave us—and will give you—a fresh perspective on all that lies below.

Who—or what—are you running to when burdens, fear, or weariness closes in like an enemy's siege? God is waiting in that strong tower. It is safe there. But the choice is yours. Will you turn to the world's quick fixes—temporary bandages that dull pain for a moment? Or will you run with intention to the eternal God, to His name and His Word of life that are ever-present, whatever the place, whatever the circumstance?

Run to His safety!

Prayer

Dear God, my strong tower, I accept Your invitation today to sit with You awhile—high above the worries of the world—and lay my burdens before You. Help me be still and listen to Your voice as You fill me with Your Word, not only to carry it in my heart but to courageously walk in it.

December 19

Reconciling Back to Peace
By Amy Leigh Hughes
Today's Scripture: Matthew 5:23-24

Jesus is The Prince of Peace. While there are many types of peace, I want to consider relational peace: being in right relationships with others. To be in communion with God requires us to be in communion with one another, because we are all one body with Christ as our head. In Him, all is well.

If we are not at peace with each other, we cannot be at peace with God. Jesus tells us to seek reconciliation with our brothers before offering our gifts to God. We can't just pretend nothing is wrong when there is a gaping wound in the body of Christ. This doesn't mean we gloss over hurt and pretend everything's okay when it's not; instead, we tend to the wounds and come to a truly restored relationship.

Of course, we will hurt and be hurt by others, but we must always seek forgiveness and restoration. If you have a grievance against someone, it must be addressed directly and promptly, without involving additional parties or allowing bitterness to fester. If you believe you may have wronged someone else, you must go to them and do everything in your power to make amends.

Sometimes this feels like an impossible task. Our own selfishness and pride get in the way of repentance and forgiveness. We may never even give our offenders the chance to reconcile because we are convinced that they will never own up to what they did.

It is only by the power of the Spirit living in us that we can forgive, because through Christ, God has forgiven us. No forgiveness we offer can exceed what God has extended to us. Jesus came to make a way for us to reconcile back to peace-- with God and each other.

Prayer

Jesus,
We pray for unity in Your body. If there are any places where relationships are broken, bring them to light so that we may swiftly reconcile and re-enter into fellowship with You and with the entire body of believers. Empower us to repent and forgive, even when it feels impossible.

December 20

Held In The Waves
By Brittany Pennel
Today's Scripture: Isaiah 43:2

Three days before Christmas, the world went quiet in a way I'll never forget. 5:30am. My dad was gone. Quickly and without warning. While lights sparkled on trees and songs sang of joy and peace, I was drowning.

Pulled beneath the surface by a tsunami of grief. The pain came in waves. Some days I could smile. Other times, the smallest memory would crash into me and I'd be sobbing without warning, gasping for air in the middle of a car ride or curled up on the couch, leaving me deeply tired.

But even in the deep and in the dark, when it felt like no one could reach me, Jesus was there. He just held me as an infant cradled gently by its mother. He whispered peace when the tears blurred my vision. He reminded me that He, too, wept. That He, too, understands the pain of death—but also defeated it.

I came through every crashing wave reminded: I am not alone.

Long before I knew, Jesus knew. He blessed me with a village of people who have surrounded me and won't let me fall. I still ache. I still cry. I still miss my dad every day. The hurt hasn't gone away, but the anchor that holds me is unmovable. Jesus, who holds both my broken heart and the hope of eternity. My grief doesn't cancel my faith. It reveals it. Even in the darkest moments, I know who holds me, I know who holds my dad now, and I know who holds you.

The waves will come, but they won't own you. Grief doesn't take holidays off. My favorite time of year is now harder to find joy in, but I know who you and I can trust in the deep, and that is the truth of the Lord that you steady yourself with.

Prayer

Lord, In the ocean of grief, be the steady breath in my lungs and strength when I feel weak. When the waves rise, anchor me in Your peace. Remind me that I'm not alone—that You are near, holding my heart. Let hope rise in the darkest of places, and Your joy be my light.

December 21

Facing the Longest Night
By Laurie Ostby Kehler
John 8:12

Today marks the winter solstice—the longest night of the year. Earth's Northern Hemisphere tilts away from the sun at its maximum angle, receiving minimal sunlight as the sun reaches its lowest point in the sky.

In ancient and contemporary pagan circles, people observe this night with bonfires, hoping that the future will be brighter. The days will become longer, and the nights shorter.

In Christian communities, we side-eye these festivities while focusing on Advent and preparing for Jesus' birthday.

But God created this celestial event. Maybe Christians can benefit from considering the dark night of the winter solstice and take it back?

Whether Christian or pagan, we all encounter dark times in our lives. Times when the nights seem endless and devoid of hope or light. It's in these dark times that Satan uses his favorite tactic, discouragement.

When there is little sunshine outside or inside our hearts and we sigh through interminable nights, he hisses his favorite lie: "See this misery you're in? This is how it will always be. It will never get better. You have no hope."

It's his sinister plot to suck out of our hearts all the glimmering hope that lies just over the horizon for us. This lie keeps our heads down, causing us to view circumstances as permanent instead of looking up to our Savior's face for our future promise.

Let's observe and mark the longest night of the year with our heads held high and with confidence and hope. Let's remind ourselves that, no matter how dark our current time may be, when we walk with Christ, we can be free from suffocating darkness. This is the promise Jesus made in John 8:12.

Prayer

Heavenly Father, Thank You for the hope You bring in our darkest times. Some nights can be interminably long and appear really bleak indeed. But into our darkness You shine Your blazing light, and the darkness cannot overcome it. Thank You that in Christ, we always have hope, no matter how dark and long the night.

December 22

Finding Peace When Life is Uncertain
By Karen Faye Newman
Today's Scripture: John 16:33

Life brings challenges. Sometimes, it's minor hurdles, and others, major life changes that shake the foundation of our world.

I will never forget the day my husband had a heart attack, and we discovered he needed quadruple bypass surgery. Our children were only two and a half years old, and I had no idea if he would survive. Fear and uncertainty gripped every moment. Several months later, I watched my brother cling to life through an unexpected illness. This included 28 days in the ICU, 15 surgeries, and countless prayers for a miracle. I've also sat in the quiet of an office, anxiety creeping in, as I learned I was being laid off, unsure how I would provide for my family in a shaky job market.

Each of these moments brought financial, medical, emotional, and spiritual chaos, worry, and uncertainty. Yet through it all, God never abandoned me. He doesn't deny that trouble will come; in fact, He warns us that it will. But He also promises to be with us, offering a peace that surpasses understanding, even during trials. This is the peace Jesus promises in John 16:33. It does not depend on circumstances; it is stronger than fear and is available to all who turn to Him.

If you are facing uncertainty today, whether it be in your health, relationships, finances, or faith, take heart. The storms may rage, but they do not have the final word. Keep your eyes fixed on Christ, the One who has overcome the world. Give your worries to him. Let His presence calm your mind and renew your strength. No matter how fierce the storm is, you are never alone—He is with you every step of the way.

Prayer

Heavenly Father, Thank You for Your unfailing love and for never leaving my side through life's trials. Help me to trust You fully, surrender my fears, and rest in Your peace. Strengthen my heart, calm my mind, and fill me with hope that endures, knowing You will carry me through any storm that life may send my way.

December 23

Making Room for Wonder
By Hope H. Dover
Today's Scripture: Psalm 46:10

My family affectionately calls today *Christmas Eve Eve*. For years, this day was a frantic one in our house. My husband and I would race from store to store, completing last-minute Christmas shopping. By the time we made it home, we were exhausted from searching for the perfect gifts to fulfill our shopping list.

After our children were born, we started to make a shift. The rushing didn't fit the kind of Christmas we wanted to create. We wanted Christ to be at the center of Christmas. So we began to take Christmas at a slower pace. We stepped back from the noise and hurry and focused on the true meaning of the season. Instead of something to be managed or perfected, Christmas became something to be received.

Instead of running through stores on December 23, we started a new tradition. Each year on this day, we bake and decorate Christmas cookies. The stress of last-minute shopping that once filled this day has been replaced with flour-covered counters, a kitchen filled with the sound of Christmas music, and abounding laughter.

The pace of our day slowed, as did our hearts. In the stillness of rolling out dough and cutting cookie shapes, we found space to exhale. We made time to talk, to laugh, and to notice the small moments that matter. It's not about perfect cookies or a picture-perfect Christmas; it's about preparing room in our hearts for the One who came to bring peace.

Now, *Christmas Eve Eve* has become one of my favorite days of the season. It's a reminder to slow down, to be still, and to make room for wonder as we prepare our hearts for the Savior who has already come.

Prayer

Jesus, quiet my heart in this busy Christmas season. Help me be still and trade the rush for rest. I want You to be at the center of Christmas. May I find Your presence as I remember that You are near. Amen.

December 24

How A Name Brings Hope
By Noreen Sevret
Today's Scripture: Matthew 12:21

The lights on my Christmas tree reflected nostalgia for my heart on Christmas Eve, as my eyes lingered the longest on an ornament with a story—a small pair of handmade blue mittens with a single thread holding them together.

I remembered the older lady who sold me the mittens. We were in an open market in Sofia, Bulgaria, on a cold December evening. The next morning, on Christmas Eve 1998, my husband and I flew home with the precious son we had just adopted, embarking on a long journey across the ocean to our home in America. We held him tightly, grateful for the hope God gave and the prayers He used to bring us together. Our son spoke a different language, but our translator taught us just enough words to communicate with this little two-year old boy with big brown eyes and a smile that lit up the room.

While sitting by the Christmas tree reflecting on my story, I thought again about Mary and Joseph and their long journey. Months before Jesus' birth, an angel of the Lord appeared to Joseph, instructing him to name their child Jesus. What hope it must have given them!

God knows the details of our lives and goes before us on our journeys, giving us hope, even down to a name. My husband's nickname is Max, after his two great-grandfathers. Our son's birth name is Maxun, and we call him Max (of course). It still amazes me how God knew and gave our son not only his father's last name, but also the gift of sharing his nickname.

When I need fresh hope, I think back on our story of the little blue mittens and the personal gift God wrapped up in the package of a name.

Prayer

Lord, As the lights of the Christmas tree shine brightly tonight, I thank You for the eternal hope I have in Jesus. May I continue to see a reflection of Your hope as I look back on the stories of my life and how you lovingly wrapped up packages for me, leaving them where I could find them.

December 25

God Is With Us
By Hannah Louise Cox
Today's Scripture: Matthew 1:23

Merry Christmas!

Christmas is a tender day for many. The older I get, the more I both love and struggle with Christmas, and I'm reminded during this season that joy and sorrow can coexist. The beauty of Christmas is that our Savior, Jesus, was born. Emmanuel, God with us! He came to live, die, and rise again for you, me, and the whole world. And because of His birth, my life changed.

On this very day, many moons ago, I accepted Jesus as my Savior, because a baby was born who would save the whole world. Jesus saved my life from shame and despair. He gave me a new name, and I'm forgiven and free.

Today, joy and sorrow coexist because, while I celebrate the birth of my Savior and the gift of salvation, I long to be fully whole and without pain and suffering. I want to see the people whom I miss who get to celebrate this day in heaven, instead of with me. There is a joyful ache amid all the family celebrations, gift exchanges, and parties that bring us together. Emmanuel, God with us is here today. Without the baby, there wouldn't be a cross, and there wouldn't be the gift of the Holy Spirit dwelling among us today. We are not alone in the chaos of our lives and the world around us.

If you are aching for those who have passed, I hope you find comfort in the peace of our Emmanuel. If you are in the chaos and busyness of travel, wrapping paper piles, and cookies, I hope you take time to pause and remember that Jesus was born for you. He came so that you can live forgiven and free. The greatest gift of Christmas is that Jesus loves you so much.

Prayer

God,
Thank You for sending Your son in flesh and blood to rescue me. Please be with me today as I celebrate Your love with and without the people I love most. Emmanuel, You are with me in the joy and sorrow of this season. Thank You for never leaving me. I love You.

December 26

It's Still the Best Time of Year
By Sasha Abele Katz
Today's Scripture: Psalm 143:8

The most exciting time of year culminated only twenty-four hours ago! We are now in the space between Christmas and New Year's. It's a mix of a few more days off from school and work. A time to reflect on God's goodness of the past year. And it's also a time when we put some planning in place for the upcoming year. For these reasons, I believe it's still one of the best times of year!

In this brief window of time, we can seize the moment to reflect, identify themes for growth, and put our hopes for the new year into words. As you reflect, God will show you His faithfulness in the past year, increasing your gratitude and praise. He will help you choose areas of growth for the upcoming year to challenge you and bring you joy. In His kindness and sense of adventure, He will help you identify your hopes for yourself and your loved ones.

As you venture into the precious days between Christmas and New Year's, here is a framework to explore. I'm praying right now that this annual practice blesses you!

Choose a word for the year and write a few reasons why you chose it.
Choose a verse for the year and write a short prayer to go along with it.
Pick a few areas of growth. Some ideas are spiritual practices, marriage, health, friendships, finances, or hospitality.
Consider the upcoming year and write out the big themes to embrace. Will you have a high school senior graduating? Are you starting a new job? An exciting trip? Do you have an obstacle to overcome?
Create a colorful vision board including all of the areas listed above. I usually use a corkboard and hang it near my home desk.

Prayer

Lord, As we venture into the new year, help us spend time with You. Help us remember Your faithfulness. Be with us as we take time to plan for the new year. Show us how we can grow more like You. Open our eyes to our hopes and dreams as we adventure in this life with You.

December 27

Jump Now
By Trudy Bosman
Today's Scripture: Matthew 11:28

One night, I was watching a movie on television where a young woman and her two companions reached the end of a long hall and stood at a high palace window, looking out. There was nowhere left to go.

Suddenly, they heard a voice calling from below. A strong man waited there with several beautiful white horses, urging them to leap so they could ride to freedom. The woman hesitated wondering if she should stay and fight, or trust the one who promised to catch her. After a pause, she climbed onto the windowsill and jumped. Her white garments floated around her as she fell, and with a smile of relief, she landed safely in his arms.

Her two friends looked at each other, and then, one after another, they leapt as well. Together, they mounted the horses and rode joyfully into the night.

As I thought about this, I realized it is a picture of us. We have trials as we go through our lives. We stumble along, looking for a way out—trying to fight off the enemy on our own. Eventually, we reach the point where we have tried everything we can and there is nowhere left to go.

Then we hear the call. It is Jesus calling. He waits to forgive our sins and set us free from our evil enemy, Satan. Don't turn back. Don't wait to experience the joy he promises. Climb on that windowsill and jump now into his loving, waiting arms.

Prayer

Dear Jesus,
Forgive me for trying to do things in my own strength and my own way. Thank you, Jesus, for loving me and providing a way, for paying the price for my sin, and inviting me to come and rest in Your waiting arms.

December 28

New Things
By Richard Dubay Jr.
Isaiah 43:18-19

Today we find ourselves in that hazy space between the joy of Christmas and the hope of the new year. The shine of December 25th is fading, and the promise of January 1st hasn't quite arrived. It's only natural, then, that we'd take some time during this season to reflect: How did this year really go?

For a lot of us, this year probably didn't turn out the way we thought it would. Our resolutions faded by January 2nd. The goals we wanted to accomplish are on some piece of paper, under some pile of stuff, somewhere on some desk in the back room.

That's okay. Not everything we plan to do will get done. Not every day goes the way we thought it would. Not every moment is under our control.

In Isaiah, God implores us to forget the former things. He asks us to not even consider the things of old.

Did you know that everything that has happened up until this moment is a "former thing"? That we no longer have to live bound by the "things of old"?

That's good news because God is in the business of doing new things. Whether you are 2, 52, or 92, He's still doing new things in you, through you, and around you. Every day, His mercies are new. Every day is an invitation to begin again. Even now, God is making a way in the wilderness and pouring out His rivers of blessing in the desert just for you.

It might be the end of the year, but it's only the beginning of the new things the Lord wants to do in and through you. Resolve today to put the past behind you and step forward into the new things God has for you.

Prayer

Father, We praise You. Give us the courage to leave the former things behind and the strength to move forward with You. Open our eyes to see You and the new things You are doing every day.

December 29

Look Forward, Not Back
By Tyann Beenken
Today's Scripture: Isaiah 43:18-19

Two years ago, I closed the door on a significant chapter in my life and walked away from a successful private physical therapy practice that I owned and ran for 12 years. I was unsure what the next chapter held and was asking God for guidance and direction. He kept impressing on my heart, "Do not look back, I am doing something new, something different."

In the eyes of the world, closing a business seems like a failure. I wrestled with the decision for a long time before making it, and at times felt like I had indeed failed. Yet, I also knew that God was calling me to something new, and in order to move forward, I needed to let go of the past.

God, through the prophet Isaiah, told the Israelites of their coming captivity in Babylon. It would have been easy for the Israelites to become discouraged and hopeless, feeling stuck in their circumstances, dwelling on their mistakes and failures. Yet, God reminds them of who He is and what He has done, and in Isaiah 43:18-19, He tells them not to look back, but to look forward to what He will do next.

As you look back at the previous year, perhaps there were things that did not go as expected, mistakes that were made, goals that were not actualized, and you feel like a failure. Dwelling on these keeps us stuck and holds us back. Instead, let them go. Ask God to remind you of His faithfulness and provision. Let that give you the courage to obey and follow Him into the new year and the new thing He wants to do in and through you, for He will make a way in the wilderness and rivers in the desert.

Prayer

Abba, As the year draws to a close, help me not to dwell on the times I stumbled and fell short. Instead, remind me of Your faithfulness. Show me where You acted on my behalf. Let that give me the courage, confidence, and faith to follow You on to the new paths You have for me in the coming year.

December 30

Stones & Gems
By Sarah Fry
Today's Scripture: John 1:16

At the start of 2021, I grabbed a piece of paper and began listing all the difficult things from the previous year. There were plenty. 2020 was full of challenges. My paper quickly filled halfway down with hard things.

But then something shifted. I began to recall the "hidden gifts" the year held—more time at home, more birdwatching, more time with my kids. So, I started a second list, this time from the bottom of the page up. As I filled in the blessings, I realized that by the time my pen met the middle, there were just as many, if not more, beautiful things than hard ones.

Of course, 2020 held tragedy, crisis, and difficulty worldwide. It was the year the world shut down. I thought of those challenges as rocks—hard things that could make us stumble along the way. But I also pictured the good things as gems—sparkling reminders of joy, lessons learned, and unexpected beauty.

It struck me that life is like a jar filled with both rocks and gems, all mixed together. Too often, it's easy for me to group the rocks and say in a weary voice, "What a hard year (or month or day) I've had." But in doing so, I overlook the bright, glittering gifts that are scattered throughout my days.

To make this real for myself, I gathered some rocks and bought sparkly gems (not real ones, but still pretty). I mixed them in a dish shaped like open hands as a daily reminder that life is a blend of both—the rough and the beautiful.

Prayer

Lord, Teach me to see Your hand in both the stones and gems life has been bringing. Remind me not to dwell only on the hard parts, but to notice the sparkles of beauty and grace You scatter through each day. Teach me to treasure those gifts and carry them with gratitude and hope.

December 31

When God Goes Deeper
By Jennifer Hope Longenecker
Today's Scripture: Philippians 1:6

Last year, my husband and I thought we'd make a few quick updates to the century-old cottage on our property for my daughter and son-in-law. Simple plan, right? But as we opened the first wall, we discovered problems that led to opening another wall, then another. Before we knew it, the entire cottage was gutted—a complete nightmare that seemed to mock our "easy update" dreams.

Sound familiar? God often works the same way in our lives. We pray for a quick fix to a relationship issue, a minor attitude adjustment, or a small breakthrough. Instead, He begins revealing deeper problems we didn't know existed. Suddenly, areas of our lives we thought were "fine" are torn wide open, leaving us feeling exposed and wondering what we've gotten ourselves into.

But here's what we discovered in that cottage, and what God knows about us: sometimes complete renovation is the only way to create something truly beautiful and lasting. With all the walls down, we could see the full picture. We rerouted plumbing, rewired electricity, and redesigned the entire floor plan. My daughter discovered gifts she didn't know she had. What seemed like chaos was actually an opportunity.

The apostle Paul reminds us in Philippians 1:6 that God will finish the work He begins in us. God isn't interested in surface-level improvements that won't last. When He starts working in your life, He's thinking long-term renovation, not quick cosmetic fixes.

That cottage now stands strong and beautiful, ready for whatever comes. The mess was temporary; the transformation is permanent.

If your life feels gutted right now, take heart. The Master Builder sees the finished product. Trust His process—even when it looks like chaos, He's creating something beautiful that will stand the test of time.

Prayer

Lord, When You tear down walls in our lives, remind us that You're the Master Builder. Help us trust Your timing and process, even when it looks like chaos. Thank You for renovating our hearts to create something beautiful and lasting.

Looking to *connect* with a community of writers?

www.hopewriters.com

The world needs your *hope-filled* words more now than ever before.

Thinking about *writing* your own book?

www.hopebooks.com